BEN SHAHN AND THE PASSION OF SACCO AND VANZETTI

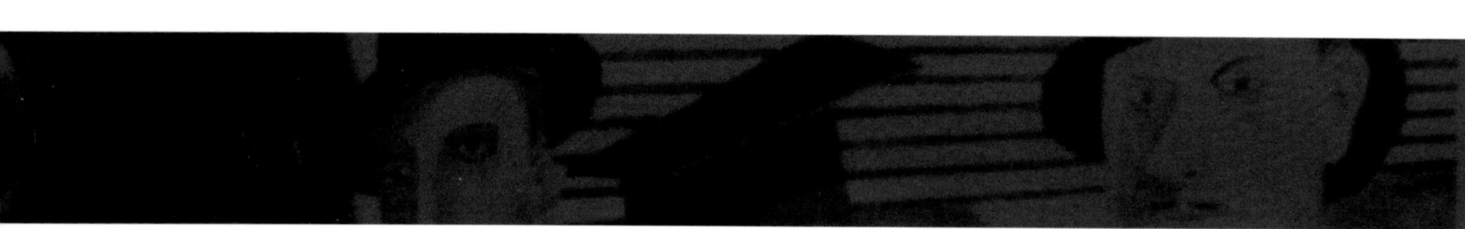

Organized by
Alejandro Anreus, Ph.D. Curator

September 12–December 16, 2001

Jersey City Museum
350 Montgomery Street
Jersey City, New Jersey 07302

This catalogue and exhibition have been made possible in part through the generous support of the National Endowment for the Arts, the Geraldine R. Dodge Foundation, and the Fleet Bank Foundation.

BEN SHAHN AND THE PASSION OF SACCO AND VANZETTI

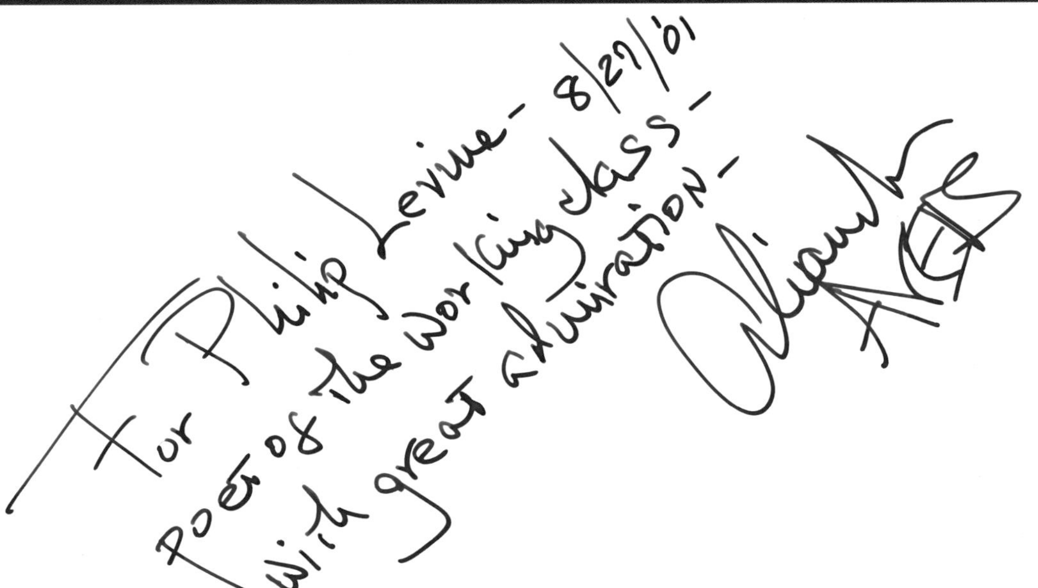

Ben Shahn and The Passion of Sacco and Vanzetti

September 12–December 16, 2001
Jersey City Museum
350 Montgomery Street
Jersey City, New Jersey 07302

Catalogue distributed by
Rutgers University Press

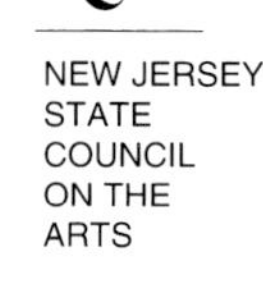

The Jersey City Museum is funded in part by the City of Jersey City and the New Jersey State Council on the Arts/Department of State, A Partner Agency of the National Endowment for the Arts. This exhibition and catalogue are partly funded through generous grants from the National Endowment for the Arts, the Geraldine R. Dodge Foundation, and the Fleet Bank Foundation.

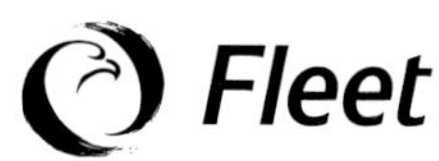

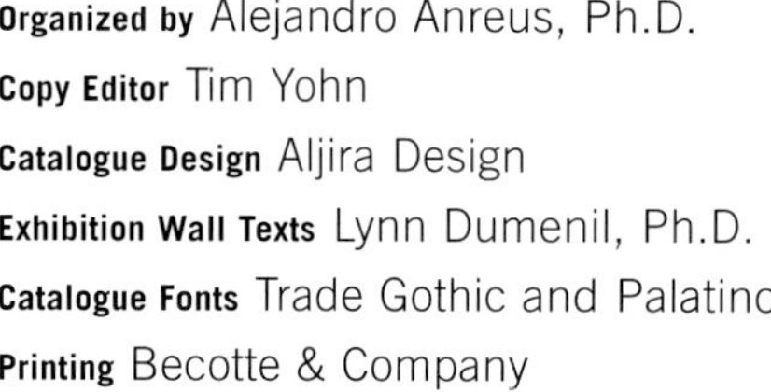
Organized by Alejandro Anreus, Ph.D.
Copy Editor Tim Yohn
Catalogue Design Aljira Design
Exhibition Wall Texts Lynn Dumenil, Ph.D.
Catalogue Fonts Trade Gothic and Palatino
Printing Becotte & Company

Cover
Vanzetti and Sacco in the Courtroom, n.d. Aldino Felicani Papers, Boston Public Library.

Ben Shahn painting The Passion of Sacco and Vanzetti (detail), 1932. Courtesy of Bernarda Bryson Shahn, Roosevelt, New Jersey

Ben Shahn
The Passion of Sacco and Vanzetti (detail)
1958. Serigraph, 25 3/4 x 17 1/2 inches
Gift of the Lessing and Edith Rosenwald Foundation. New Jersey State Museum, Trenton, New Jersey

Back cover, inside
Vanzetti and Sacco in their Coffins, 1927, Aldino Felicani Papers, Boston Public Library.

The curator and essayists wish to dedicate this catalogue to the memory of Dr. Stephen Lee Taller (1933–1997) collector and archivist of Ben Shahn material, and friend to Shahn scholars everywhere.

Contents

Ben Shahn and The Passion of Sacco and Vanzetti

This exhibition began back in 1994, when I presented a paper at the annual meeting of the College Art Association in New York, as part of the panel *Museums and the New American Art History*, which was chaired by Alan Wallach and H. Barbara Weinberg. Seven years later, with the support of the National Endowment for the Arts, the Geraldine R. Dodge Foundation, and the Fleet Bank Foundation, an academic proposal for an exhibition has been transformed into an exhibition with a substantial catalogue. These seven years have been years of research, grant writing, conceptualization of the exhibition, detective work in tracking down specific works of art, etc. These labors have not been solitary, on the contrary, they have been possible due to the team efforts of the entire staff of the Jersey City Museum. From the start the museum's administration, in the persons of former Executive Director Nina S. Jacobs and former Deputy Director Aleya Saad, supported this project, in spite of initial rejections from funders. Within the Curatorial / Exhibitions department, the following people have been very helpful and have worked very hard on this project: Tom Strider, Collections Manager; Rocío Aranda-Alvarado, Assistant Curator; and curatorial interns Barbara Modell, Carolyn Murray, and Mary Tso. Former Curator of Education Sandra Toro designed an extraordinary multi-disciplinary education program to complement the exhibition. The Development department, with Director Anne Kneuer and a succession of grant writers, has sought support for this project with great constancy and commitment. Finance Director David Silletto, has kept track of our funding, and has reminded us on an almost daily basis of the need to keep raising funds for the "S, S & V" (as it is known around here) project.

Finally, our preparators have done their usual outstanding job installing the works of art. All of the contributors to the catalogue, historian Nunzio Pernicone, art historians Frances Pohl, Laura Katzman, and Diana Linden, have been consultants, authors, supporters, and most of all friends. The high level of scholarship evident in this catalogue speaks volumes of their intellectual depth and rigor. The late Stephen Lee Taller, M.D., shared his archives with all of us, encouraged us, and rooted for all of the Shahn exhibitions that have been taking place since 1998. We dedicate this catalogue to his memory. I want to thank Professor Lynn Dumeniel, who teaches history at Occidental College in California, for writing the wall texts throughout the exhibition. Historian Paul Avrich, a leading authority on the subject of anarchism, has been a friend and supporter of this project.

Lastly, my wife Debra Blehart, and my children David and Isabel, have put up with great humor and patience with seven years of our lives where I have "eaten, breathed, slept and dreamed" Ben Shahn and Sacco and Vanzetti.

The following public collections and private collectors have been very generous in lending to this exhibition:

The Art Museum, Princeton University, Princeton, NJ
Fogg Art Museum, Harvard University, Cambridge, MA
The Montclair Art Museum, Montclair, NJ
The Museum of Modern Art, New York, NY
New Jersey State Museum, Trenton, NJ
Frederick R. Weisman Art Museum,
University of Minnesota, Minneapolis, MN
Whitney Museum of American Art, New York, NY
Kennedy Galleries, New York, NY
Private Collector and R.D. Schonfeld & Co., Inc., NY
Private Collector
Private Collector, Plainfield, NJ
Alfredo Sinibaldi, Montclair, NJ
Dr. Nunzio Pernicone, Newtown, PA
Mr. and Mrs. Harry Spiro, NY
Mr. and Mrs. Jonathan Wittenberg, NY

Thank you, one and all.

Alejandro Anreus, Ph.D.
Curator

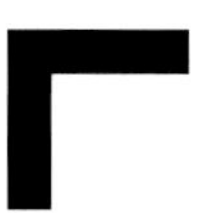

Foreword

Throughout the 1920s the Sacco and Vanzetti case dominated the judicial and political stage in the United States. Since their execution by electrocution on August 23, 1927, their lives, the lives of two Italian immigrants and rank and file anarchists, have been transformed into *the case that will not die*. Beginning in the early 1930s, the work of artist Ben Shahn has exemplified the balance between formal rigor and political commitment. Shahn is also a son of our state, having lived and worked in Roosevelt, New Jersey for most of his life.

The subjects of Nicola Sacco and Bartolomeo Vanzetti were Shahn's vehicles for developing his own visual vocabulary as a mature artist. This exhibition contextualizes Shahn's work with the Sacco and Vanzetti case; it also illuminates the case through Shahn's visual narrative.

It is fitting that this exhibition is one of the three exhibitions that inaugurates our new facility. The exhibition is the end product of over six years of planning. Our new facility began as a dream of the Trustees, staff, and community back in 1992. With eight spacious galleries, education classrooms, a theater, a resource room, museum shop and coffee bar, the Museum will serve as a cultural center where local residents, artists, students and educators, and visitors will feel at home.

The Jersey City Museum could not have attempted such an ambitious capital project without the support of our Board of Trustees, the City of Jersey City, particularly the office of The Mayor, and the members of the City Council, and the New Jersey State Council on the Arts. We are most grateful to the National Endowment for the Arts, the Geraldine R. Dodge Foundation, and the Fleet Bank Foundation for their generous support of this exhibition and catalogue. We thank the New Jersey Council for the Humanities and the National Italian American Foundation for their support of the exhibition's public programs. We also thank the lenders, both private and public, for generously sharing Shahn's work with us. Special thanks to Leslie Mitchner, Editor-in-Chief at Rutgers University Press, the distributors of this publication.

The Staff of The Jersey City Museum

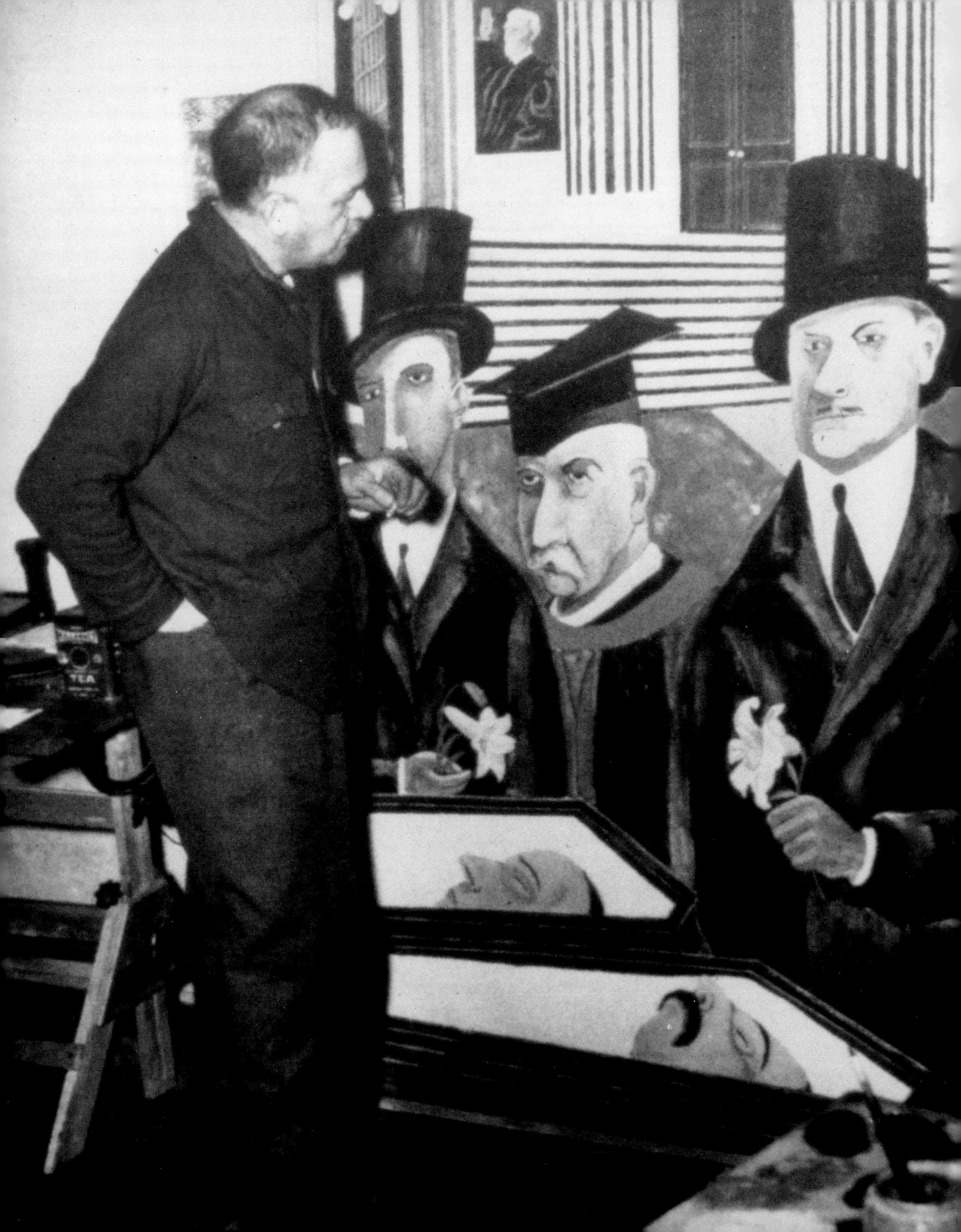
TEA

Frances K. Pohl

Ben Shahn, Politics, and Art

As I was completing my doctoral dissertation on Ben Shahn, I had the following dream:

I was on a baseball field, close to first base. Ben Shahn was up to bat. He was a small, wizened old man, very unlike the tall, barrel-chested Shahn I had known from photographs. On the pitcher's mound was a member of my dissertation proposal defense committee. This professor proceeded to throw the ball at the fence, then at a telephone pole, anywhere but across the plate, thus intentionally walking Shahn. Shahn arrived at first base very upset. "Why didn't he give me a chance to hit the ball?" he asked me. "Well," I answered, "he can handle the way you deal with war, but he can't handle the way you deal with peace."

Ben Shahn painting *The Passion of Sacco and Vanzetti*, 1932. Courtesy of Bernarda Bryson Shahn, Roosevelt, New Jersey

This dream is revealing of both my own interest in Shahn and of the way in which he has been perceived over the years by both art historians and critics. The professor in the dream, a Marxist art historian, believed Shahn did his most politically and aesthetically radical work in the 1930s and early 1940s. His move away from the depiction of specific historical events and his turn to a more symbolic language and to religious imagery after the end of World War II represented, for this professor, Shahn's abandonment of his earlier leftist politics. Therefore, the older Shahn, a mere shadow of his earlier robust self, was not "given a chance to hit the ball" in the game of leftist art history.

My own research on Shahn at the time of my dream focused not on the 1930s, but on the late 1940s and early 1950s.[1] I was not interested in the artist for his turn away from images with clear references to historical events that were of importance to the Left. Rather, I was interested in examining the manner in which his work changed in response to both the rise of the Right and the development of the Cold War, as well as to the growing popularity within the art world of a nonfigurative form of abstraction. For me Shahn had not become any less political, or even any less "radical" in his politics. Instead, I saw Shahn, like other artists whose work drew direct inspiration from their political activities, struggling to find a way to maintain his reputation and livelihood as an artist while simultaneously protesting the increasing political repression resulting from McCarthyism and the Cold War.

From the moment Shahn decided to address the political in his art, scholars and critics have argued over the exact nature of his politics, as well as the significance of his art. The reviews of the original exhibition of his Sacco and Vanzetti paintings in 1932 reveal the range of this debate. While the critic for *Art News* described the show as "one of the most arresting and vital pictorial documents of our immediate time," Walter Gutman, critic for the leftist publication *The Nation* found the work "disappointing" and "flippant."[2] For Gutman, Shahn had "failed to realize any of the emotional or idealistic significance of the martyrdom." The *Art News* critic approved of the satire, simplicity, and poignancy of the series, while Gutman wanted a more aggressive and idealistic presentation. "Until his feelings are more passionate, more spontaneous, and more partisan," writes Gutman, "[Shahn] cannot create those eloquent symbols which are typical of an art deeply concerned with affairs."

Such debates over passion and partisanship continued to dog Shahn's work during the 1940s. Hank Brennan, head of the Office of War Information's graphics bureau, found that the central figure in Shahn's 1942 poster *We French Workers Warn You* "simply wasn't an appealing-looking guy," which, for Brennan, meant that it would not make good propaganda. He also found that Shahn's image of two welders, one black and one white, "didn't mean anything" as a poster and therefore refused to use it. The Congress of Industrial Organizations' Political Action Committee (CIO-PAC), however, had no trouble turning it into a successful poster in 1944, with the caption *For Full Employment After the War, Register/Vote.*[3] In 1946 the art critic Walter Abell wrote in *Magazine of Art*: "Shahn's *Welders* can speak to a factory worker much as a *Holy Family* spoke to a medieval monk. It is of the tissue of his soul's experience; a symbol of his world and of his impulse toward a fuller life."[4]

Yet Gutman's sentiments also reappear in the late 1940s in a review of Shahn's retrospective exhibition at the Museum of Modern Art (MoMA) in New York by Ann Leonard, the critic for the Communist publication *People's World*. Leonard wrote that while Shahn had "assimilated a rich variety of experiences" and had responded "with an honest sensitivity attuned to the working people from whom he comes," his workers often became "object[s] of dismay, almost to the point of revulsion." This tendency may have originated in "a somewhat unhealthy adjustment to his subjects" or in "a little too much pity, a little too much concern over what he may feel to be weak and helpless elements in society."[5] James Thrall Soby, on the other hand, in his essay for the catalogue that accompanied the MoMA exhibition, wrote that Shahn's work was "as inspired in structure as in humanistic content" and that as a propagandist, Shahn was "involved in mass appeal on the far-flung scale peculiar to our times."[6]

Not surprisingly, in an era of increasing paranoia and persecution, Soby also emphasized Shahn's Americanness. He may well have been anticipating the attacks of individuals like Republican Representative George Dondero of Michigan, who charged in 1948 that all modern art was communistic and thus anti-American, and that Shahn was a "proponent of social protest in art" and a "Communist-fronter."[7] This emphasis on Shahn's nationality, if not his patriotism, peaked in 1954, when he was sent along with Willem de Kooning to represent American painting at the Venice Biennial. A summary of the press reaction compiled by MoMA, the organizer of the exhibition, noted: "One of the most striking and possibly surprising aspects of Shahn's appeal was the fascination that he exerted as a distinctly 'American' painter of 'American' subjects."[8] Yet Shahn did not represent just any America. For some it was "the myth of America—the America of Washington, of Ford, of gangsters; of the America that grew so rapidly out of the courage, the simplicity and the struggles of the early pioneer"—and, one might add, of the early immigrants from Europe, many of whom were Italian.[9] For others it was "America as an ideal and a potential of liberty."[10]

These differing opinions of Shahn's work and politics are due, in large part, to the political sympathies of the writers. Advocates of a workers' revolution wanted a more uplifting, celebratory depiction of workers, while those who promoted reform rather than revolution as the solution to working-class problems in America often were drawn to the pathos, lyricism, and/or satire of Shahn's works. Right-wing politicians disliked Shahn not because he failed to celebrate workers, but because the style and content of his work undermined what they saw as the very moral, political, and economic foundations of the country. Liberals, on the other hand, were more likely to see Shahn as representative of the best the country had to offer in terms of the rights of individuals and freedom of expression.

Thus, while many have argued over the exact nature of Shahn's politics and the way in which these politics are expressed in his art, none have denied that Shahn's political beliefs, however they may be interpreted, informed his art. Shahn may well have told those who asked which political side he was on that he was a supporter of justice and democracy, wherever it might be found. Democracy was, in his own words, "the most appealing idea that the world has yet known."[11] Yet Shahn also would have pointed out that ideas, no matter how appealing, are not enough and that democracy can only be achieved and maintained through action by individuals. One such action is direct participation in the electoral process. "Where the voting booth is present," he wrote, "government cannot for long pursue ends other than those of the public good." Of course, that public must also be an informed public. "The uninformed vote," argued Shahn, "the emotionally partisan vote, the intimidated vote may lead to disaster."[12] Shahn joined many organizations and argued forcefully for an involved citizenry. He saw art as an important tool for informing the public about the importance of justice, compassion, and political action. This was one of his primary goals in creating the series of paintings on the case of Sacco and Vanzetti. The significance of this series for us today is best captured in the words of Matthew Josephson, who wrote in *The New Republic* in April 1932: "Judge Thayer, the Lowell Committee, won out in 1927. But what of 1937 and 2027? One senses, at this point, the enormous, latent power of artists and poets over human events—if they would but use it. The statesmen propose; the artists, poets, historians, dispose, in the long run."[13]

List of endnotes on page 124

Vanzetti and Sacco in the Courtroom (detail), n.d.
Aldino Felicani Papers, Boston Public Library.

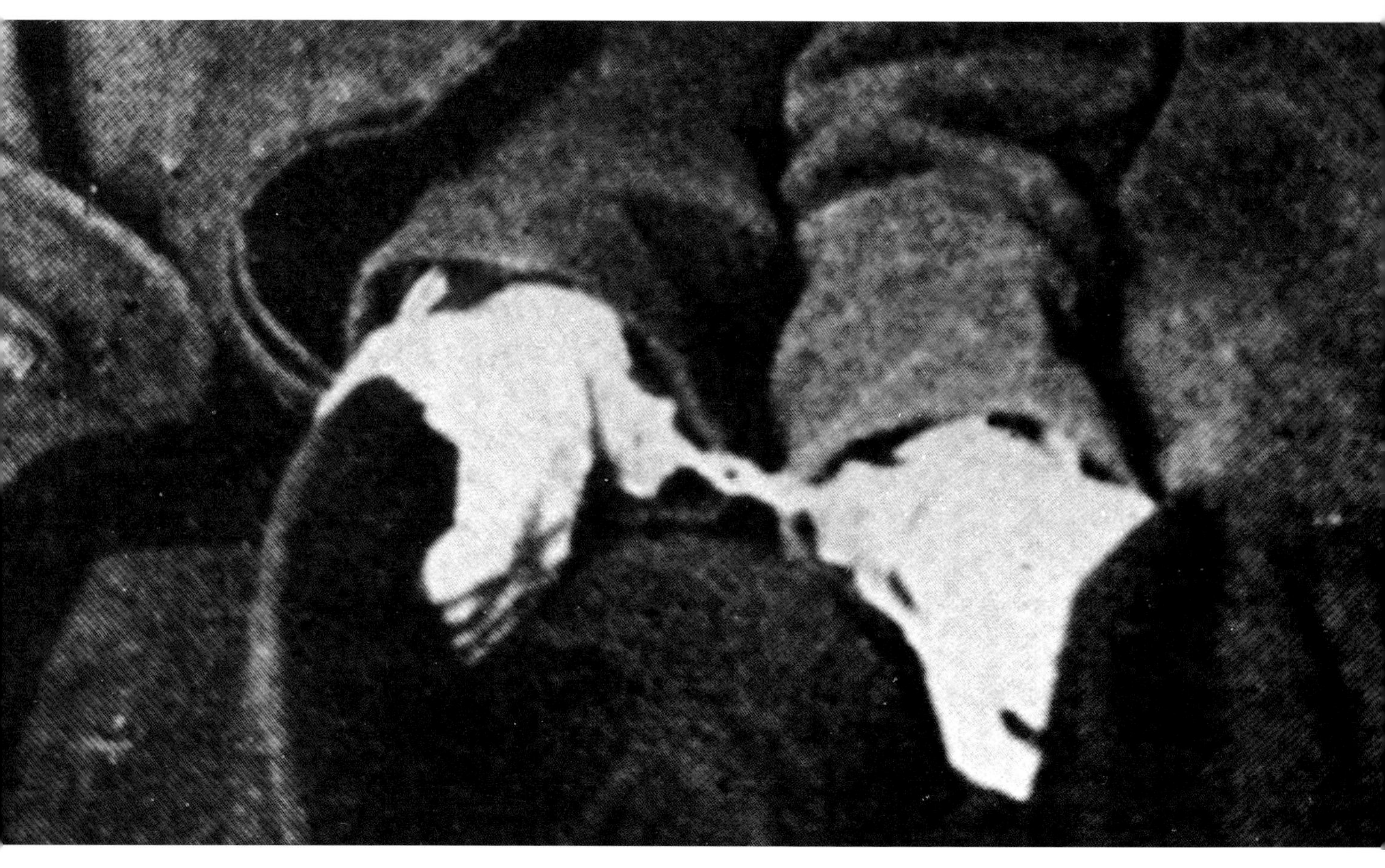

Nunzio Pernicone

The Sacco-Vanzetti Case: An Overview

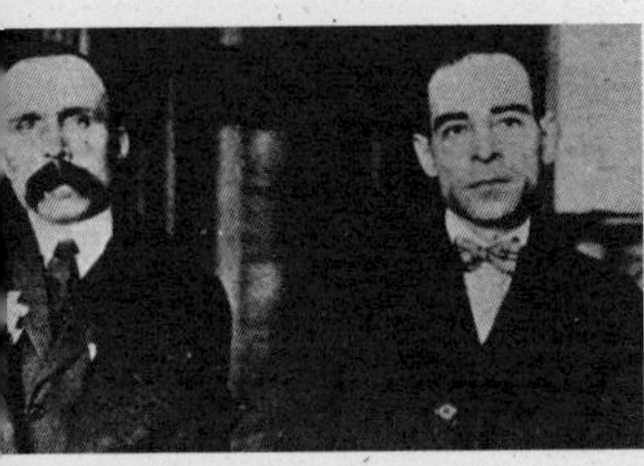

Shortly after midnight, on August 23, 1927, two Italian anarchists, Nicola Sacco and Bartolomeo Vanzetti, were electrocuted at Charlestown State Prison in Massachusetts for their alleged participation in a payroll robbery that had left two men dead seven years earlier. An international cause célèbre in the 1920s, the Sacco-Vanzetti case—as Edmund Wilson astutely observed—"revealed the whole anatomy of American life, with all its classes, professions, and points of view and all their relations, and it raised almost every fundamental question of our political and social system."[1] Opinion concerning the case split millions of Americans into hostile camps, much as the Dreyfus Affair had done in France during the 1890s. Defenders of Sacco and Vanzetti argued that two working-class immigrants were innocent men, that their trial and conviction had been a travesty of justice, resulting from ethnic prejudice and political intolerance. Their detractors rallied behind the judicial and political institutions of the Commonwealth of Massachusetts, insisting that the men had been guilty as charged and fairly tried.

If their ordeal had not captured world attention, Sacco and Vanzetti would probably have lived and died in obscurity, like the vast majority of the 2.5 million Italians who immigrated to the United States during the fifteen years preceding World War I. Both men came from the peasant stock that comprised the majority of Italian immigrants, although neither was motivated to leave Italy by the desperate poverty that drove most of their countrymen to America. The third son in a family of seventeen children, Nicola Sacco (his given name was Ferdinando; he adopted the name Nicola in 1917 to honor an older brother who had died) was born on April 22, 1891, in Torremaggiore, a small town located in the Puglia region of southern Italy. His father was an enterprising peasant who had acquired a large vineyard and an olive oil business. Sacco's childhood was happy and relatively free of economic hardship. Rather, it was his vision of a "free country, the country that was always in my dreams"[2] that convinced Sacco to emigrate to the United States in April 1908.

"We came," he explained to Governor Alvan T. Fuller before his execution in 1927, "because we heard that it was a land of freedom—freedom not merely to gain wealth, for which we cared little, but freedom of the mind and of ideas."

His future comrade Bartolomeo Vanzetti emigrated three months later. Born on June 11, 1888, in Villa felletto, in the northern region of Piedmont, Vanzetti, too, came from moderately prosperous peasant stock and experienced a happy childhood. Whereas Sacco had exhibited little interest in school, preferring to work with machines, Vanzetti was a bright and introspective boy who might have become a fine teacher or even a priest, as he was a devout Catholic in his youth. At the age of thirteen, however, his father apprenticed him to a pastry shop owner in Cuneo, and for the next six years he lived a wretched existence, working as much as eighteen hours a day in bakeries and restaurants. His only pleasure was books. The worst tragedy of Vanzetti's young life occurred at the end of 1907, when his mother died of cancer. He was emotionally devastated by the loss and immigrated to the United States "to put the seas between me and my grief."[3] His expectations were similar to

Sacco's. "We came," he explained to Governor Alvan T. Fuller before his execution in 1927, "because we heard that it was a land of freedom—freedom not merely to gain wealth, for which we cared little, but freedom of the mind and of ideas."[4]

Sacco and Vanzetti experienced very different circumstances after their arrival. Within two years, Sacco found steady work as an edge-trimmer in a Milford (Massachusetts) shoe factory, earning good wages and the respect of his employers. He married Rosina Zambelli in 1912, had a son named Dante the following year; he also fathered a daughter, Ines, born after his arrest. A devoted family man, whose hobby was tending his garden of vegetables and flowers, Sacco seemed destined for a tranquil and happy life . Vanzetti, in contrast, had difficulty finding his niche in American society. Wandering from New York through New England, he suffered long periods of unemployment, poverty, and even homelessness. When he did find work, he toiled long hours at unskilled jobs in restaurants, a brick factory, a stone quarry, a railroad pick-axe crew, a construction gang, and several factories. Leading a solitary and lonely existence, Vanzetti found solace in books on history, philosophy, literature, science, and religion. In 1913, he settled in Plymouth, Massachusetts, renting a room with the family of Vincenzo Brini, who treated him as one of their own. After working as a gardener and handyman, Vanzetti found a job with the Plymouth Cordage Company in the spring of 1914. He quit after less than a year and resumed construction work for the next two years. Finally, In the spring of 1919, Vanzetti began peddling fish, a job that suited his gregarious nature and his preference for working outdoors.

What Sacco and Vanzetti shared in common during these years—and what distinguished them from most Italian immigrants—was their belief in the revolutionary doctrines of anarchism. For decades Sacco and Vanzetti were mistakenly portrayed as "philosophic anarchists"—defined by John Dos Passos as "an anarchist who shaves daily, has good manners and is guaranteed not to act on his beliefs."[5] Thanks to the research of Professor Paul Avrich and Mr. Robert D'Attilio, however, it has been conclusively established that Sacco and Vanzetti were militant disciples of Luigi Galleani, an intransigent anarchist communist who believed that capitalism and the state must be destroyed by violent means, including bombs and assassination.[6] Like so many Italian immigrants who subscribed to Galleani's revolutionary credo, Sacco and Vanzetti had become radicalized after living in the United States for several years. Their conversion resulted from the hardships and inequities of working-class life they had directly experienced and observed, and the propaganda absorbed from Galleani's charismatic oratory and his newspaper, *Cronaca Sovversiva* (Subversive Chronicle), published in Lynn, Massachusetts. Anarchism for Sacco had an ethical and emotional appeal. His heart went out to "the weak ones that cry for help," the "prosecuted and the victim," and "all the legion of the human oppressed."[7] The primary catalyst for his conversion was the 1912 textile workers' strike led by the Industrial Workers of The World (IWW) in Lawrence, Massachusetts. Sacco collected money to help feed the strikers and contributed later to the defense fund for Arturo Giovannitti and Joseph Ettor, the two strike leaders falsely accused of murder. By 1913, Sacco had become an active associate of the anarchist Circolo di Studi Sociali of Milford, helping to raise funds for striking mill workers in nearby Hopewell. He participated in various strikes during the next few years and was arrested for disturbing the peace (charges later dropped) in 1916, while demonstrating in sympathy for the Mesabi Range strikers and their imprisoned leaders.

Vanzetti was described by Upton Sinclair as "an idealist if ever I knew one—a gentle, quiet, simple man, with a wonderful dream of justice for the working class and peace on earth; a dreamer and a religious man in the true sense of that word."[8] Having experienced hardship and exploitation directly, Vanzetti proved highly receptive to the antistatist and anticapitalist doctrines expressed in the works of the anarchist intellectuals he read, including Peter Kropotkin, Elisée Reclus, Francesco Saverio Merlino, and Errico Malatesta. Siding with the poor and the oppressed, Vanzetti, like Sacco, vowed to wage class war against capitalism and government. His political activities dated from the Lawrence strike of 1912, when he became active in an anarchist group in Worchester and began subscribing to Galleani's *Cronaca Sovversiva*. Vanzetti's militancy intensified during the period of his employment as a manual laborer for the Cordage Company in 1914–1915, and when a big strike broke out at Cordage in January 1916, he participated in the action, making speeches, collecting money, and picketing.

That Sacco and Vanzetti were rank-and-file militants rather than leaders of the Italian anarchist movement provided no exemption from repression, when in 1917 the federal government launched a campaign to eliminate radicalism from American society. Indeed, in the eyes of Anglo-Saxon America, Sacco and Vanzetti represented the worst of all possible combinations—they were both Italians and anarchists. Racial prejudice against Italians was all-pervasive during pre-and-post World War decades. Embracing a form of racism known as Nordicism, mainstream Americans generally conceived of Caucasians in hierarchical terms, with the Anglo-Saxons, Germans, and Scandinavians of northern Europe considered racially superior to ethnic groups originating in southern and eastern Europe. Italians occupied the lowest rung of this Caucasian hierarchy. Southern Italians, in particular, were deemed not only inferior to Nordic groups, they were also often considered not truly "white." For example, when the Italian-American IWW leader Joe Ettor was arrested during the Lawrence strike of 1912, the *Boston Evening Transcript*—the voice of Brahman Boston—rejoiced with headlines declaring that the "Passing Out of Ettor Means Ascendancy of the White-Skinned Races at Lawrence," in contrast to the newspaper's gloom of the previous three weeks, when Ettor had successfully led the strikers and "the dark-skinned races were in the ascendancy."[9] Nordicism's worst manifestations of anti-Italian sentiment resulted in vigilante violence: thirty-nine Italians were lynched or shot between 1874 and 1915, mainly in the South and the Far West.[10] More commonly, Italians were looked upon with undisguised contempt and subjected to every sort of social and economic discrimination. Disparaging terms such as "Dagoes," "Wops," and "Guineas" were used openly in everyday parlance, by the educated and uneducated alike. In the popular press, magazines, school books, and even government documents, Italians were depicted as unintelligent, dirty, lazy, and prone to violence and criminality. Stereotypes associating Italians with the "Mafia" and the "Black Hand" were more common in the period before and after World War I than in the modern era of the "Godfather" movies. The view that Italians constituted an inferior and undesirable element would fuel the long campaign to terminate emigration from southern and eastern Europe that finally culminated with the racist immigration laws of 1921 and 1924, with their quota system that virtually ended mass immigration from Italy to the United States.

Vanzetti was described by Upton Sinclair as "an idealist if ever I knew one—a gentle, quiet, simple man, with a wonderful dream of justice for the working class and peace on earth; a dreamer and a religious man in the true sense of that word."

Belief in Italians' proclivity for violence and crime was reinforced by the widespread misperception that Italy produced an inordinate number of dangerous anarchists, the most feared subversives of the epoch. After Gaetano Bresci, an anarchist silk worker from Paterson, New Jersey, assassinated King Umberto of Italy in 1900—the last of four European heads of state felled by Italian anarchists since 1894—the *New York Evening Journal* proclaimed that "no matter where one hears of the life of some ruler or royal personage being attempted, one may always be sure to find that the assassin bears an Italian name."[11] Most Americans, like most Europeans, did not recognize the political nature of the *fin-de-siècle* assassinations. Rather, they lumped anarchist terrorists together with the criminally insane. This viewpoint had already been popularized and "scientifically" validated in the 1890s by the famous Italian criminologist Cesare Lombroso, whose quack theories deemed most anarchists to be innately criminal. *The New York Times* reflected this attitude, declaring after Bresci's deed that "a perversion of faculty, a criminal instinct or tendency to evil, unbalanced by a moral sense, a cerebral state amounts to disease, or something not far short of it, are the antecedent conditions of an assassination."[12]

In 1901, the assassination of President William McKinley by Leon Czolgosz, a self-professed anarchist of Polish extraction, demonstrated that Italians possessed no monopoly on political violence. Nevertheless, the deed crystallized the public's image of anarchists as maniacal sociopaths bent on destroying society. Theodore Roosevelt proclaimed that "the anarchist is the enemy of humanity, the enemy of all mankind, and his is a deeper degree of criminality than any other."[13] During the anarchist-labor scare of 1908–1909, the *Washington Post* demanded the death penalty for all anarchists, whether or not they had committed acts of violence, arguing that "an avowal of anarchy has been found to be equivalent to an intention to commit murder"; therefore, "an anarchist is, in fact, a murderer, even before he has done the deed."[14] Identifying anarchists with violence and criminality had now become automatic in American society.

Efforts to bar anarchists from immigrating to the United States and to deport those already settled resulted in the immigration laws of March 1903, February 1917, and October 1918, each more repressive than its predecessor. The immigration laws, the Espionage Act of June 1917, and the Sedition Act of May 1918, provided the federal government with the weapons needed to suppress foreign subversives and other internal enemies. Following America's declaration of war against Germany on April 7, 1917, federal and local authorities, assisted by superpatriotic organizations and giant corporations, launched a brutal campaign of repression that would continue for at least three years. Its ultimate objective was to suppress subversive political elements, cripple the labor movement, restrict immigration of undesirable ethnic groups, and enforce "100 percent Americanism" among the "new immigrants" whose traditional culture and lifestyle were considered alien and un-American. By the end of the war, the antiradical campaign intensified under the influence of President Woodrow Wilson and Attorney General A. Mitchell Palmer. During the so-called "Red Scare" of 1919–1920, the Constitution and Bill of Rights were systematically violated, as federal and local authorities across the nation raided the homes and offices of suspected radicals (most of them aliens) without search warrants, destroying office equipment, printing presses, and other private property. Over four thousand individuals were arrested and held in custody for weeks and months without due process. Many were marched in chains through city streets; hundreds were beaten, and more than a few were lynched by local vigilantes. Ultimately, around six hundred alien radicals were deported before the "deportations delirium" abated in 1921.

Together with the IWW, the Socialist Party of America, and the Russian Union of Workers, the Galleanisti were ranked at the top of the government's list of dangerous subversives, after having been selectively targeted by the Deportation Law of October 1918. The Justice Department deemed Galleani "the leading anarchist in the United States" and considered his newspaper *Cronaca Sovversiva* to be "the most rabid, seditious and anarchistic sheet published in this country."[15] Efforts to suppress Galleani's newspaper began soon after passage of the military conscription act of May 18, 1917. In an article entitled "Matricolati!" (Registrants!), Galleani issued an oblique warning to his followers not to register for the draft and to put themselves beyond the reach of the authorities. The following month, *Cronaca Sovversiva* was banned from the mails and its office in Lynn, Massachusetts, raided by federal agents. Galleani and his printer, Giovanni Eramo, were arrested and charged with conspiracy to obstruct the draft. Pleading guilty, Galleani and Eramo were fined $300 and $100, respectively. Although Galleani sought to sustain the life of his newspaper, first by irregular and then clandestine publication, *Cronaca Sovversiva* was effectively suppressed by July 1918.

Meanwhile, between the spring and fall of 1917, around sixty Galleanisti—including Sacco and Vanzetti—had heeded their leader's recommendation by taking refuge in Mexico. The purpose of their flight, however, was not merely avoidance of military service or imprisonment for draft resistance. Remaining at liberty would enable the Galleanisti to return to Italy and participate in the revolution they expected to erupt there, following the March 1917 revolution that overthrew czarism in Russia. Among the group in Mexico were several of the most militant Galleanisti: Umberto Postiglione, Emilio Coda, Giovanni Scussel, Mario Buda, Umberto Colaarossi, and Carlo Valdinoci, *Cronaca*'s publisher, who had eluded capture in June.

But Italy never erupted in social revolution as the anarchists and other leftists had hoped. So the Galleanisti in Mexico drifted back into the United States, fully anticipating a struggle with the American government, especially now that scores of their comrades were being arrested. Exercising necessary caution, Sacco and Vanzetti returned in September 1917 and led a semiclandestine existence for more than a year. Sacco found work as an edge-trimmer at the Three-K Shoe Company in Stoughton, Massachusetts, in November 1918, and Vanzetti began peddling fish in Plymouth in the spring of 1919. Both men resumed their political activities as associates of the Gruppo Autonomo of East Boston, despite the risk of arrest and deportation. By now, they must have suspected that their identities were known to the Justice Department because a federal raid of *Cronaca Sovversiva*'s office in February 1918 had uncovered more than 3,000 mailing labels with names and addresses.

The government's determination to eliminate the "Red Menace" had increased after the war ended, as economic recession, a wave of major strikes, and official propaganda fueled America's paranoia about revolution. Indeed, "Red Scare" of 1919–1920 would mark the height of antiradical hysteria and the nadir of civil liberties in America. Now equipped with the immigration law of October 1918, which was specifically tailored to deal with the Italian anarchists, the federal government escalated its campaign of repression, deporting Galleani and eight of his closest comrades on June 24, 1919. This last act of repression virtually guaranteed a counterreaction from the Galleanisti.

Following his teachings on revolutionary violence, some sixty of Galleani's disciples, including most of those who had gone to Mexico, embarked upon a campaign of retaliatory terrorism that began in October 1917 and continued intermittently for the next three years. The chief protagonists of the campaign included the movement's principal men of action: Valdinoci, Buda, Coda, Scussel, and Nicola Recchi among others. Sacco and Vanzetti were probably peripheral players in this bombing conspiracy, but their specific activities have not been determined. The Galleanisti rarely practiced indiscriminate terrorism. Believing themselves locked in class warfare with the state and capitalism, their principal targets—aside from famous symbols of capitalism like John D. Rockefeller and J.P. Morgan—were mainly judges, prosecutors, legislators, and other politicians who had played a significant role in the suppression of radicals, antimilitarists, and labor leaders during and after the war. Intended for delivery on May 1, 1919, some thirty package bombs were mailed to these prominent personages. However, with the exception of one explosion that caused serious injury to a maid rather than the intended target, none of the bombs reached their destination. Some thirty bombs in all were intercepted after an alert postal clerk in New York remembered a number of packages resembling the one described in a newspaper account of the first bombing. Sixteen of the package bombs had been set aside because they lacked sufficient postage! Growing more determined, the Galleanisti carried out another series of bombings on

The only reason given for their arrest was that they were "suspicious characters."

June 2, 1919, this time planting the devices at the doorstep of their intended victims. Within an hour of midnight, explosions took place in Boston, New York, Paterson, Philadelphia, Pittsburgh, and Washington. Property damage was substantial, but fatalities were limited to one security guard and one perpetrator, Carlo Valdinoci, blown to pieces together with the Washington, D.C. home of Attorney General A. Mitchell Palmer, the chief architect of the "Red Scare."

The bombing of Palmer's home set into motion a chain of events that led eventually to the arrest of Sacco and Vanzetti. A leaflet entitled "Plain Words," declaring the intentions of the "American Anarchists" to resist repression with violence, was found at the scene of Palmer's home and other bomb sites on June 2, 1919. In fact, the leaflet had been written by the Galleanisti, and after a lengthy search aided by Italian spies planted in the movement, the Justice Department's Bureau of Investigation, headed by J. Edgar Hoover, traced the leaflet to a Brooklyn print shop, where two Galleanisti, Roberto Elia and Andrea Salsedo, published the anarchist magazine *Domani* (Tomorrow). The two Galleanisti were taken into custody on February 25, 1920, and held incommunicado for several weeks at the Justice Department's offices on Park Row in New York. Beaten repeatedly, Salsedo finally revealed what he knew about the bomb conspiracy; then, on May 3, he jumped (radicals believed he was pushed) to his death, evidently in despair over having betrayed his comrades.

Knowing from the daily press that Salsedo had named names, the Galleanisti scrambled to hide any material that might identify them as anarchists. On the night of May 5, 1920, Sacco and Vanzetti, together with their comrades Mario Buda (alias Mike Boda) and Riccardo Orciani, arrived at Simon Johnson's garage, where Boda had previously left his Overland for repairs. The men would later claim that Buda's car was needed to transport anarchist literature, which they had been advised to hide by Carlo Tresca, the anarchist editor of *Il Martello* (The Hammer) in New York. However, if literature was indeed the material they wished to hide, it is very possible that the incriminating bomb manual, *La Salute é in Voi*, was included among the usual propaganda pamphlets and books. Or, as some writers have speculated, their real mission that night might have been to hide dynamite.

In either case, when the four anarchists arrived, Johnson—as previously arranged with Bridgewater Police Chief Michael Stewart—informed them that the vehicle was missing its license plates and should not be driven, while his wife went next door to telephone the police. Unaware that they had just sprung a trap, Buda and Orciani departed on the motorcycle they had driven to the garage. Sacco and Vanzetti walked away on foot to board the Bridgewater-Brockton trolley at around 9:40 P.M.: A half-hour later, they were arrested on the trolley by Brockton police officer Michael Connolly. When searched, both men were found to be carrying weapons and an assortment of ammunition: Sacco a .32 Colt automatic, Vanzetti a .38 Harrington and Richardson revolver. The only reason given for their arrest was that they were "suspicious characters." Later that night, Sacco and Vanzetti were interrogated by Chief Stewart, who questioned them about their comrades and their political affiliations and beliefs. Both men denied knowing Buda or Ferruccio Coacci, another comrade in their group, and they lied when asked whether or not they were anarchists or communists. The next day Sacco and Vanzetti were interrogated by Frederick G. Katzmann, the district attorney for Norfolk and Plymouth counties, whose questions were largely routine and nonspecific as to the reason for their arrest. Still suspecting that their arrest was politically motivated, they again provided false and evasive answers. Sacco and Vanzetti were only partly correct in assessing their plight. That the two men were anarchists definitely had accounted for their becoming suspects in the eyes of the authorities; however, the crimes for which Sacco and Vanzetti would soon be indicted did not involve political activities.

Thursday, April 15, 1920, was payday at the Slater and Morrill shoe factory in South Braintree, Massachusetts. A few minutes after 3:00 P.M., as the paymaster, Frederick Parmenter, and his guard, Alessandro Berardelli, approached the factory carrying a the payroll of $15,776, two men who had been standing by a fence opened fire on them with pistols, killing Berardelli outright and mortally wounding Parmenter. The assailants grabbed the money bags, fired several shots at the factory windows and a nearby observer, jumped into an awaiting car containing two or three confederates, and then sped away. The entire shooting and escape transpired in less than one minute.

State police and Pinkerton detectives were immediately summoned to investigate, but they uncovered no clues suggesting the identity of the perpetrators. Three weeks later Chief Stewart developed his own theory, attributing the South Braintree crime to Italian anarchists. Suspicious of "foreigners," like many second-generation Irish-American policemen in Massachusetts, Stewart epitomized the law-enforcement officer who considered anarchism synonymous with criminality. When he and other policemen examined an abandoned automobile believed to be the getaway car for the South Braintree holdup, Chief Stewart declared to his fellow officers that "the men who did this job knew no God."[16] Since most radicals were atheists, ipso facto the perpetrators must have been radicals. Chief Stewart considered himself an expert on the subject, because he had been involved in rounding up alien radicals for deportation, one of them an Italian anarchist named Ferrucio Coacci. On the night of April 16—one day after the robbery and murder—an immigration official sent

"consciousness of guilt"

"radicals to be watched"

to conduct Coacci to the Immigration Service for processing found him with suitcases packed and anxious to depart. He also seemed unconcerned about the wife and children he would have to leave behind. Now suspicious of Coacci, Stewart learned that the deportee shared his house with another Italian anarchist, Mario Buda, who kept an automobile in a garage near Bridgewater, the scene of a botched holdup of the L.Q. White Shoe Co. on December 24, 1919, at which shots were exchanged but no one injured. Chief Stewart, meanwhile, had leaped to the conclusion that a gang of Italian anarchists had committed both the Bridgewater and the South Braintree crimes. And since Sacco and Vanzetti had been seen in Buda's company on the night of May 5, they, too, must have been members of the anarchist gang. Furthermore, since eyewitnesses had seen as many as five men in the getaway car, Chief Stewart deduced that Sacco, Vanzetti, Buda, Coacci, and Orciani comprised the gang. District Attorney Katzmann immediately accepted Chief Stewart's theory of Italian anarchist highwaymen as an incontrovertible fact. Their lies and possession of weapons was positive proof for Katzmann that Sacco and Vanzetti had exhibited "consciousness of guilt" on the night of their arrest. For the next seven years, Katzmann never wavered in his belief that Sacco and Vanzetti were guilty. He refused to investigate any leads pointing to other culprits and ignored all evidence supporting their innocence. On the contrary, in pursuit of a conviction, Katzmann proved himself a ruthless and unscrupulous prosecutor, doing whatever was necessary to achieve his objective, even if it meant trampling justice in the process.

In his search for proof that Sacco and Vanzetti committed the Bridgewater and South Braintree crimes, District Attorney Katzmann requested the Justice Department to determine whether the Italian anarchists in New York had received any large sums of money. Justice Department agents in New York, by means of informers, learned that no large sums of cash had been received by local anarchists. This discovery strengthened the conclusion already reached by Justice Department agents in Boston, namely, that professional highwaymen, not anarchists, were responsible for the crimes. Belief in the innocence of Sacco and Vanzetti, however, did not prevent the Justice Department from colluding with District Attorney Katzmann to obtain a conviction. The Justice Department was very interested in the Sacco-Vanzetti case. Both of the anarchists were listed in its files as "radicals to be watched;" moreover, they were suspected of being comrades of Carlo Valdinoci, the dead bomber of Attorney General Palmer's house. Hereafter, the Justice Department assisted Katzmann in several ways: keeping him informed of Italian anarchist activities, placing a spy in a cell next to Sacco's in Dedham jail, and infiltrating one or more informants into the Sacco-Vanzetti Defense Committee formed after their arrest.

Although the Stewart-Katzmann theory presupposed that a gang of five Italian anarchists had committed the crimes, prosecuting the comrades of Sacco and Vanzetti's would prove impossible. Coacci already had been deported. A search of his former domicile in West Bridgewater revealed nothing, as did an examination of his trunk, conducted by Italian authorities upon his arrival in Italy. Orciani had a strong alibi: time-clock records substantiated his presence at work on the days of both crimes. Buda, who stood only five feet tall and had a conspicuously large nose, fitted none of the descriptions offered by eyewitnesses. No matter. Buda did not wait for the outcome of Katzman's investigation. After Sacco and Vanzetti were arrested, he went underground for several months and then escaped to Italy, but not before exacting terrible revenge for the prosecution of his comrades—the Wall Street bombing of September 16, 1920.

Thus, only two members of the alleged Italian anarchist gang were vulnerable to prosecution. Proving that Sacco and Vanzetti had committed both crimes, however, posed a serious problem for Katzmann. Physical evidence was meager. The stolen payroll had disappeared without a trace. Fingerprints taken from the suspected getaway car did not match those of Sacco or Vanzetti, an important fact Katzmann withheld from the defense. Sacco's confirmed presence at work on December 24, 1919, gave him a solid alibi for the Bridgewater crime. On the day of the South Braintree crime, April 15, 1920, however, Sacco had missed work. He claimed to have visited the Italian Consulate in Boston that day, to apply for a passport. Vanzetti had difficulty establishing an alibi for both dates because he was self-employed; however, the evidence linking him to the South Braintree crime was negligible. This did not deter Katzmann, who wanted to obtain a double conviction for the capital crime. The strategy he devised was to prosecute Vanzetti first for the lesser of the two crimes. Although this was contrary to established procedure in Massachusetts, Katzmann reasoned that a conviction for the Bridgewater crime would bring Vanzetti into court for the South Braintree crime as a proven criminal, a fact that would be known to the local community and destroy any presumption of innocence the jurors might have entertained.

Vanzetti was brought to trial in Plymouth on June 22, 1920, charged with assault with intent to murder and assault with intent to rob for the Bridgewater attempt. He was defended by John P. Vahey and James M. Graham, Massachusetts attorneys hired for their presumed influence within the local legal establishment. The presiding judge was Webster Thayer, a Yankee bigot who saw himself as St. George in black robes, doing his patriotic duty by battling the red dragon. Thayer's prejudice against foreigners and radicals had already been demonstrated that April, when he angrily censured a Norfolk jury for acquitting an admitted anarchist, Serge Zagroff, charged under the Criminal Anarchy Statute for advocating the violent overthrow of the government. Thayer's hatred for alien radicals would spell doom for Sacco and Vanzetti.

During the six months that passed between the Bridegwater attempt and the Plymouth trial, eyewitnesses to the crime proved highly malleable in the hands of Chief Stewart, Katzmann, and his assistants. Indeed, the prosecution might just as well have provided them with a written script. Descriptions of the perpetrators furnished at Plymouth bore little resemblance to those given to the Pinkerton detectives immediately after the robbery attempt in Bridgewater. The "short croppy mustache" reported initially now became long and droopy, as they identified Vanzetti. A newsboy who had caught a glimpse of one of the criminals "knew by the way he ran he was a foreigner." The getaway vehicle identified first as a Hudson now became a Buick, because the abandoned car Chief Stewart believed had served as the getaway vehicle at South Braintree was a Buick. Vanzetti's lawyers could not contradict these newly tailored accounts because the Pinkerton reports had not been furnished to the defense. The only witnesses who testified in Vanzetti's behalf were sixteen Italians, who swore mostly through interpreters that they had seen him selling eels (a Christmas Eve specialty among Italians) on the day of the Bridgewater attempt. Among them was Beltrando Brini, a thirteen-year-old boy who had accompanied Vanzetti on his rounds that day. But the Italian witnesses made no impression on the Anglo-Saxon jurors. On the contrary, Katzmann's openly contemptuous attitude toward them reinforced the belief—clearly shared by the judge and the jurors—that "all Wops stick together." Also weighing heavily against Vanzetti was his failure to testify in his own defense, a decision influenced by the fear that his appearance in the dock would give Katzmann the opportunity to expose his radical beliefs to the jury. At the Plymouth trial, the issue of Vanzetti's anarchist beliefs was not flagrantly exploited by Katzmann, as it was during the Dedham trial that followed, but the prosecutor succeeded nonetheless in making the jury aware that Vanzetti was a subversive.[17] Judge Thayer, too, conveyed this information by declaring in his charge to the jury that "the defendant's ideals are cognate with crime."[18] Predictably, on July 1, 1920, the jury found Vanzetti guilty of all charges. His lawyers did not appeal the verdict.

Judge Thayer's bias against Vanzetti also was revealed during the sentencing phase of the proceedings. First he ensured that the guilty verdict would stand. During the trial, he and Katzmann became aware that the jurors had acted improperly by surreptitiously opening shotgun shells found on Vanzetti at the time of his arrest. (They believed that buckshot as opposed to birdshot would indicate

"the defendant's ideals are cognate with crime."

whether Vanzetti's intent had been to commit murder as well as robbery.) But neither the judge nor the prosecutor revealed the jurors' transgression to the defense, knowing full well that evidence tampering constituted grounds for a mistrial. Furthermore, at sentencing, Thayer "filed" (quashed) the jurors' conviction of Vanzetti on the charge of assault with intent to commit murder, a clever maneuver that precluded any future appeal on these grounds because the issue of the shotgun shells was now moot. Finally, on the second charge of assault with intent to commit robbery, Thayer condemned Vanzetti to a term of twelve to fifteen years, a sentence that greatly exceeded the usual term of imprisonment for that crime, especially in the case of a defendant who had no previous criminal record.

With Vanzetti now branded as a common criminal, Katzmann proceeded on September 11, 1920, to indict him and Sacco for the South Braintree robbery and murders. Because his case against the two anarchists was still weak, however, Katzmann left the trial date open in order to have more time to find or fabricate more evidence. He had already begun preparations for a frame-up two days after Vanzetti's conviction, when he removed Captain William H. Proctor, senior officer of the Massachusetts State Police, as the head of the South Braintree investigation, replacing him with Chief Stewart of Bridgewater. An officer with the state police for twenty-three years and a captain for sixteen, Proctor had far more expertise than Stewart, a rural policeman whose experience with serious crime was virtually nil. But Proctor had concluded from his investigation that Sacco and Vanzetti were innocent, whereas Stewart remained unalterably convinced of their guilt. Together, they made an effective team. Neither would investigate a single lead suggesting innocence; neither was burdened by ethical scruples in their zealous pursuit of a conviction.

Meanwhile, the Sacco-Vanzetti Defense Committee, correctly interpreting Vanzetti's conviction and Thayer's harsh sentence as a portent of worse to come, decided to hire a new legal team for the next trial. Aldino Felicani, the committee's treasurer, turned to his anarchist friend Carlo Tresca in New York for advice. Tresca and his lover, Elizabeth Gurley Flynn, the IWW's former strike leader, recommended Fred H. Moore, a socialist lawyer from Spokane who had been involved in a number of labor cases for the IWW, including the successful defense of Joe Ettor and Arturo Giovannitti in Lawrence in 1912. For the Lawrence proceedings, Moore had functioned as a "leg lawyer" or investigator, whereas in the Sacco-Vanzetti trial he would serve as chief counsel.

The Sacco-Vanzetti Defense Committee had no way of knowing at the time that selecting Moore would prove to be a disastrous mistake.

Everything about Moore's personality and demeanor, from his long hair and sandals to his habit of taking naps in his shirt-sleeves outside the courthouse, offended the starched-collar club that comprised the local legal community. But intolerance of Moore's bohemian life-style soon escalated into outrage and hatred aimed at Sacco and Vanzetti. Basing his strategy on the premise that justice was unattainable in a capitalist court, Moore would politicize the case by putting the Massachusetts judicial system on trial before the bar of world opinion, and demonstrating that the real issue behind the prosecution was not robbery and murder but the defendants' anarchist beliefs and the desire of local officials to assist the federal government's crusade against radicalism. His strategy succeeded brilliantly in so far as it transformed the case into an international *cause célèbre* supported by liberals, intellectuals, labor unions, radicals, and even conservatives devoted to upholding justice. However, the avalanche of protest and condemnation that descended upon the political authorities and judicial establishment of Massachusetts provoked a furious reaction from conservative and patriotic forces within the Commonwealth and the rest of the country, spurring them to rally in defense of traditional institutions and the "American way of life" against a mortal threat perceived as emanating from foreigners and Reds. Ultimately, defense of the status quo would require that the Commonwealth of Massachusetts sacrifice Sacco and Vanzetti for what Europeans called *raison d'état*—reasons of state.

This viewpoint was certainly shared by Judge Thayer, who wrote to Judge John Aiken, the Chief Justice of Massachusetts and a fellow Dartmouth alumnus, requesting that he be appointed presiding magistrate at the trial of Sacco and Vanzetti. Although Thayer's request was highly irregular, Aiken appointed him trial judge because he sensed the importance of the case and wanted the right man on the bench. To Thayer he wrote: "I am assigning you to hear the most important murder case tried in Massachusetts since the last century, if not in all time."[19] Thayer's appointment precluded any chance of a fair trial. Before the jury was even impaneled, Thayer developed a loathing for Moore that was palpable. Determined to eliminate anyone he considered a "capitalist," (i.e., middle-class), Moore rejected scores of potential jurors on the most trivial of pretexts, infuriating Judge Thayer. After a contentious session, Judge Thayer stated to a friend, "I'll show them that no long-haired anarchist from California can run this court."[19] On a similar occasion, during one of

To Thayer he wrote: "I am assigning you to hear the most important murder case tried in Massachusetts since the last century

his many moments of pique, Thayer told reporters, "You wait till I give my charge to the jury. I'll show 'em."[21]

Shortly before the trial began, three local attorneys, John, Jeremiah, and Thomas McAnarney, were hired by the Defense Committee to assist Moore. The McAnarneys immediately became apprehensive about the blatant antagonism existing between Judge Thayer and Moore. They tried to have Moore replaced by William G. Thompson, a conservative Boston lawyer, and asked him first to observe the interaction between the judge and chief counsel. A dismayed Thompson reported: "It wasn't what he [Thayer] said, it was his manner of saying it. It looked perfectly straight on the record; he was too clever to do otherwise. I sat there for a while and I told John McAnarney 'Your goose is cooked.' You will never in this world get these men acquitted. The judge is going to convict these two men and see that nothing gets into the record; he is going to keep his records straight and you have no chance.'"[22] But Thompson did not replace Moore until 1924, when the fate of Sacco and Vanzetti had already been sealed.

The trial of Sacco and Vanzetti for robbery and murder began in the Dedham courthouse on May 31, 1921, amidst lurid publicity and extraordinary security. On the first day of the trial and everyday thereafter, the defendants were marched in handcuffs from the jail to the courthouse under the vigilant eyes of well-armed state police and deputies who lined the streets and surrounded the courthouse. The message this small army transmitted was unequivocal: Sacco and Vanzetti were dangerous men, precisely the impression District Attorney Katzmann wanted Massachusetts citizens and selected jurors to retain. Up to now, seven months after the indictment, Katzmann still lacked a strong case with which to convict Sacco and Vanzetti fairly. No matter. To achieve his ends, Katzmann would violate prosecutorial procedure, suppress and withhold exculpatory evidence, tailor testimony of prosecution witnesses and experts, and even suborn perjury. In fact, Katzmann and his associates may even have gone so far as to manufacture incriminating evidence.

Katzmann's case rested upon three categories of evidence:

1. eyewitness testimony,
2. ballistics tests, and
3. "consciousness of guilt."

This evidence was supplemented with as much prejudicial information about the defendants' radical beliefs and unpatriotic behavior as he could interject into the proceedings.

Eyewitness testimony is problematic under the best of circumstances. It becomes almost worthless, however, when the prosecution relies upon improper procedures and manipulates the witnesses. For starters, Sacco and Vanzetti were never properly observed by eyewitnesses to the Bridgewater and South Braintree crimes. During the first few days subsequent to their arrest, they were displayed not in a line-up, as was customary even in 1920, but individually and together. They were forced to mimic the criminal behavior of the perpetrators by pulling up their coat collars and pointing their fingers, as if holding a gun. Testimony offered by several witnesses at Dedham revealed how remarkably acute the human memory can become after fourteen months, as they now identified Sacco and/or Vanzetti with absolute certainty, despite having been unable to do so just hours and days after the crimes were committed. The defense, however, could not detect the discrepancies between what these witnesses had reported to the Pinkerton detectives in April 1920, and what they were now saying in court at Dedham. The prosecution had withheld these reports precisely for that reason. It is also indisputable that witnesses had been directly coached and cajoled by Katzman and Stewart.

The alibis offered by Sacco and Vanzetti were highly plausible but not easily substantiated, at least not to the satisfaction of an Anglo-Saxon and Irish jury. Vanzetti claimed he had been selling fish on April 15, 1920, just as he had been on December 31, 1919. Thirteen witnesses testified that they had seen him in Plymouth selling fish that day. Since most of his corroborating witnesses were Italian, however, Katzmann subjected them to brutal cross-examination calculated to make them appear untrustworthy. An additional thirty-one witnesses testified that Vanzetti was not one of the bandits they had seen commit the crime. Sacco's alibi rested on his claim that on April 15, 1920, he had gone to the Italian Consulate in Boston to obtain a passport to return to Italy with his family. His visit was corroborated by several Italian comrades and acquaintances, as well as by a deposition from Giuseppe Andrower, a former clerk at the Italian Consulate who remembered that, on April 15, he could not process Sacco's request for a passport because he had brought an unsuitable, oversized family photograph. Besides his usual condescension toward Italians, Katzmann vigorously challenged the credibility of Sacco's defense witnesses by demonstrating their inability to associate specific dates with various inane activities of everyday living. How could they be certain, therefore, of having seen Sacco on April 15, 1920.

Evidence concerning weapons possession and ballistics was probably a more important determinant of the final verdict than eyewitness testimony. Since the four bullets extracted from Berardelli's body and the two from Parmenter's were all .32 caliber, the prosecution could not claim that Vanzetti's .38 caliber Harrington and Richardson revolver was one of the murder weapons, and during his opening statement Assistant District Attorney Harold Williams did not try to link the weapon with the crime. Failure to do so, however, would mean that the prosecution had no physical evidence to incriminate Vanzetti, thereby making an already weak case against him even more feeble. But a few weeks into the trial, the prosecution offered a clever theory, claiming that Vanzetti's revolver had been taken from the dead guard Berardelli during the shooting. No matter that none of the eyewitnesses had seen any of the bandits pick up Berardelli's gun, or that the caliber of his weapon was uncertain, or that there was no proof the guard was even carrying a weapon that day, or that the serial number of Berardelli's revolver matched Vanzetti's, G-82581. The prosecution never furnished the serial number of Berardelli's weapon, preferring to allow the jury to assume a match in the absence of corroborating evidence. However, a memorandum written by Chief Stewart on February 18, 1920, but not released by the Massachusetts State Police until 1977, revealed that Stewart's investigation had indeed discovered the true caliber and serial number of Berardelli's weapon: a .32 caliber Harrington and Richardson, serial No. 394717. This exculpatory evidence was never furnished to the defense during the trial nor to the Lowell Committee that investigated the proceedings shortly before the execution in 1927.

Katzmann's handling of the ballistic evidence was equally unethical. Tests had determined that five of the six bullets taken from the bodies of Berardelli and Parmenter could not have been fired from the guns Sacco and Vanzetti were carrying at the time of their arrest. Only the famous Bullet III which killed Berardelli was a possibility. Two experts for the defense, James Burns and J. Henry Fitzgerald, testified that there was no match between Sacco's gun and the fatal bullet. One expert for the prosecution, Charles Van Amburgh, testified that he was "inclined to believe" that Sacco's gun was the murder weapon. A second expert for the prosecution, Captain William Proctor of the Massachusetts State Police, did not believe that Sacco's gun had fired Bullet III. He was certain only that the bullet had been fired from a Colt .32 automatic. Nevertheless, at the Dedham trial, when asked whether Bullet III had been fired from Sacco's weapon, Captain Proctor responded: "My opinion is that it is consistent with being fired by that pistol."[23] As he later acknowledged in an affidavit supporting an appeal, the wording of his statement had been prearranged with Katzmann. But the defense failed to request that Proctor elaborate further about his opinion. Thus Katzmann's subterfuge went undetected, and the judge and jurors concluded that Sacco's Colt was indeed the murder weapon. Katzmann's willingness to manipulate ballistics evidence may not have ended with Proctor. Several authorities have advanced the theory that the prosecution fired a test bullet from Sacco's gun and substituted it for the real fatal bullet, which had been fired from a different weapon. This theory cannot be proven beyond a doubt, but given all the other instances of the prosecution's willingness to distort the facts, it is entirely plausible.

The third category of evidence was "consciousness of guilt." As explained earlier, Sacco and Vanzetti were carrying weapons when arrested, lied during the first round of interrogations, and appeared generally "suspicious" to the authorities. The key question, of course, is whether "consciousness of guilt" reflected their knowledge of having committed the South Braintree murders or their fear that they had been arrested because they were anarchists. Caught between the proverbial rock and a hard place, Sacco and Vanzetti risked certain conviction if they remained silent about their activities on April 15, 1920; however, to admit that they were anarchists and had been trying to hide subversive literature (much less dynamite) might prove equally fatal. John F. Moors, a prominent Boston banker and a Sacco-Vanzetti supporter, thus described the atmosphere of prejudice and fear that pervaded Massachusetts: "the hysteria against 'the reds' was so great, at the time when these men were convicted, that even the most substantial bankers in this city were carried away to the extent of paying for full-page advertisements about the red peril."[24]

Because the defense had opened up the question of their radicalism, Sacco and Vanzetti had not only to explain the cause of their suspicious behavior but also to submit themselves to cross-examination on this issue by Katzmann. This provided the district attorney with the opportunity to crucify the defendants and clinch his case. On the one hand, Katzmann was able to argue against all logic that the suspicious behavior and lies of the defendants had no connection with their anarchist beliefs, representing instead their consciousness of guilt in regard to the South Braintree crime. On the other hand, Katzmann was able to depict Sacco and Vanzetti as unpatriotic and ungrateful foreigners, who repaid American hospitality by evading the draft and engaging in subversive activity. In his final summation, Katzmann ended on a patriotic note, exhorting the jurors to close ranks against the enemy represented by Sacco and Vanzetti: "Gentlemen of the jury, do your duty. Do it like men. Stand together, you men of Norfolk!"[25] Assessing Katzmann's performance, Harvard law professor and future Supreme Court Justice, Felix Frankfurter, wrote in 1927: "by systematic exploitation of the defendants' alien blood, their imperfect knowledge of English, their unpopular social views, and their opposition to the war, the District Attorney invoked against them a riot of political passion and patriotic sentiment; and the trial judge connived at—one had almost written, cooperated in—the process."[26]

Attorney William Thompson's prediction regarding Judge Thayer was realized to the letter. He had been careful throughout the trial not to commit any errors of law which might provide the basis for a new trial, although in numerous ways not evident in the trial record, his prejudice against Sacco and Vanzetti had been abundantly clear. Judge Thayer's charge to the jury amounted to a total endorsement of the prosecution's case, with similar reliance on the emotions of patriotism and nativism. The flag was unfurled with his opening words: "The Commonwealth of Massachusetts called upon you to render a most important service Although you knew that such service would be arduous, painful, and tiresome, yet you, like the true soldier, responded to that call in the spirit of supreme American loyalty. There is no better word in the English language than 'loyalty.'"[27]

Thereafter, Judge Thayer essentially recapitulated the prosecution's case. He ignored all the alibi evidence crucial to the defense, focusing instead on incriminating evidence most likely to sway the jurors. His discussion of the ballistics tests indicated that he had misunderstood Captain Proctor's cryptically worded testimony, declaring to the jury that "it was his [Sacco's] pistol that fired the bullet that caused the death of Berardelli."[28] Most important, however, was his discussion of "consciousness of guilt," which took up seven pages in the transcript and supported Katzmann's version. Thayer's mission to convict Sacco and Vanzetti was fulfilled on July 12, 1921, when the jury returned a verdict of guilty on all counts after only five hours of deliberation.

The legal struggle to save Sacco and Vanzetti did not cease with their conviction. Between 1921 and 1927, eight motions for a new trial were filed. In many states, the evidence revealed by several of the motions would probably have resulted in a new trial. However, the judicial system of Massachusetts (later changed because of the Sacco-Vanzetti case) required that motions for a new trial be heard by the same judge who had presided at the defendant's conviction.

The first motion, filed a few days after the trial , asserted that the jury's verdict was not supported by the evidence and had resulted from prejudice. Judge Thayer heard the motion on November 5 and denied it on December 24, 1921, declaring that "I cannot—as I must if I disturb these verdicts—announce to the world that these twelve jurors violated the sanctity of their oaths, threw to the four winds of bias and prejudice their honor, judgment, reason and conscience...."[29] Better to send Sacco and Vanzetti to the electric chair than besmirch the reputation of Yankee jurors.

The next five supplementary motions were filed in rapid succession by Fred Moore. Although mediocre as a trial lawyer, Moore was highly adept as an investigator, tracking down witnesses and uncovering new evidence. The first supplementary motion—the Ripley motion—was filed on November 8, 1921, the result of Jeremiah McAnarney's having learned that the jury foreman at the Dedham trial, Walter H. Ripley, a former chief of police and firemen in Quincy, had violated procedure by bringing three cartridges into the jury room to compare them with five cartridges found on Vanzetti.

The second supplementary motion—the Gould-Pelzer motion—filed on May 4, 1922, revealed that Roy E. Gould, a peddler, had stood closer to the bandits at South Braintree than any other witness, so close that one of the bandits fired a shot at him which grazed his overcoat. Gould had been interviewed by police and stated categorically that neither Sacco or Vanzetti resembled the man who shot at him. Katzmann failed to relate this bit of exculpatory evidence to the defense and never summoned Gould to testify at the trial. Louis Pelser, a young shoe worker at the Rice-Hutchins factory, claimed he had looked out the window after hearing shots and saw the gunman who killed Berardelli. Now, two years later, Pelser signed an affidavit obtained by Moore, stating that he had told police right after the crime that he could not positively identify the gunman. He further maintained that Assistant District Attorney Williams pressured him to identify Sacco as the murderer. At the trial Pelser heeded the prosecution's bidding, testifying that "I wouldn't say he is the man, but he is the dead image of the man I saw."[30] Pelser's credibility was also undermined by three of his fellow workers, who informed the defense that he had not been looking out the window at the time of the shooting. But two days after giving his statement to Moore, Pelser wrote to the district attorney, repudiating everything he had just related, claiming he had been drunk at the time.

The third supplementary motion, filed on July 22, 1922, pertained to Carlos Goodridge, a career criminal who testified at Dedham that when he emerged from a nearby poolroom to investigate the shooting, a man he identified as Sacco pointed a gun at him. Four of his friends, however, related that Goodridge had told them that he could not identify the man. Moore also learned that Goodridge had been granted probation for a larceny charge pending in the Dedham court. That Katzmann had treated Goodridge with leniency in exchange for incriminating testimony against Sacco was obvious.

The fourth supplementary motion, filed on September 11, 1922, pertained to Lola Andrews, the only prosecution witness who actually had spoken with one of the bandits. Seeking employment at the Rice & Hutchins factory, Andrews asked directions to the factory from one of the bandits, who was feigning repairs under the getaway car while awaiting the payroll. At the trial Andrews identified Sacco as the man with whom she had spoken. Moore, having learned that Andrews had a shady past she wished to keep secret, charged that the district attorney's office intimidated her into identifying Sacco. Andrews subsequently retracted her allegations, claiming that Moore had coerced her with threats to reveal her past.

The fifth supplementary motion, filed on April 30, 1923, pertained to Albert H. Hall and Augustus H. Gill, ballistics experts who, using a high-magnification compound microscope, had concluded in 1923 that Sacco's gun had not fired the fatal Bullet III and its matching shell. Experts retained by Harold Williams, who had replaced Katzmann as district attorney, countered their findings, one of them, Captain Van Amburgh, asserting that he was more positive now than he had been during the trial. The issue was complicated further when someone, Hamilton or Van Amburgh, switched the barrel of Sacco's gun with another Colt .32 that was being examined with it. The defense charged that the prosecution had made the switch in order to prevent additional test firings. The prosecution claimed that the defense had switched barrels in order to secure a new trial.

The issue of ballistics testing was raised again on November 5, 1923, when the defense filed its last supplementary motion, exposing the collusion between Captain Proctor and District Attorney Katzmann. Proctor asserted that prior to the trial he and Katzmann had "repeatedly" discussed the manner of how he would testify about Sacco's gun. According to Proctor, he had "repeatedly" told the prosecutor that he could not identify Sacco's gun as the murder weapon if so asked directly in court. Katzmann could only say in rebuttal that he had not asked Proctor "repeatedly" to identify Sacco's Colt as the gun that killed Berardelli.

On October 1, 1923, the defense filed a supplement to the Ripley motion, otherwise known as the Daly motion. The motion asserted that after being called for jury duty, Ripley had discussed the case with his friend William H. Daly. Daly did not believe the "Guineas were guilty," to which Ripley allegedly replied, "Damn them, they ought to hang them anyway."[32]

That the prosecution might have engaged in subornation of perjury, suppression of exculpatory evidence, and unethical collusion with police authorities made no impression whatever on Judge Thayer. He willfully rejected any suggestion that the state might have crossed the border of legality or erred by convicting the two anarchists. Indeed, Judge Thayer's determination to send Sacco and Vanzetti to the electric chair seemed to increase with each passing year and every new motion filed. He denied all supplementary motions for a new trial on October 1, 1924. A few days later, while attending a football game at Dartmouth, his alma mater, Judge Thayer boasted to Professor James Richardson, "Did you see what I did with those anarchistic bastards the other day. I guess that will hold them for a while. Let them go to the Supreme Court now and see what they can get out of them."

The slowness and the frustration of the appeals process took a psychological toll on Sacco and Vanzetti. Sacco suffered greatly from his confinement. Whereas Vanzetti, as a convicted felon, was able to work in prison and occupy the rest of his time reading and writing, Sacco was prohibited from engaging in labor of any sort and could not find solace in books. For a man who had thrived on work and social contact, the enforced idleness and loneliness of Dedham jail were heavy burdens. More than anything, Sacco missed his wife Rosina and their two children, Dante and Inez (born during his imprisonment). Nor did he derive any hope from the appeals process, believing more deeply than Vanzetti that anarchists could never receive justice from a capitalist legal system. Starting on February 14, 1923, Sacco began a hunger strike, which lasted more than a month. Physical weakness only aggravated his mental state. Examined by psychiatrists, Sacco was judged to be mentally disturbed, with suicidal behavior and episodes of paranoiac delusion. His physical and mental condition continued to deteriorate, and on April

Indeed, Judge Thayer's determination to send Sacco and Vanzetti to the electric chair seemed to increase with each passing year and every new motion filed.

23, with the approval of Fred Moore, he was committed to the Bridgewater State Hospital for the Criminally Insane. Contact with other inmates, polishing floors, and tending a garden on the prison farm gradually restored Sacco's mental stability. On September 29, 1923, having been judged sane, Sacco was released from the state hospital and returned to Dedham jail.

Vanzetti, too, experienced an emotional breakdown. Having entertained greater hope for a new trial than Sacco, he became deeply depressed when Thayer denied all of the supplementary motions. He started exhibiting paranoiac behavior in jail and was committed to Bridgewater Hospital early in January 1925. He continued to act in this fashion until April, when he showed signs of returning to his normal self. He was certified sane and released from the hospital on May 25, 1925.

Meanwhile, the long simmering conflict between Sacco and Fred Moore had come to a head. Sacco and his wife Rosina had disliked Moore from the outset, and after his release from the state hospital (he and Rosina were furious when Moore signed the commitment papers), Sacco demanded that Moore withdraw from the case. Sacco's decision to be rid of Moore was heartily endorsed by the Italian anarchists of the defense committee, whose relationship with the attorney also had been strained from the start. Moore's strategy of politicizing the case required a great deal of money, as did his ongoing and relentless investigations. His incessant demands for more and more money antagonized the Italian anarchists on the defense committee, who, unlike Moore, were always mindful of the fact that the defense funds had came mainly from the contributions of thousands of poor workers. Furthermore, the defense committee anarchists, as well as Sacco and Vanzetti, were greatly disturbed by Moore's efforts to apprehend the real culprits. Helping Moore play a policeman's role seriously violated their antistatist beliefs. Finally, in August 1924, Moore yielded to Sacco's demand that he withdraw from the case.[33] But it was far too late to repair the damage Moore had done.

Moore's role as chief counsel was assumed in November 1924 by William G. Thompson, an aristocratic Boston conservative who took on the case because he wanted to prove that justice for two Italian anarchists was really possible in Massachusetts. Thompson completely rejected Moore's strategy of

His 25,000-word document cannot accurately be described otherwise than as a farrago of misquotations, misrepresentations, suppressions, and mutilations.

politicizing the case, preferring instead to put trust in the legal system and utilize its mechanism to save his clients. During the next three years, Thompson would be assisted by Arthur D. Hill, Herbert B. Ehrmann, and Michael A. Musmanno. Despite Thompson's Brahmin status, the anarchists on the defense committee reacted more positively to him than they ever had to Moore. Aldino Felicani, the defense committee's treasurer expressed the widely held belief that the trial might have ended differently if Thompson had been chief counsel from the beginning.

Thompson argued a new appeal (based on the first, second, and fifth supplementary motions) before the Supreme Judicial Court of Massachusetts in January 1926. In reality, he had no chance of success. Under the existing system, the Supreme Judicial Court considered only questions of law rather than the facts of the case, meaning that nothing short of discovering some egregious errors on Judge Thayer's parts could his rulings be reversed. Accordingly, on May 12, 1926, the Supreme Judicial Court of Massachusetts rejected Thompson's appeal and confirmed the convictions.

The disappointment caused by the ruling would have been crushing if a Dedham prisoner named Celestino Madeiros had not confessed to participating in the South Braintree robbery and murders. A young thief, awaiting a new trial for a murder he had committed while robbing a bank in Wrentham the previous year, Madeiros claimed to have been part of a gang of professional criminals that really committed the crime. When interviewed by Thompson, Madeiros furnished many details of the crime which tended to corroborate his story, but he refused to name his accomplices. That task of investigating Madeiros' story was assigned to Herbert B. Ehrmann, Thompson's young associate. Ehrmann concluded that the murders had been committed by a gang from Providence led by a hardened thug named Joe Morelli. Interviewed by Ehrmann in Levenworth Penitentiary, Morelli—who bore a striking resemblance to Sacco—denied all knowledge of the events. In 1931, however, Morelli boasted to attorney Morris Ernst that he and his gang had been responsible. The defense continued to believe in Morelli's guilt, especially after several eyewitnesses who previously identified Sacco now examined photos of Morelli and swore he was one of the bandits. Unfortunately, the new district attorney, Winfield M. Wilbar, was unwilling to conduct a thorough investigation of this alternative theory.

The Morelli gang theory and new revelations concerning Katzmann's collusion with the Justice Department formed the basis for

Thompson to file a seventh supplementary motion for a new trial. Affidavits from two former Justice Department agents in Boston, Fred J. Weyland and Lawrence Letherman, revealed that the Justice Department wanted to deport Sacco and Vanzetti, but was perfectly content to see them convicted of murder, despite believing them innocent. Weyland's affidavit stated that

> *... I am also thoroughly convinced, and always have been, and I believe that it is and always has been the opinion of such Boston agents of the Department of Justice as had any knowledge on the subject, that these men had nothing whatever to do with the South Braintree murders, and that their conviction was the result of co-operation between the Boston agents of the Department of Justice and the district attorney. It was the general opinion of the Boston agents of the Department of Justice having knowledge of the affair that the South Braintree crime was committed by a gang of professional highwaymen.*[34]

Former agent Letherman corroborated Weyand's allegation, adding in part:

> *The Department of Justice in Boston was anxious to get sufficient evidence against Sacco and Vanzetti to deport them, but never succeeded in getting the kind and amount required for that purpose. It was the opinion of the Department of Justice here that a conviction of Sacco and Vanzetti for murder would be one way of disposing of these two men.*[35]

Neither the Morelli gang theory nor the affidavits confirming collusion between the district attorney and the Justice Department made the slightest impression on Judge Thayer, who denied the motion on October 23, 1926. He dismissed Madeiros's confession on the grounds that he "is, without a doubt, a crook, a thief, a robber, a liar, a rum-runner, a 'bouncer' in a house of ill fame, a smuggler, and a man who has been convicted and sentenced to death."[36] As for the collusion between the district attorney and the Justice Department, Judge Thayer suggested that Thompson was suffering from "hysteria" for even suggesting such a thing, and that the Justice Department's secret files on Sacco and Vanzetti had "no present existence" because the department had refused to open them to the defense.[37] Judge Thayer's denial of this appeal outraged many legal experts. Professor Frankfurter, who was now the principal advisor to the defense, wrote the following:

> *I assert with deep regret, but without the slightest fear of disproof, that certainly in modern times Judge Thayer's opinion stands unmatched, happily, for discrepancies between what the record discloses and what the opinion conveys. His 25,000-word document cannot accurately be described otherwise than as a farrago of misquotations, misrepresentations, suppressions, and mutilations. The disinterested inquirer could not possibly derive from it a true knowledge of the new evidence that was submitted to him as the basis for a new trial.*[38]

Nevertheless, Thayer's denial of Thompson's motion was upheld by the Massachusetts Supreme Judicial Court on April 5, 1927. Four days later, in a Dedham courtroom surrounded by policemen armed with rifles, Sacco and Vanzetti would face their nemesis for one last time. In accordance with Anglo-Saxon legal procedure, Judge Thayer asked if Sacco and Vanzetti had anything to say before he pronounced sentence. Both defendants, in their fractured English, followed in the long tradition of anarchists pitted against the state, denouncing their conviction as a class decision and a travesty of justice. Sacco declared in part:

> *I never know, never heard, even read in history anything so cruel as this Court. After seven years prosecuting they still consider us guilty....*
>
> *I know the sentence will be always between two classes, the oppressed class and the rich class, and there will always be collision between one and the other. We fraternize the people with the books, with the literature. You persecute the people, tyrannize over them and kill them. We try the education of people always.... That is why I am here today on this bench, for having been the oppressed class. Well, you are the oppressor....*
>
> *You forget all the population that has been with us for seven years, to sympathize and give us all their energy and all their kindness. You do not care for them. Among that peoples and the comrades and the working class there is a big legion of intellectual people which have been with us for seven years, but to not commit the iniquitous sentence, but still the Court goes ahead....*
>
> *As I said before, Judge Thayer know all my life, and he know that I am never been guilty, never,—not yesterday nor today not forever.*[39]

Vanzetti spoke in the same defiant manner as Sacco:

> *What I say is that I am innocent, not only of the Braintree crime, but also of the Bridgewater crime. That I am not only innocent of these crimes, but in all my life I have never stole and I have never killed and I have never spilled blood... but I have struggled all my life, since I began to reason, to eliminate crime from the earth....*
>
> *Now, I should say that I am not only innocent of all these things, not only have I never committed a real crime in my life—though some sins but not crimes—not only have I struggled all my life to eliminate crimes, the crimes that the official law and the official moral condemns, but also the crimes that the official moral and the official law sanctions and sanctifies—the exploitation and the oppression of the man by the man, and if there is a reason why I am here as a guilty man, if there is a reason why you in a few minutes can doom me, it is this reason and none else....*
>
> *We have proved that there could not have been another Judge on the face of the earth more prejudiced and more cruel than you have been against us.... Still they refuse the new trial. We know, and you know in your heart, that you have been against us from the very beginning, before you see us. Before you see us you already know that we were radicals, that we were underdogs.... We were tried during a time that has now passed into history. I mean by that, a time when there was a hysteria of resentment and hate against the people of our principles, against the foreigner, against*

slackers, and it seems to me—rather, I am positive of it, that both you and Mr. Katzmann has done all what it were in your power in order to work out, in order to agitate still more the passion of the juror, the prejudice of the juror, against us....

This is what I say: I would not wish to a dog or to a snake, to the most low and misfortunate creature of the earth—I would not wish to any of them what I have suffered for things that I am not guilty of. But my conviction is that I have suffered for things that I am guilty of. I am suffering because I am a radical and indeed I am a radical; I have suffered because I was an Italian, and indeed I am an Italian; I have suffered more for my family and for my beloved than for myself; but I am so convinced to be right that if you could execute me two times, and if I could be reborn two other times, I would live again to do what I have done already.[40]

The moment for which Judge Thayer had so long awaited was finally at hand, the fulfillment of his holy mission against the Reds. With silent malevolence exuding, Judge Thayer now sentenced Sacco and Vanzetti to death in the electric chair. News of the death sentences spread throughout the world within hours, provoking a transcontinental hurricane of outrage and protest. Awareness and concern about Sacco and Vanzetti, originally generated by Fred Moore's publicity campaign in 1921, had subsided during the years following the trial. However, by the spring of 1927, when it seemed that the defendants were doomed, saving Sacco and Vanzetti had become a great crusade, as literally millions of people—high and low, rich and poor, educated and uneducated—raised their voices to challenge the verdict and to prevent the execution. Among the individuals who rallied to the defense were renowned men and women from every field of endeavor: writers, musicians, artists, journalists, scientists, lawyers, theologians, academicians, and even politicians. Some of the more recognizable figures included Albert Einstein, George Bernard Shaw, Thomas Mann, Upton Sinclair, John Dos Passos, H. L. Mencken, Felix Frankfurter, Samuel Eliot Morrison, and Fiorello LaGuardia. Collective protest took the form of mass demonstrations in New York, Paris, Berlin, London, Buenos Aires, Moscow, and other cities, many of them organized by the Communists, who exploited the Sacco-Vanzetti case for their own ends, chiefly to anoint them as proletarian martyrs and symbols of capitalist oppression.

As the protest wave gained momentum worldwide, the conservative and patriotic elements in Massachusetts and elsewhere—working class as well as middle and upper class—dug in their heels and rallied around "American" institutions and beliefs, ready to battle the perceived threat from "un-American" and anticapitalist enemies, local and foreign. So while pro-Sacco and Vanzetti forces demanded the liberation of the two men, anti-Sacco and Vanzetti forces campaigned for their execution. Defense of God, country, and apple pie required that the death sentences be carried out.

Recourse to the Massachusetts judicial system having already proved futile, demands to spare Sacco and Vanzetti were now directed towards the governor of the Commonwealth, Alvan T. Fuller, a millionaire car salesman with aspirations for higher office. At the beginning of April 1924, a few days before the Supreme Judicial Court upheld Thayer's latest denial for a new trial, Thompson beseeched Governor Fuller to appoint a commission to reconsider the entire case. While Fuller was pondering the idea of a commission, Thompson, on May 4, convinced Vanzetti to petition the governor for clemency—clemency instead of a pardon because the latter would connote guilt. Sacco refused to sign the petition. He believed it useless. The Commonwealth, he remained convinced, was determined to execute him. And besides, an appeal to the state for mercy would violate his anarchist principles. Vanzetti, too, harbored few illusions that his petition would gain their freedom. In a letter to Mrs. Glendower Evans, the benevolent dowager who defended the two men throughout their ordeal, Vanzetti urged her not "to expect that Fuller will stand against the judiciary, the middle class, the big money in behalf of two damned dagos and anarchists."

On June 1, 1924, Governor Fuller appointed an advisory committee composed of Abbot Lawrence Lowell, the president of Harvard University, Samuel W. Stratton, the president of the Massachusetts Institute of Technology, and Robert Grant, a former probate court judge. The dominant figure of the committee was Lowell, whose family fortune derived from the exploitation of immigrant workers in the mill towns of Lawrence and Lowell. The notion that Lowell and his associates would conduct a thorough investigation of the case and render an unbiased opinion was absurd. The banker John Moors, a friend of Lowell and a member of the Harvard Corporation, told Felix Frankfurter that Lowell was "incapable of seeing that two wops could be right and the Yankee judiciary wrong."[41] Herbert Ehrmann, the young attorney who dealt directly with the committee, related that "like the jury in Dedham, they knew the answers before their deliberations began: Sacco and Vanzetti were guilty.... The Committee members gave us the impression that they regarded themselves as prosecutors, whose duty it was to expose or discredit anything pointing to the innocence of the men."[42]

Indeed, the Lowell Committee's true purpose was not to determine whether Sacco and Vanzetti were guilty or innocent, or had been fairly tried and convicted. Rather, its function was to vindicate the Commonwealth of Massachusetts. Thus, after conducting its "investigation" for only ten days, the Lowell Committee issued a report to Governor Fuller on July 21, affirming the fairness of the judicial proceedings and the guilt of Sacco and Vanzetti. Accordingly, the committee recommended against clemency. Many supporters of the condemned anarchists, especially those who until now had retained their faith in the judicial and political institutions of Massachusetts, were outraged and dispirited by the Lowell Committee's sham deliberations. Others more realistic shared the cynical sentiments of journalist Heywood

Defense of God, country, and apple pie required that the death sentences be carried out.

Broun, who wrote: "What more can immigrants from Italy expect? It's not every prisoner who has the President of Harvard throw the switch on him."[43]

Governor Fuller, meanwhile, had been conducting his own "investigation," an undertaking that proved more of a farce than that conducted by the Lowell Committee. There was never the slightest chance that Fuller would reach any conclusion other than that Sacco and Vanzetti were guilty and had been fairly tried. Despite the appearance of serious concern and involvement feigned for public consumption, Fuller approached every issue with intellectual and political blinders that caused him to see the prosecution's arguments and nothing else. His ignorance of vital new evidence astonished Thompson and Ehrmann. For example, after finally receiving the Pinkerton reports that Katzmann had withheld from the defense during the Plymouth and Dedham trials, Thompson and Ehrmann submitted a thirty-three page analysis of the discrepancies between what eyewitnesses had reported originally to the Pinkertons and the testimony given at the trials. When the defense received no reply, an intermediary, John Moors, queried the governor about his opinion of the reports. Fuller replied: "What are the Pinkerton reports?" When Fuller asked his secretary, Herman MacDonald, to enlighten him about the Pinkerton reports, the latter replied: "Oh, something about a cropped mustache." Ignorance was compounded by indifference and incompetence. After Fuller demanded tangible proof to corroborate Vanzetti's claim that he had received eels for sale on Christmas Eve, 1919, Ehrmann and defense committee treasurer Aldino Felicani discovered an American Express Company receipt confirming the sale. This vital piece of new evidence, which greatly strengthened Vanzetti's claim that he was selling eels on the day of the Bridgewater crime, was entrusted to Joseph Wiggin, Fuller's personal lawyer, rather than to MacDonald, whose primary responsibility was to examine the governor's Sacco-Vanzetti mail, most of which he discarded. The precaution failed. Nothing more was ever heard about the receipt. Finally, on August 3, 1927, his "investigation" completed, Governor Fuller denied clemency.

In desperation, the defense team submitted petitions for a writ of habeas corpus to the United States Supreme Court and several lower courts. All were rejected, meaning that every avenue of legal action had been exhausted.

Meanwhile, the news of Fuller's denial of clemency had reverberated throughout the world, sparking public demonstrations that mobilized literally millions of protesters. Various radical elements, including anarchists and Communists, called for workers to prevent the executions by means of general strikes and other forms of direct action, including terrorism. But nothing could save them now. Sacco and Vanzetti were executed on August 23, 1927.

The most fitting epitaph for the two Italian anarchists was spoken by Vanzetti himself, several weeks earlier in an interview with journalist Philip Stong:

> *If it had not been for these thing, I might have live out my life talking at street corners to scorning men. I might have die, unmarked, unknown, a failure. Now we are not a failure. This is our career and our triumph. Never in our full life could we hope to do such work for tolerance, for joostice, for man's understanding of man, as now we do by accident.*
> *Our words—our lives—our pains—nothing! The taking of our lives—lives of a good shoemaker and a poor fish peddler—all! That last moment belong to us—that agony is our triumph.*[44]

Debate over the Sacco-Vanzetti case has continued intermittently for nearly three-quarters of a century, with disputants frequently dividing along political lines, much as they had in the 1920s. Authors who argued that Sacco and Vanzetti were innocent men whose conviction and execution had constituted a grave miscarriage of justice—Felix Frankfurter (1927), Osmond K. Fraenkel (1931), and Michael A. Musmanno (1939), Louis G. Joughin and Edmund M. Morgan (1948)—went largely unchallenged until 1960, when Robert H. Montgomery, a friend of Judge Thayer and an associate of the reactionary John Birch Society, published a study contending that the two Italian anarchists had been guilty and fairly tried. That Montgomery's book appeared at the height of the Cold War was hardly coincidental. For almost twenty-five years, Sacco and Vanzetti had reigned supreme as symbols of capitalist injustice in America. Accordingly, they were hated by right-wing politicos and intellectuals like William F. Buckley, Jr., who greeted Montgomery's study with jubilation and denounced the case as "a human vehicle through which to indict the existing order, condemn our institutions, dramatize the cause of proletarian socialism, scrape away at the Puritan ethic, tear and wrench the nation and cause it to bleed across the pages of history."[45] Not surprisingly, therefore, Montgomery's book initiated a "reconviction process" calculated to destroy the Sacco-Vanzetti legend by retrying them and thereby seal the original verdict. Accordingly, the primary issue of the case, the unfairness of the trials and subsequent proceedings, was relegated to a secondary status, as though a guilty verdict nullified the claim of justice crucified.

The "reconviction process" received a big boost from the writings of Francis Russell, an amateur historian who portrayed himself as the only writer who ever changed his mind about Sacco and Vanzetti. Between 1955 and 1986, in two books and a half-dozen articles, Russell executed a 180 degree turnabout, arguing first that both men were innocent, second that Sacco was guilty but Vanzetti innocent, and finally contending that Sacco was definitely and Vanzetti possibly guilty. The principal basis for Russell's thesis is hearsay evidence attributed to Carlo Tresca and some other anarchists.[46] Meanwhile, another reconvictionist, David Felix, had come into the field. His 1965 study of Sacco-Vanzetti and the intellectuals declared both men guilty and fairly tried. The pendulum swung in the opposite direction in 1969, when attorney Herbert B. Ehrmann's weighty volume (far and away the best treatment of the case) pronounced both of them innocent victims of a legal system that had egregiously erred. Sacco-Vanzetti defenders considered themselves vindicated in 1977, when Massachusetts Governor Dukakis commemorated the fiftieth anniversary of the execution by issuing a proclamation declaring that "the atmosphere of their trial and appeals was permeated by prejudice against foreigners and hostility toward unorthodox political views," and that "the conduct of the many officials involved in the case shed serious doubt on their willingness and ability to conduct the prosecution and trial of Sacco and Vanzetti fairly and impartially."[47] The Dukakis proclamation took no stand on the issue of innocence or guilt; nevertheless, it deeply offended many public officials and private citizens in Massachusetts. The State Senate expressed this outrage by voting, 21-14, to condemn the governor's act as illegal and without constitutional authority.

Naturally, the Dukakis proclamation was heralded by liberal and radical supporters of Sacco and Vanzetti as a significant triumph. For example, Carey McWilliams, former editor of *The Nation* and a veteran defender of Sacco and Vanzetti, declared confidently that the proclamation would thwart "'neo-conservative intellectuals" like Buckley from conducting "still another campaign ... to reconvict the innocent."[48] Such expectations were naive. Russell's later publications continued the "reconviction process," buttressed by ballistics tests he ordered in 1961. The tests concluded that Sacco's gun had fired the fatal Bullet III and an accompanying shell. The value of these tests was seriously undermined, however, when it was discovered that the two experts had advanced the same conclusion in an essay

Sacco and Vanzetti were executed on August 23, 1927

published before they had examined the weapon and bullets. Another coup for the reconvictionist cause was seemingly struck in 1983, when new ballistics tests commissioned by a Boston television station determined that Sacco's Colt .32 was the murder weapon. Those findings were vigorously challenged in 1986 by the work of William Young and David E. Kaiser, who argued (like Thompson in 1927) that Bullet III and its shell (Shell W) were substituted for the real items by the prosecution, thereby demolishing the basis of all the ballistics tests ever conducted on Sacco's gun. That same year, on the basis of the firearms evidence revealed in the 1883 tests, forensic scientist James E. Starrs dismissed the substitution theory, insisting instead that Sacco was probably guilty as a perpetrator or conspirator in the crime.[49] As for Vanzetti, Starrs concludes that "the firearms record is as inadequate today as it was at his trial in 1921."[50] The last work worthy of attention, published by Joseph B. Kadane and David A. Schum in 1996, is a probabilistic and statistical analysis of the trial evidence. The authors concluded that Vanzetti was innocent and the case against Sacco unproven.

The likelihood that the question of guilt or innocence will someday be conclusively resolved is highly doubtful. But even without a definite answer, the Sacco-Vanzetti case will continue to rank as the most notorious political trial in twentieth-century American history, "the case that will not die."

List of endnotes on page 124

If it had not been for these thing, I might have live out my life talking at street corners to scorning men. I might have die, unmarked, unknown, a failure. Now we are not a failure. This is our career and our triumph. Never in our full life could we hope to do such work for tolerance, for joostice, for man's understanding of man, as now we do by accident. Our words—our lives—our pains—nothing! The taking of our lives—lives of a good shoemaker and a poor fish peddler—all! That last moment belong to us—that agony is our triumph.

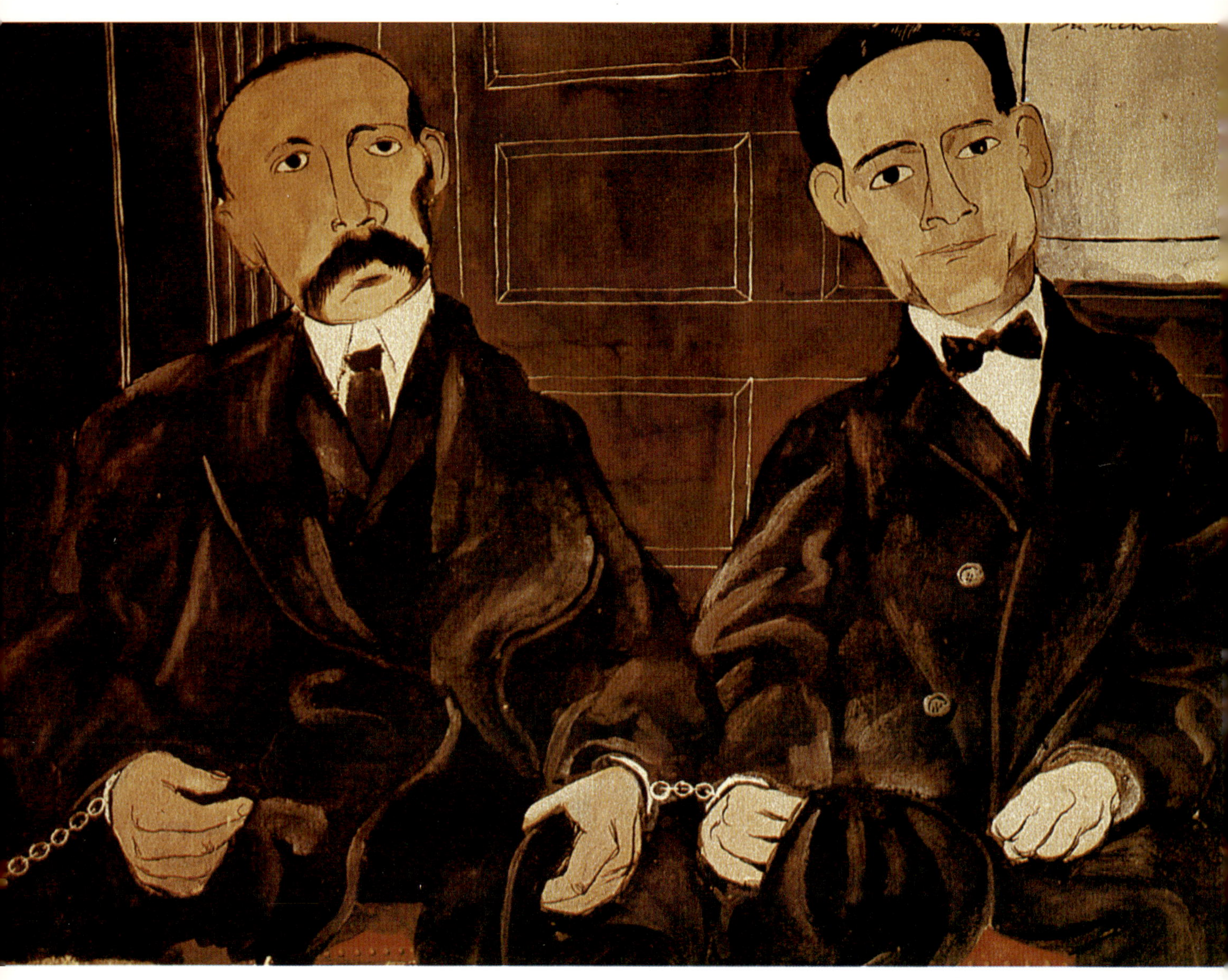

Ben Shahn
Bartolomeo Vanzetti & Nicola Sacco, 1931–32.
Gouache on paper mounted on composition board
$10^{7}/8$ x $14^{5}/8$ in.
The Museum of Modern Art, New York,
New York. Gift of Abby Aldrich Rockefeller

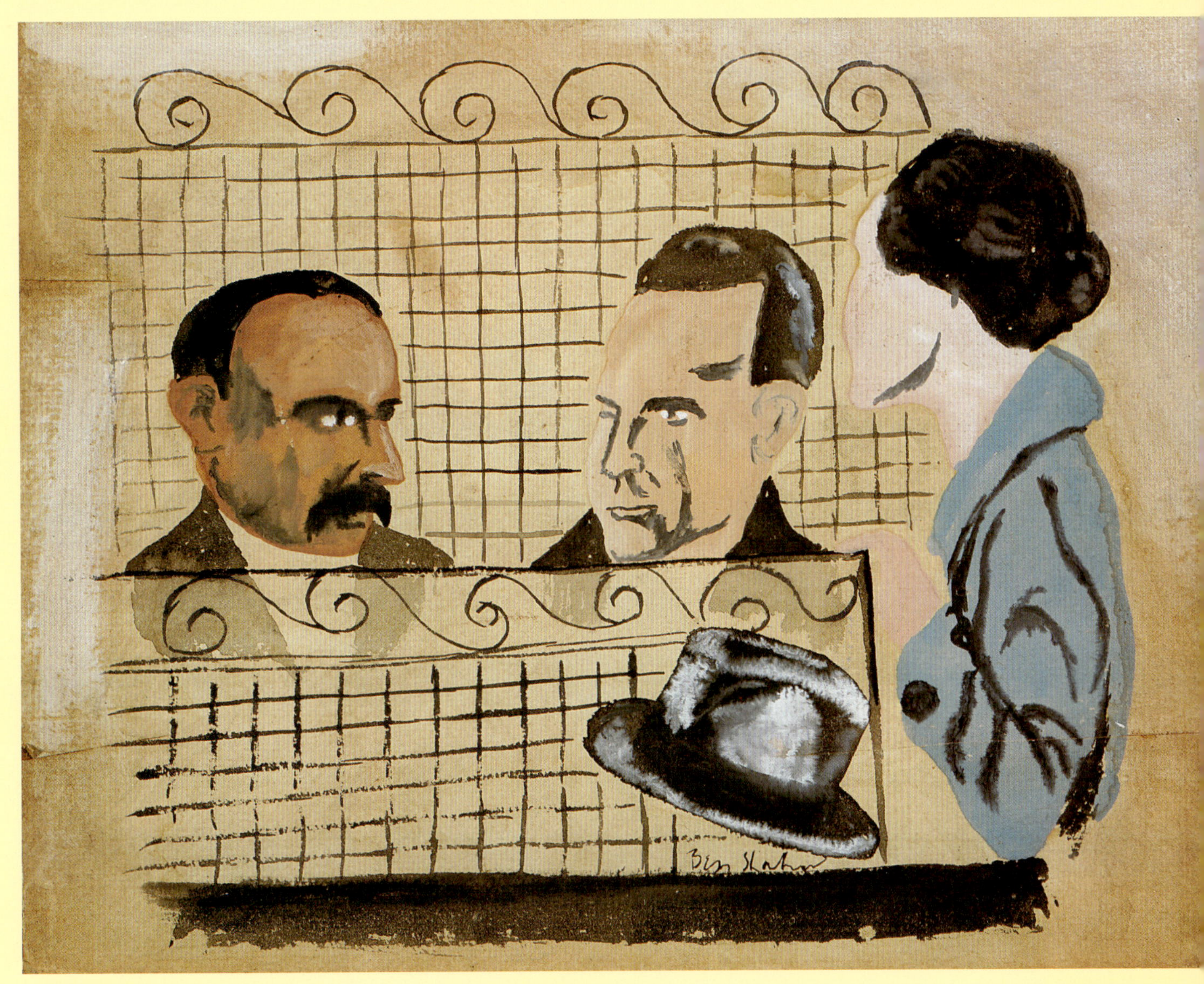

Ben Shahn
In the Courtroom Cage, 1931–32.
Gouache on paper, 11 1/2 x 14 1/2 in.
The Art Museum, Princeton University,
Princeton, New Jersey
Gift of Dr. Walter E. Rothman

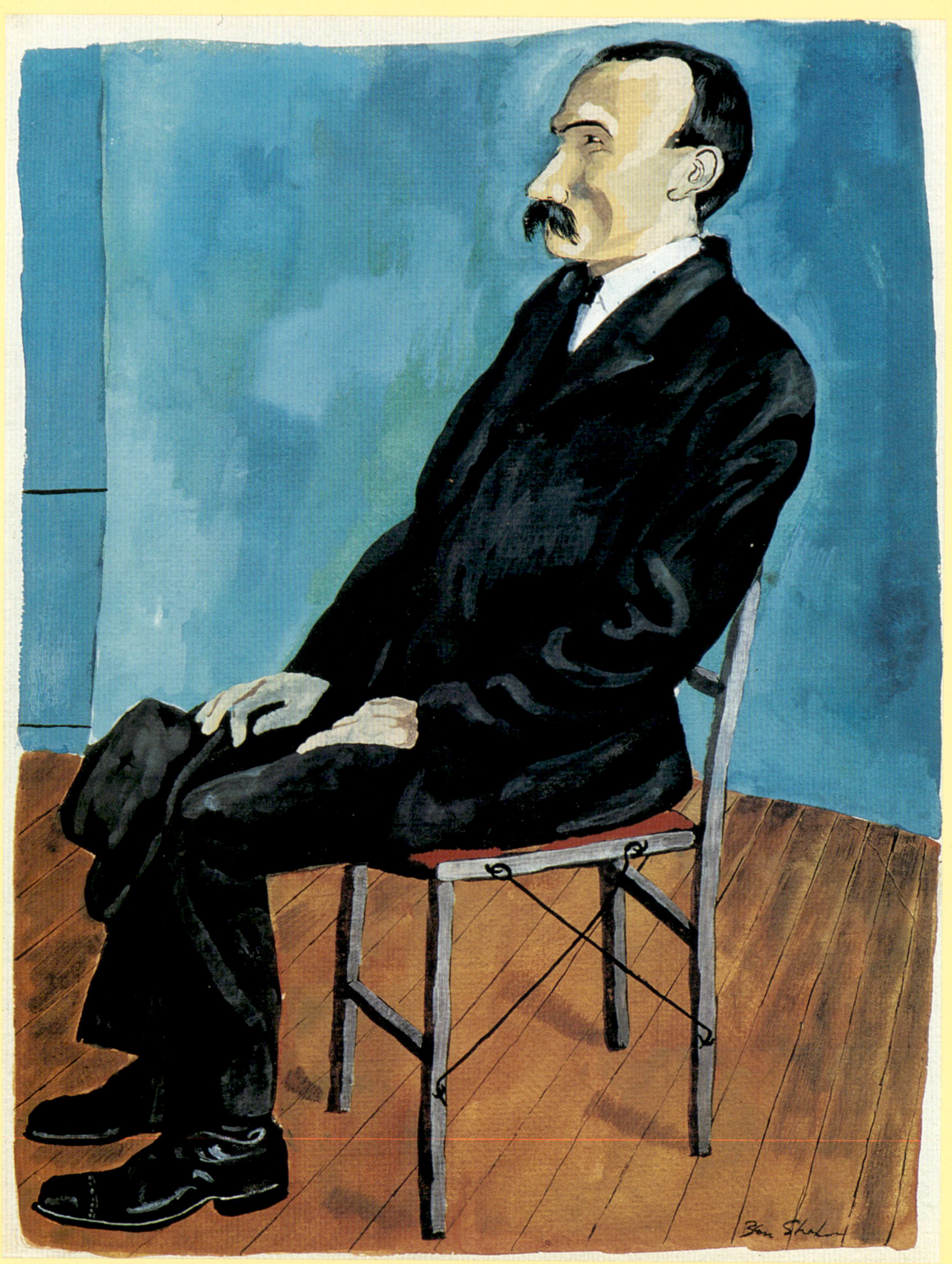

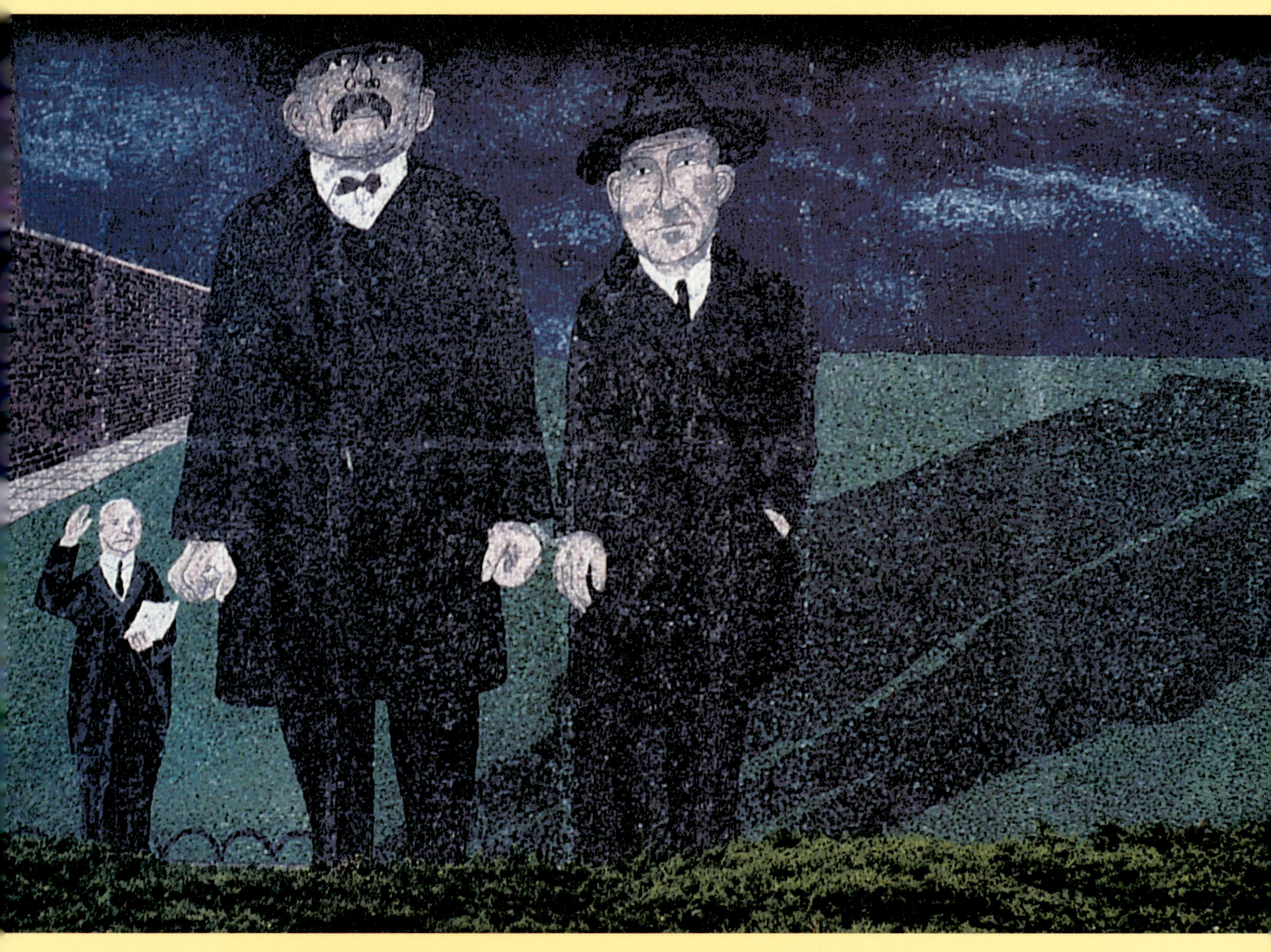

LEFT
Ben Shahn
Bartolomeo Vanzetti, 1931–32.
Gouache on paper, 14 1/2 x 11 1/2 in.
Private Collector, and R.D.Schonfeld & Co., Inc.

Ben Shahn
The Passion of Sacco and Vanzetti, 1967.
Middle panel. Mosaic. Syracuse University, Syracuse, New York
Gift of Mr. and Mrs. Jacob Schulman, and Mr. and Mrs. Richard Evans, III

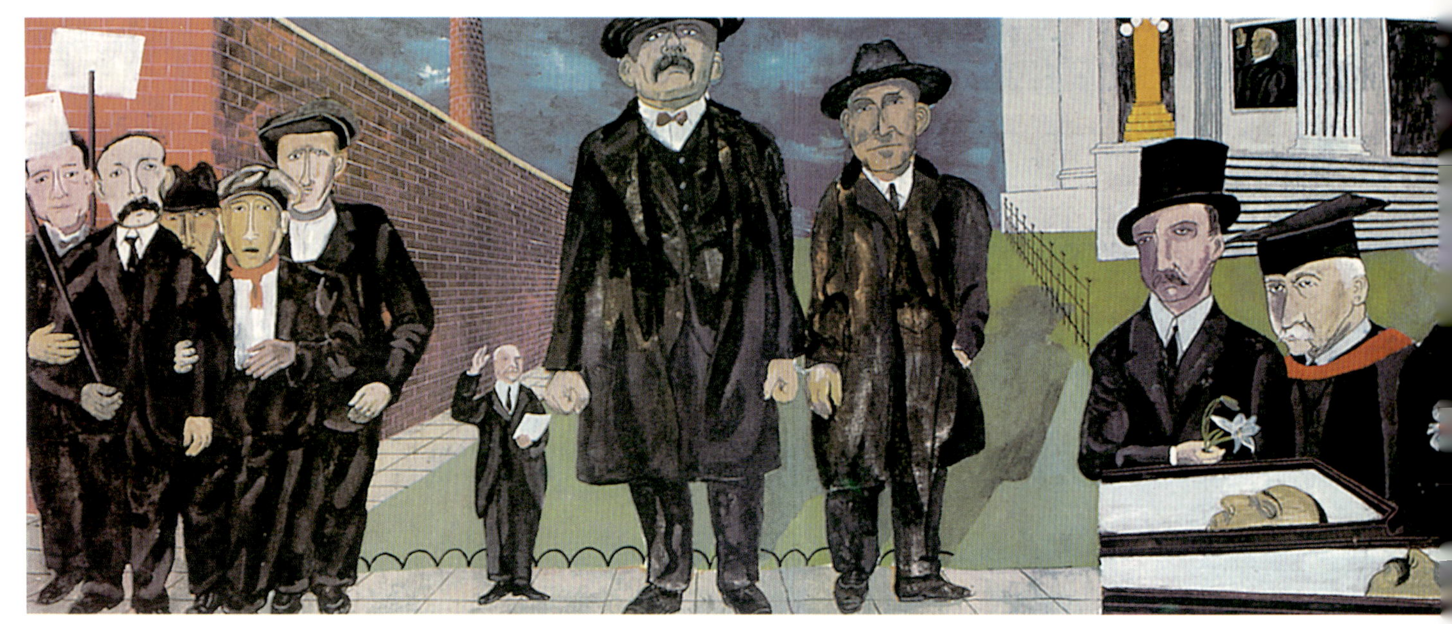

Ben Shahn
The Passion of Sacco and Vanzetti, 1932.
Tempera on board, 21 x 48 in.
Private Collection
(not in exhibition)

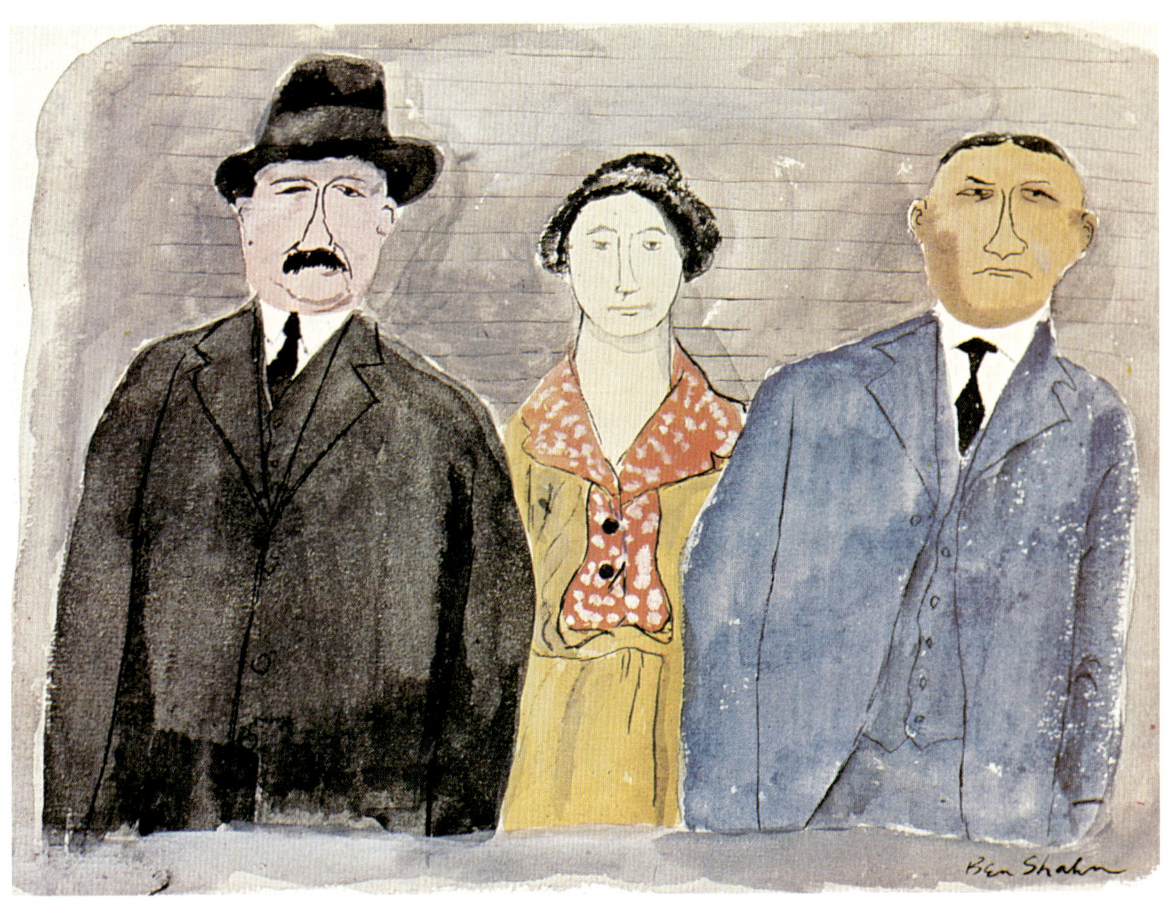

Ben Shahn
Three Witnesses, 1931–32.
Gouache and watercolor on paper,
9 1/2 x 13 in.
The Montclair Art Museum,
Montclair, New Jersey.
Bequest in memory of Moses
and Ida Soyer

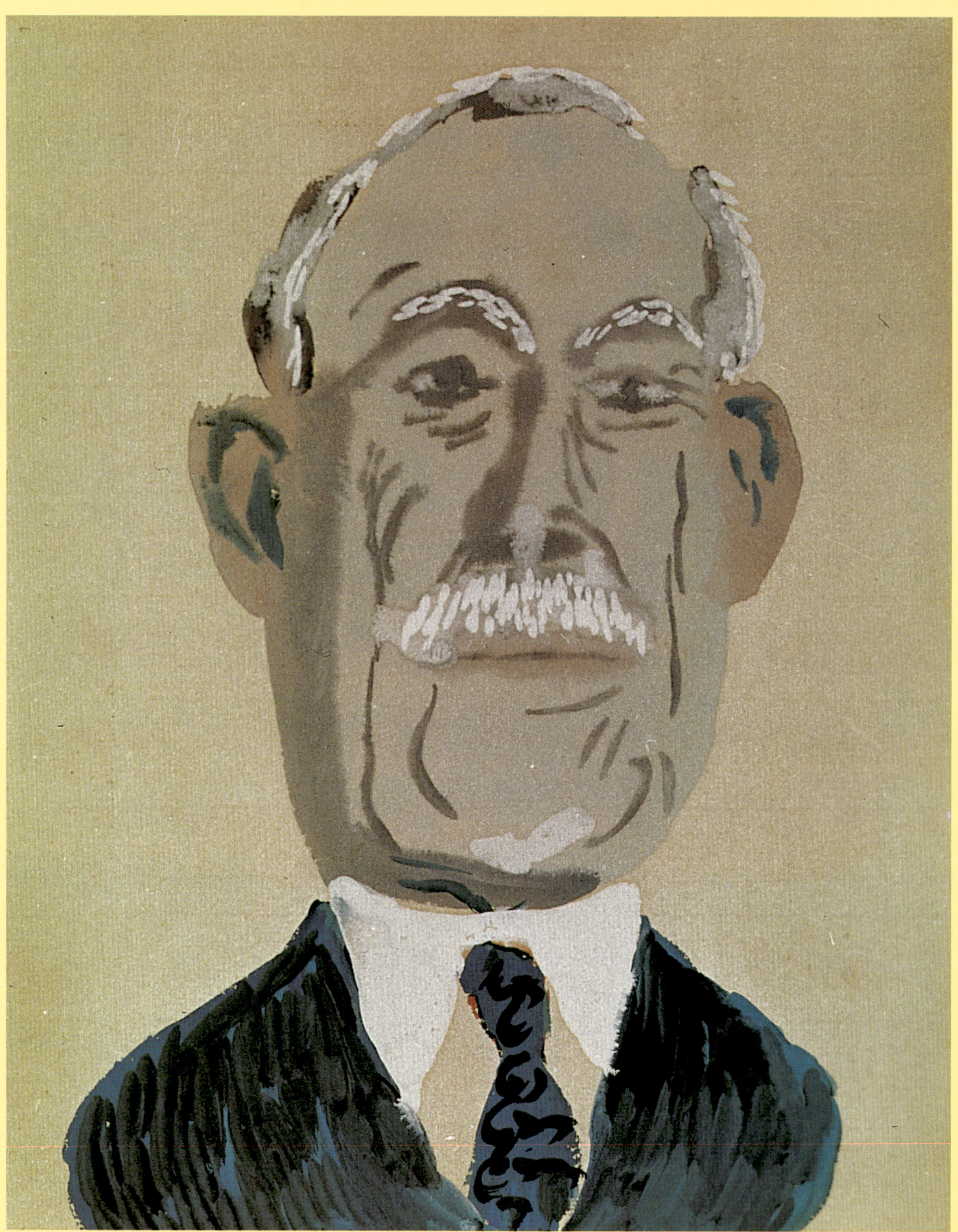

LEFT
Ben Shahn
Judge Webster Thayer, 1931–32
Gouache on paper, 13 x $6^{1}/_{2}$ in.
Collection of Mr. and Mrs.
Jonathan Wittenberg, New York

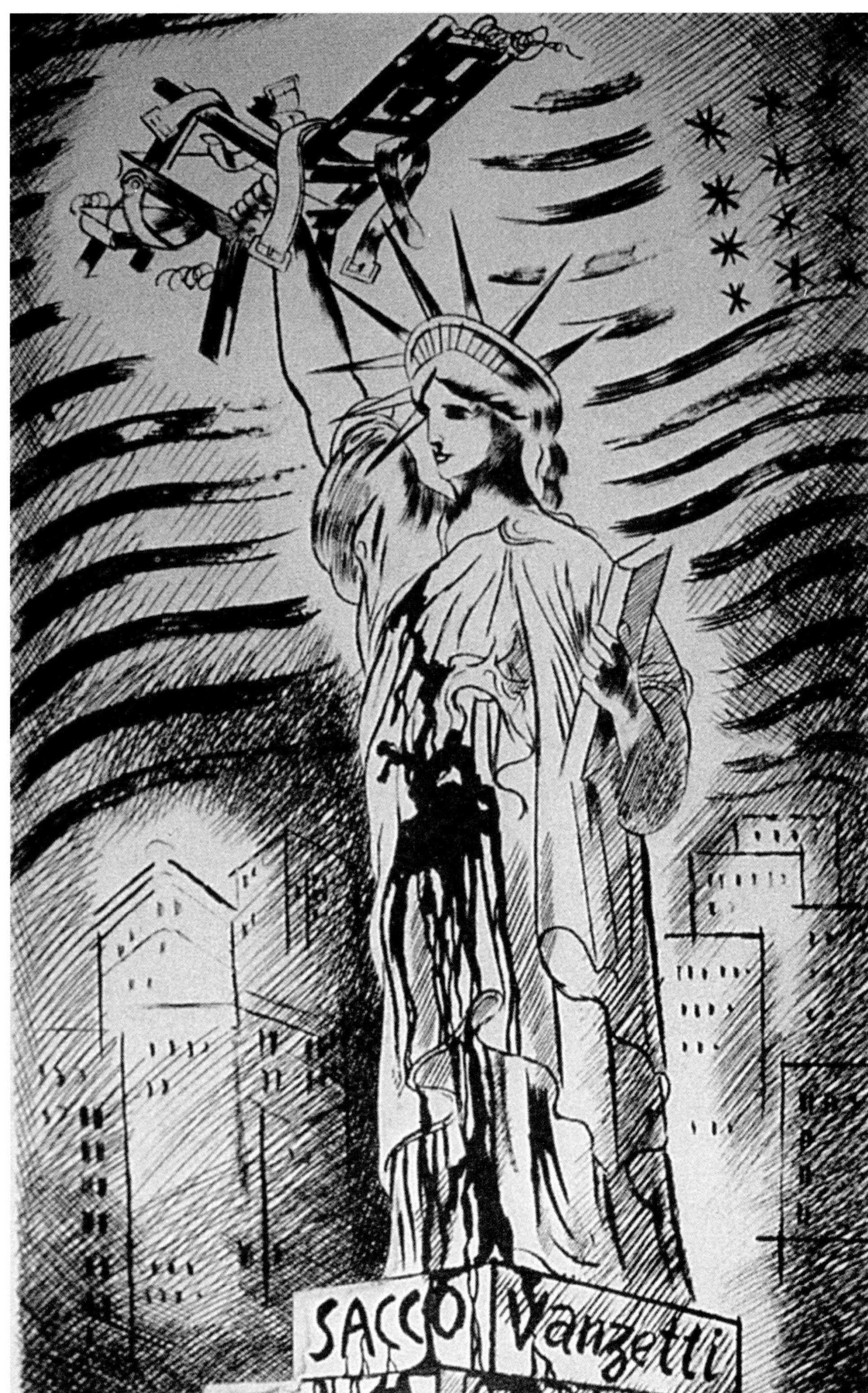

George Grosz
Sacco & Vanzetti, 1927
Ink on paper, 12 x 9 inches
Courtesy of Peter Grosz,
Princeton, New Jersey

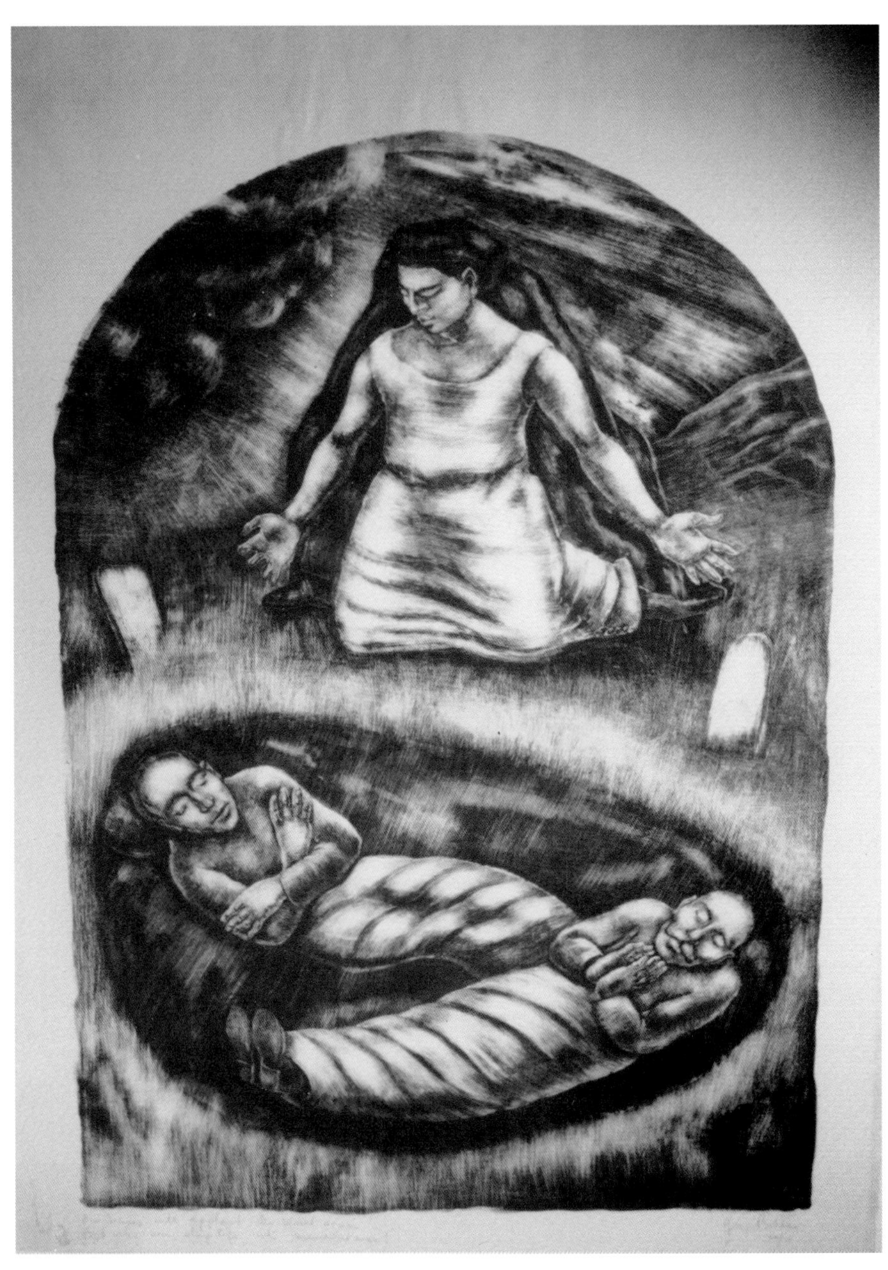

George Biddle
Our senses will applaud this world again, But who can clap life with murdered men?, 1930
Lithograph, 24 x 18 in.
Private Collection, New Jersey

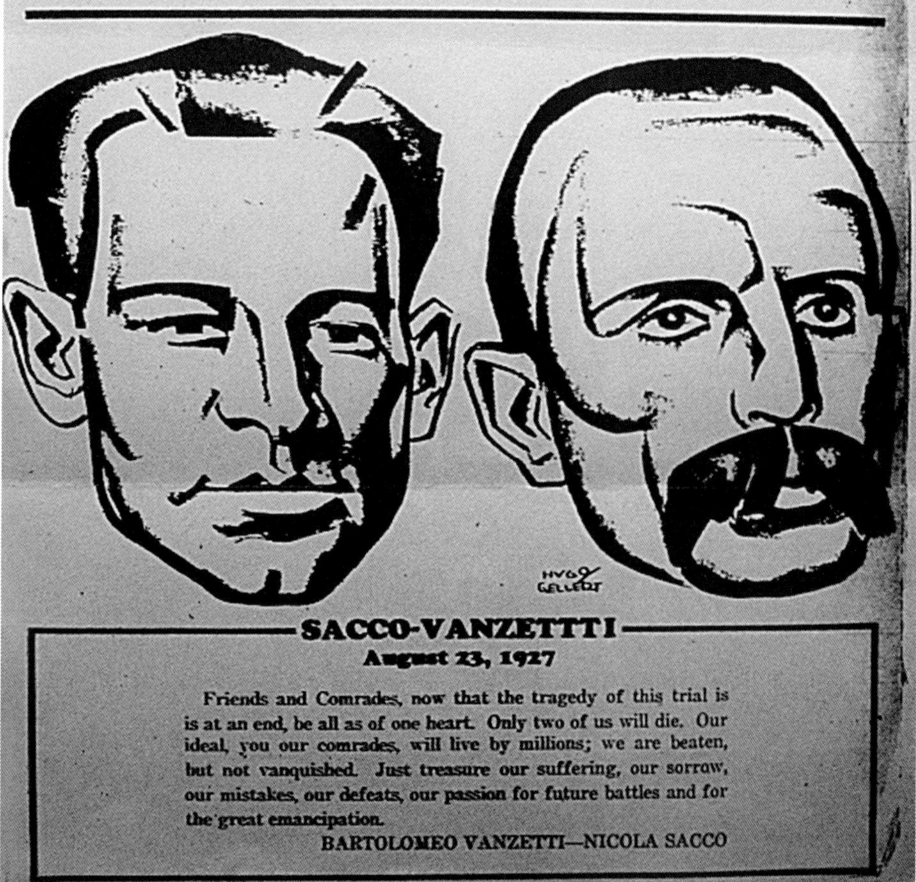

New Masses

AUGUST, 1932

proletarian culture. The world is divested of mystery. The universe cannot strike fear into proletarian hearts. Armed with science, the worker will change the world. Therefore he cannot be sad. He has no misgivings. He loathes decay. He considers swamp-lights as hideous as the swamp itself despite their alluring brilliance. He handles wounds of the spirit like wounds of the flesh. He is all impact, all dynamics. He knows no hesitation. He despises "doubts." He will rather err and correct his error than "meditate" in indecision. He is extremely realistic, extremely practical, but for this very reason he has a width of horizon denied the bourgeoisie. He sees the outlines of the future. He has discovered the laws of development of all human society. He is therefore universal. At the same time he knows his own place in the sum total of the creative collective.

This of necessity finds expression in fiction and poetry, in the theatre and in music, in painting and sculpture. The very term "fiction" is abhorrent to the Russian worker. Not tales that are fictitious, unreal, untrue, but the facts of life seen through class imagination and co-ordinated in a skilful ("artistic") manner with a view to organizing the reader's mind in the direction required by the class struggle. Not material for amusement but armament for battle. Not harps vibrating in the breeze but trumpets in the storm, arrows thrust into the future, showing the way, mobilizing for conquest of new worlds. Not mental trifles for the aged who never knew youth, but things of historic importance for a whole youthful class changing the world.

There is still a struggle on between this new proletarian culture and the remnants and the worshippers of the old. But the old recedes—to the museums and textbooks. There are still hybrid creatures to be encountered here and there. But the new is winning all along the front. Victory is assured.

SACCO-VANZETTI

August 23, 1927

Friends and Comrades, now that the tragedy of this trial is is at an end, be all as of one heart. Only two of us will die. Our ideal, you our comrades, will live by millions; we are beaten, but not vanquished. Just treasure our suffering, our sorrow, our mistakes, our defeats, our passion for future battles and for the great emancipation.

BARTOLOMEO VANZETTI—NICOLA SACCO

Hugo Gellert
Sacco and Vanzetti, 1932
Dimensions unknown
Crayon on paper
Location unknown

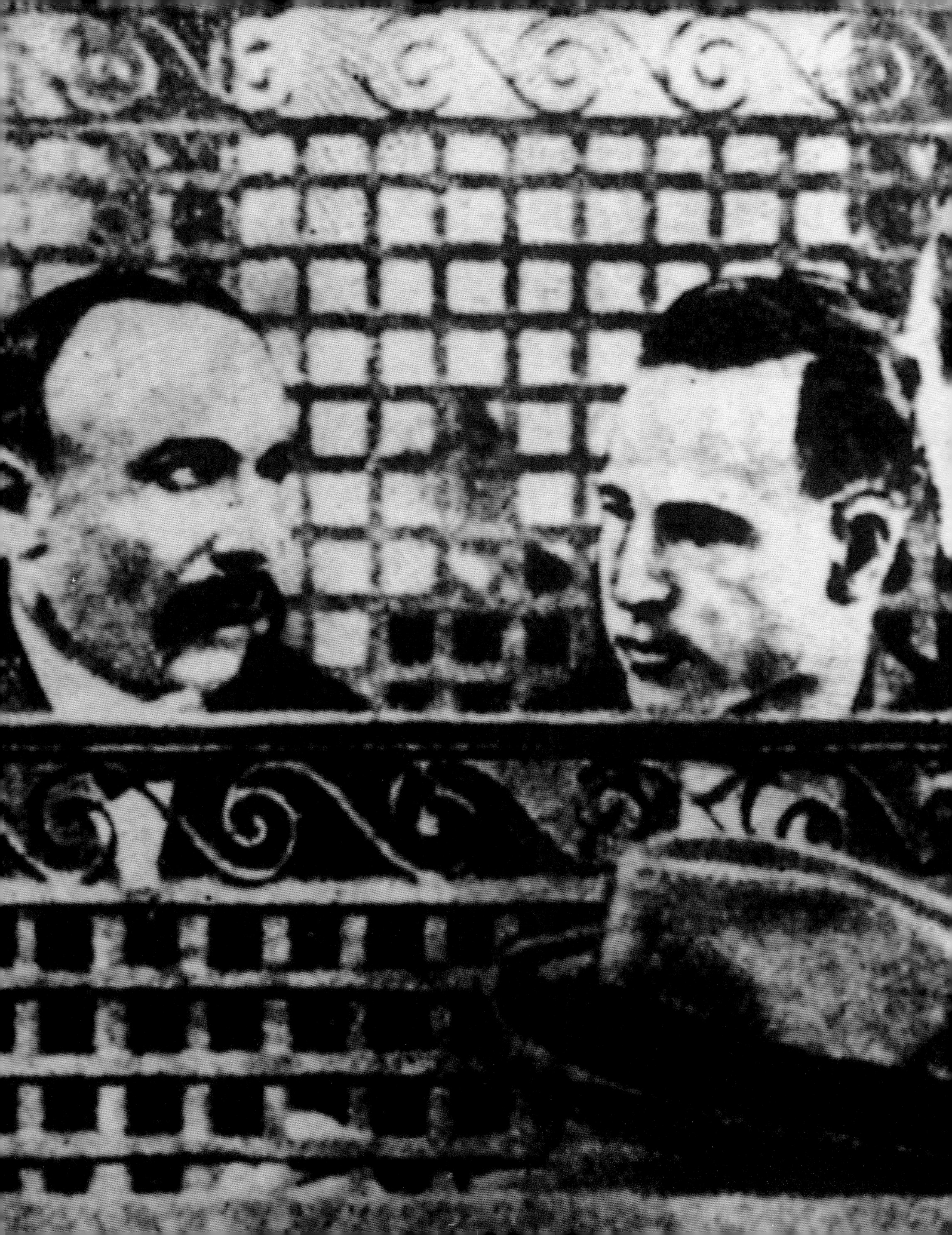

Laura Katzman

"Mechanical Vision:" Photography and Mass Media Appropriation in Ben Shahn's Sacco and Vanzetti Series

The photograph teaches us to see—it sees what the eye fails to discern. In the future it will not be the model for the painter in the old sense of academic models, but his documentary aid in the same sense in which, in our day, files of daily newspapers are indispensable to the novelist....I will assert that the painting of tomorrow will use the photographic eye as it has used the human eye.—Louis Aragon, 1937[1]

There has been some interaction of course between the two mediums but this has led most frequently to misconception and sterility on both sides. An Utrillo painted from an Atget print...is not one-hundredth as good a work of art as the photograph. Moreover it is a kind of spiritual theft...I believe that all vital arts result from the artist's direct and actual involvement with the real world. If painters want to use the heroic life and death struggle of the Spanish people as material for their art they should go to Spain as Bresson has done, not borrow from his photographs.

—Paul Strand, 1937[2]

LEFT
"Vanzetti and Sacco In The Cage in the Court Room" (detail), n.d., photograph, United Press International, mounted photostat in Ben Shahn Papers, Archives of American Art, Smithsonian Institution, Washington DC. Repr. in Elizabeth Glendower Evans, *Outstanding Features of the Sacco-Vanzetti Case* (Boston: New England Civil Liberties, 1924), p.4. Copy photograph by Lee Ewing.

INTRODUCTION

The Sacco and Vanzetti case stands as one of the great *cause célèbres* of the early twentieth century. Liberals and intellectuals worldwide were among the groups who believed deeply in the innocence of the two working-class Italian-American immigrants convicted and executed in 1927 for the murder of a paymaster and his guard in South Braintree, Massachusetts.[3] American artists, poets, novelists, playwrights, historians, labor leaders, civil libertarians, and legal scholars protested and devoted professional work to the cause out of sympathy, grief, and outrage for what they perceived as a tragic miscarriage of justice in a climate of antiradical hysteria and brutal "Red" deportation.[4] Ben Shahn's series of paintings, *The Passion of Sacco and Vanzetti* (1931–1932), is arguably the most vital and extensive visual treatment of the case from the time.[5] It received enthusiastic acclaim as well as more critical response in the mainstream, left, and liberal press when it was shown at Edith Halpert's Downtown Gallery in April 1932.[6] According to Halpert's exhibition press release, the series represented a "turning to theme painting again" as '[t]he accent of 'art for art's sake' is slowly being lessened."[7] This was socially relevant art that responded to the crisis of the Great Depression.

The Sacco and Vanzetti series also became Shahn's most famous work. Even though it was his commercial production of the 1950s and 1960s that brought him widespread public popularity, his Sacco and Vanzetti series is touted as a turning point in his career, signaling his artistic maturity. Indeed, the work defined Shahn's subsequent pictorial style, which achieved incisive characterization with an economy of means. It affirmed his leftist political status in the 1930s as a communist-involved artist and secured his liberal affinities for virtually the rest of his career.[8] From extant letters of the time, we learn that the series meant a lot to Shahn himself, and that both he and his dealer Halpert reveled in the lively scandal it caused in New York City and in Cambridge, Massachusetts.[9]

Despite the status and scholarly visibility of the Sacco and Vanzetti series, key aspects of the work remain unexplored. Shahn's use of news photographs, and the relationship of the series to the mass media, have yet to be analyzed closely. While many contemporary scholars of American art know that Shahn worked from newspaper photographs and have juxtaposed his paintings and source photographs in major monographs and exhibition catalogues, little interpretive scholarship exists on this subject. According to the art historian Morris Dorsky, "[a]lthough his use of photos was known at the time, the full extent of Shahn's reliance on them was not understood."[10] The few critics in 1932 who did mention Shahn's use of photographs did so casually.[11] And even though later biographers such as James Thrall Soby and Selden Rodman recognized the photographic foundation for the Sacco and

Vanzetti series, no extensive effort has been made to investigate the formal and conceptual relationship between the paintings and the photographs.[12]

This essay examines the news photographs Shahn used to construct his Sacco and Vanzetti series, with the premise that the ways in which he employed his sources—that is, how he appropriated and altered information from photographs—necessarily bears upon the meanings of individual paintings, affecting our interpretation of the series as a whole. This enterprise challenges the traditional view that photographs lose their significance once they are used by artists.[13] It attempts to expand the useful but limited formalist analysis of earlier scholars with more probing, analytical sociohistorical interpretation. Such investigation also compels us to ask why Shahn would have used news photographs in the first place. How were newspapers popularly perceived in his day, and what could news images have brought to his painting? Finally, if using photographs was such an important and integral part of Shahn's working process, then why has the subject been so neglected or cursorily treated in the Shahn literature?

PHOTOGRAPHS AND THE SHAPING OF CONTENT[14]

It is rather amazing to see how Shahn makes his effects. He has depended upon photographs, naturally, and he reflects the photographic feeling in a way that is practically burlesque and at the same time attains to extraordinary sincerity. As an artist he half laughs at his distortions, and yet the feeling back of the work is that of the zealot.—**Henry McBride, 1932**[15]

Shahn's treatment of many details in the Sacco [and Vanzetti] paintings could be compared to the effect of looking at a bad foreign film with stilted subtitles. He superimposed his pseudo-documentary style of drawing on the straight-forward record made by the lens. This often brought Shahn close to artistic failure, as he attempted to excerpt from and add meaning to his sources, which in their raw state were more convincing than his paintings when it came to communicating the essential ideas with which he was concerned—**Van Deren Coke, 1972**[16]

Photographs constituted a major part of Shahn's research on the subject of Sacco and Vanzetti; in fact, they were employed for every painting in the series. Shahn had used photographs earlier—in his Dreyfus Affair series of 1930—but the scope, breadth, and depth of the photo-usage in the Sacco and Vanzetti pictures were more far-reaching, establishing future working patterns.[17] In the early 1930s, Shahn began collecting news photographs, along with documentary images for clipping and source files that have only recently come to light in a public repository.[18] Since Shahn valued the communicative aspect of photography more than matters of technique, he thought newspaper photographs were the best kind of picture in terms of image content, even taking irreverent delight in these and other non-"art" photographs, which necessarily lose much of their print quality in reproduction and enlargement. He remembered disagreements with Paul Strand over the significance of tonal quality and sharpness in photography. Shahn also loved newsreels, which he said influenced his work, and felt movies were the "master medium."[19]

The documentary detail provided by film and photographic media was important to Shahn, who at the time was interested in how class and character could be conveyed in the "difference in the way a twelve-dollar coat wrinkles from the way a seventy-five-dollar coat wrinkles." He even took up street photography himself as an adjunct to painting, providing an aide memoire, an efficient sketchpad to arrest movement, to give what he called "those details of forms that you think you'll remember but don't," the kind of "endless details you may need for reference."[20] His government-commissioned photographs for the New Deal's Resettlement Administration/Farm Security Administration (RA/FSA), which he also used as "raw materials" for paintings, were intended to document poverty for public policy purposes. This documentary mode, common in much 1930s art, literature, music, and film, brought authenticity to one's work, and what scholar William Stott has called "the texture of reality." It "ma[de] it possible to see, know and feel the details of life, its styles in different places, to feel oneself part of some other's experience," according to cultural historian Warren Susman, and provided a way to make order out of the chaos endemic to hard times.[21]

Shahn began clipping, collecting, classifying and taking pictures at a time when documentary photographs enjoyed great popularity. The 1930s saw the contagion of "picture journalism" in American newspapers and magazines (inspired by European news photography that had already expanded in the 1920s). According to art historian Bruce Robertson:

> *The uses of photography dramatically increased in all media throughout the period, as new technology made good quality photo-reproduction increasingly cheap. For example, during the 1930s, newspapers increased their use of photographs 57%, with the average large newspaper using over 1 1/3 photographs per page, spending (all newspapers combined) perhaps $8,000,000 annually to provide them.*[22]

With the availability of 35mm cameras, the flash bulb, the perfection of "fast " films, wirephotos, and newsreels, this period experienced an explosion of mass media technologies. So pervasive and influential were technologies facilitating mass communication—press, movies, radio, telegraph, telephone, and photograph—that Warren Susman characterized the 1930s as "a culture of sight and sound." Although these technologies were not exactly new, according to Susman, they were put to subtle and refined uses "to document in art, reportage, social science, and history the life and values of the American people" as part of a "complex effort to seek and to define America as a culture."[23] Shahn at once embraced the form and content of what print media in particular could offer, and with his own photographs, especially the government-sponsored work, he actively participated in the self-conscious and widespread documentation of American life in the spirit of social reform.

In order to obtain photographs for the Sacco and Vanzetti series, Shahn wrote to Gardner Jackson, a devoted member of the Sacco and Vanzetti Defense Committee since 1927, its Secretary during the Committee's last period, and co-editor of *The Letters of Sacco and Vanzetti* (1928). Shahn asked for "pamphlets and photographs on every possible angle of the Sacco-Vanzetti affair." Jackson suggested he contact Aldino Felicani, the anarchist and Treasurer of the Committee, for firsthand impressions of Sacco and Vanzetti and for access to pictures at the moving picture office in Boston. He also mentioned how Shahn could get in touch with the National Sacco-Vanzetti Committee, another source for films and material.[25] Shahn went to the New York Public Library (42nd Street branch) to look for photoengravings in newspapers and pamphlets published by the various defense committees kept on file there. The New York Public Library Picture Collection, run by Romana Javitz, was an invaluable picture resource for fine and commercial artists, advertisers, and designers in the 1930s. The library of the Socialist Rand School offered yet additional visual data.[26] Furthermore, images of the case had been imprinted on Shahn's mind from having witnessed the Sacco and Vanzetti protests in Paris, and from his own participation in Boston demonstrations.[27]

Shahn's selection of photographs, according to Morris Dorsky, appeared "haphazard," based simply on documentation available to the artist at the time.[28] He also believes Shahn's choice of images created a look of detachment, and noted that "[t]he news photos of the period have a deadpan effect, the result of reportage without comment or emphasis." Dorsky elaborated:

> *Shahn managed, through the use of photographs, to create an aura of "objectivity" and picturesqueness. This characteristic, along with the arbitrariness of Shahn's selections, lent to them a kind of "objectivity," as though one were looking at a series of unconnected photos in a newspaper or pamphlet. Arranged in no particular order, without highlight or*

> *dramatic incident leading towards a climax, the Sacco and Vanzetti series had an air of historical and psychological detachment somewhat at odds with the emotional freight carried by its subject matter.*[29]

Yet despite such arbitrary and objective looking effects, subjective choices and careful decisions on Shahn's part were involved in the making of his series. First, the fact that many of the news photographs came from Sacco and Vanzetti defense pamphlets and radical/progressive publications necessarily indicates a leftist bias. Second, while Shahn had access to photographs of members of both the defense and the prosecution in the case, he deliberately chose to use more photographs (and thus make more paintings) of the defense side. Further, Shahn left out some key figures on both sides—figures whose presence may have diluted his intended message. For example, he avoided Sacco and Vanzetti's first chief counsel Fred Moore, the outrageous Californian who used melodramatic tactics to gain publicity and promote speculation on the case, and whom Sacco and Vanzetti disdained as one who did great damage to their cause.[30] Thus, analysis of both the photographic sources, and the process by which those sources were selected over others, provides insight into *how* Shahn constructed his seemingly nonpartisan vision, while still remaining true to his leftist sympathies and firm convictions about the men's innocence.[31]

THE DEFENSE PICTURES

Sacco and Vanzetti actually appear in only six of the twenty-three pictures in the series, but are alluded to in many more. One of the most famous, *Bartolomeo Vanzetti and Nicola Sacco,* is often reproduced with its United Press International source photograph. This popular image was featured as the frontispiece in Eugene Lyons's The *Life and Death of Sacco and Vanzetti* (1927), an important sympathetic biography that was translated into Russian, Italian, German, and Yiddish, and which Shahn likely owned **(figs.1 & 2)**.[32] Lyons published the photograph with the caption "Bartolomeo Vanzetti and Nicola Sacco in Court," while *The Letters of Sacco and Vanzetti* (1928), which also printed the photograph as its frontispiece, used the caption: "Bartolomeo Vanzetti After Three Years of Imprisonment," which would date the photograph circa 1923. Since Sacco and Vanzetti were separated for most of their seven years in prison, this photograph documents one of the few times the men saw each other when motions for a new trial were being heard.[33]

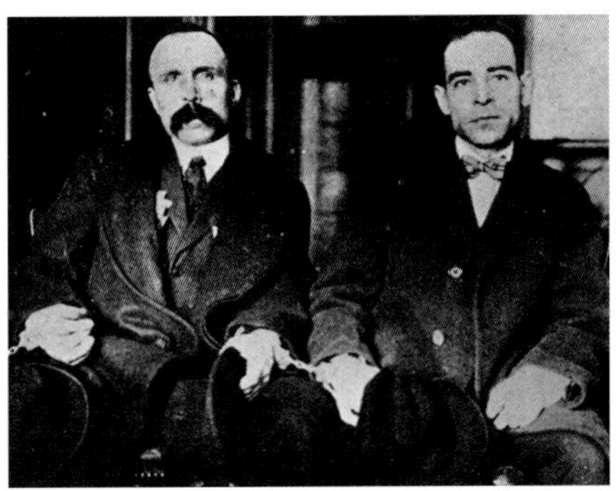

fig. 1

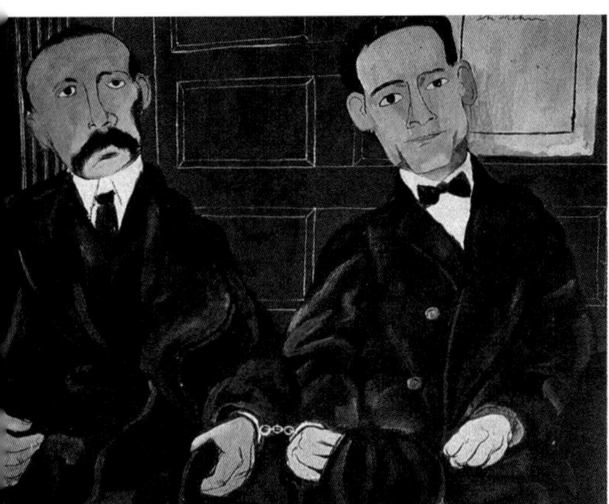

fig. 2

Shahn's painting depicts Sacco and Vanzetti frontally seated and handcuffed to one another before an impersonal, shallow architectural setting. Their somber expressions are reinforced by the rectilinear geometry and unadorned surfaces of the wall behind them. The painting bears close resemblance to the photograph, which Shahn used as inspiration for the overall composition, as well as for details such as Vanzetti's bushy mustache, Sacco's buttons and bow tie, the studs on the chairs, and the links of the handcuff chain, which at once connect the prisoners as double martyrs and call attention to their hands—icons of manual

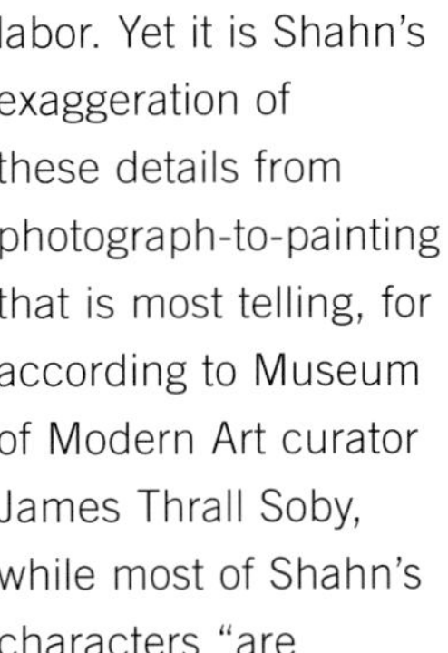

labor. Yet it is Shahn's exaggeration of these details from photograph-to-painting that is most telling, for according to Museum of Modern Art curator James Thrall Soby, while most of Shahn's characters "are depicted much as they appeared in stark press photographs... gradually we become aware how skillful has been the painter's intensification of truth."[34]

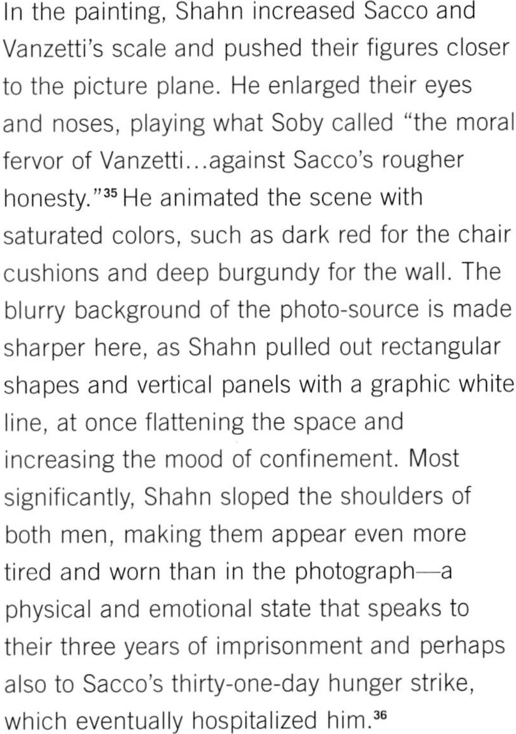

In the painting, Shahn increased Sacco and Vanzetti's scale and pushed their figures closer to the picture plane. He enlarged their eyes and noses, playing what Soby called "the moral fervor of Vanzetti...against Sacco's rougher honesty."[35] He animated the scene with saturated colors, such as dark red for the chair cushions and deep burgundy for the wall. The blurry background of the photo-source is made sharper here, as Shahn pulled out rectangular shapes and vertical panels with a graphic white line, at once flattening the space and increasing the mood of confinement. Most significantly, Shahn sloped the shoulders of both men, making them appear even more tired and worn than in the photograph—a physical and emotional state that speaks to their three years of imprisonment and perhaps also to Sacco's thirty-one-day hunger strike, which eventually hospitalized him.[36]

Shahn lowered both the chains of the handcuffs that link the men and Vanzetti's right arm and hand (the latter connected to a guard who is cropped out of this version of the source photograph). This results in more resigned body language, reinforced by the elimination of the paper sticking out of Vanzetti's coat pocket in the photograph. The paper suggests Vanzetti's habitual writing and reading in prison, his work on articles for anarchist newspapers, letters to supporters and to Judge Thayer, a petition to Governor Fuller, translations of books from Italian to English, and an autobiography.[37] (Vanzetti was known as the more articulate and eloquent in English of the two, the one who held out hope longer, and the one with the better claim to some degree of innocence). Shahn softened Vanzetti's agitated posture and expression as well as the intense, even angry (if not crazed) look in his eyes, making them sadder in the painting. Shahn may have been stressing Vanzetti's oft-noted self-control, calmness, and public composure. As for Sacco, his jaw protrudes more strongly here, while his lower cheeks are sunken more deeply. His eyes are widened, and his tightly pursed lips appear to be holding back emotion.[38]

Shahn tilted Sacco and Vanzetti's heads in the painting, creating more wistful, sympathy inspiring figures than those found in the news photograph. Like many of the intellectuals of his generation who embraced the Italian immigrants' cause, Shahn did not emphasize the men's revolutionary, militant activities, their unstinting belief in anarchism and in the complete destruction of government, law, and private property under the capitalist system—views they expressed quite openly and consistently in their letters.[39] By stressing their humbleness as "the poor fish peddler" and "the good shoemaker," respectively, Shahn avoided certain disturbing realities. According to historian Paul Avrich,

> *Far from being the innocent dreamers so often depicted by their supporters, [Sacco and Vanzetti] belonged to a branch of the anarchist movement which preached insurrectionary violence and armed retaliation, including the use of dynamite and assassination.*[40]

Changes made from the photograph to the painting speak to Shahn's emphasis on Sacco and Vanzetti's universal human qualities. Dorsky noted that by tempering the physical distinctions between the men in the painting, Shahn rendered them "more appealing," and "as victims," with "their sympathetic expressions."[41] Shahn was, in fact, conscious of presenting the sides of Sacco and Vanzetti that would elicit the greatest support for the larger cause. He said:

> *I was trying to take advantage of the spectator's existing feeling and set fire to that. I didn't try to convince Judge Thayer, or those who believed them guilty. But I do think that by presenting the two anarchists as the simple, gentle people they essentially were, I increased the conviction of those who believed them innocent.*[42]

This focus on "simple" and "gentle" virtues is apparent in Shahn's pictures of Sacco and Vanzetti's supporters, friends, and respective families and witnesses. Deadpan news photographs were used here to render folksy, cartoonlike figures, which reinforces the plainness and unpretentiousness of those who testified in favor of the defense. This, in turn, was designed to encourage a stronger public perception of the men's honesty and credibility.[43] According to the eminent Harvard law professor and future U.S. Supreme Court Justice Felix Frankfurter, the alibi for Vanzetti was "overwhelming" in his favor. Shahn supported this view in pictures like *Six Witnesses who bought eels from Vanzetti*, where he brought out from the blurry photograph the individual features of the women who testified to buying fish from Vanzetti the day of the Braintree murder **(figs. 3 & 4)**. This sharpening of details intensifies our direct engagement with the customers, who were among the many eyewitnesses who corroborated Vanzetti's testimony.[44]

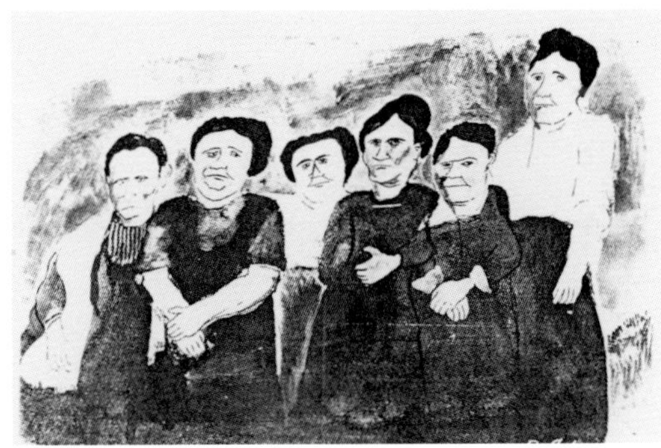

fig. 3

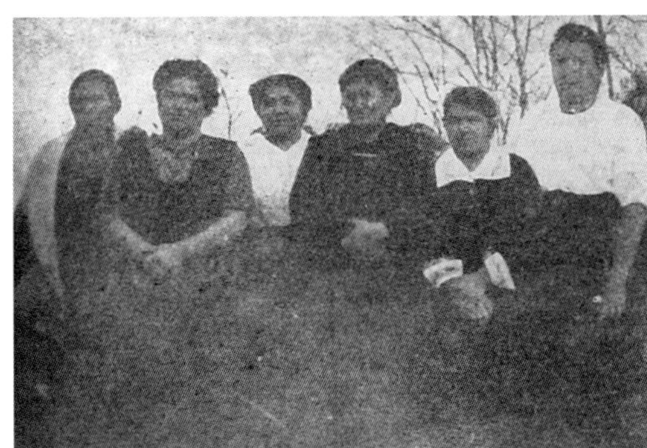

fig. 4

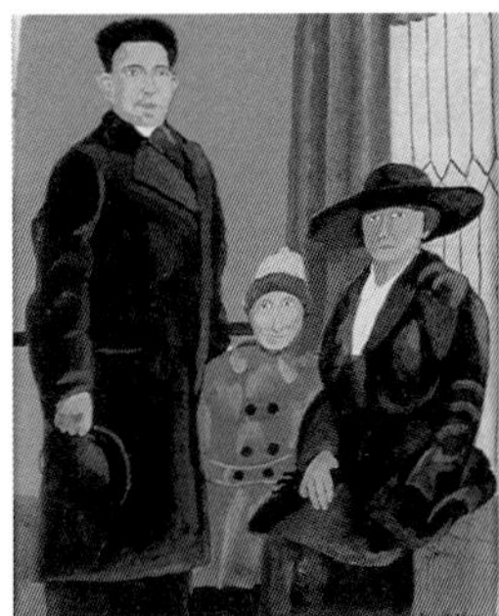

fig. 5

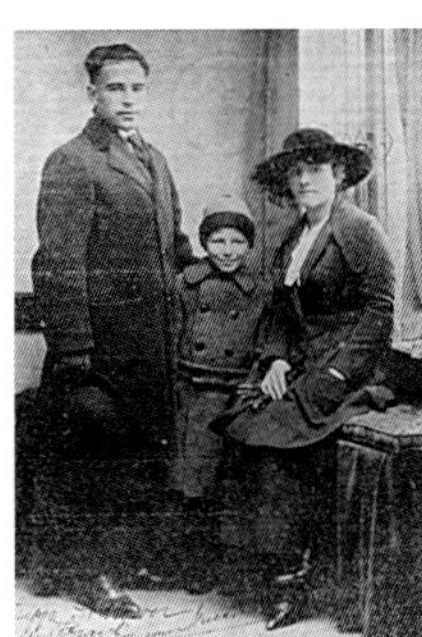

fig. 6

The painting *Nicola Sacco and his Wife and their Son, Dante*, compared to the United Press International photograph that inspired it, shows how Shahn aged Sacco and his family **(figs. 5 & 6)**. All three figures appear heftier, the wife looks matronly, and their seven-year-old son serious. Sacco stands slightly farther from his son, and against the largest patch of the bright blue background. This, along with the wispy red feather in his wife's hat, is incongruent with their somber faces—more somber here than in the photograph. These changes gain greater potency in light of the fact that the source photograph was taken in Boston shortly before Sacco's 1920 arrest. It was rejected at the Italian consulate for being too large for passport purposes. The photograph conveys more hope than the painting, the happier expressions reflecting perhaps the subjects' feelings about seeing their family in Italy, even if the trip was apparently for the purpose of visiting Sacco's recently bereaved father.[45] Shahn transformed the painting into a sadder, more foreboding picture, rendering it with the knowledge and hindsight of what he perceived as his subjects' tragic fate.

Similar effects are found in *Sacco's Family after the Verdict*, a picture of Sacco's extended family at his boyhood home in the southern Italian village of Torremaggiore. Here Shahn exploited the head-on seriousness and severe frontality of the figures in the source photograph, whose caption informs us that Sacco's brother recently had become mayor of the town and that Sacco regularly had been sending money to his parents until his arrest.[46] Shahn reinforced the mother's matriarchal presence and aged the nieces, intensifying their already somber expressions. In *Mrs. Sacco and Elizabeth Glendower Evans*, Shahn likewise exaggerated his subjects' countenances, compared to the United Press International photograph on which the double-portrait was based. In this painting, Shahn amplified the already sweetly animated expression of Sacco's wife Rosina, who smiles sincerely in a warm side embrace with her sturdy, bespectacled friend, Elizabeth Glendower Evans, the wealthy Bostonian and civil rights activist who was one of Sacco and Vanzetti's most loyal supporters **(figs. 7 & 8)**. Shahn stressed Rosina Sacco's white-toothed smile and the lattice design on her stylish hat, opening her eyes wider, elongating her face, and endowing her with pinkish toned skin.[47] Her youthful vitality

fig. 7

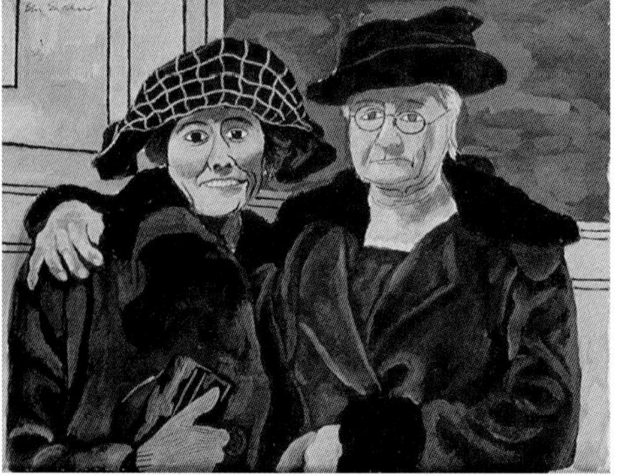

fig. 8

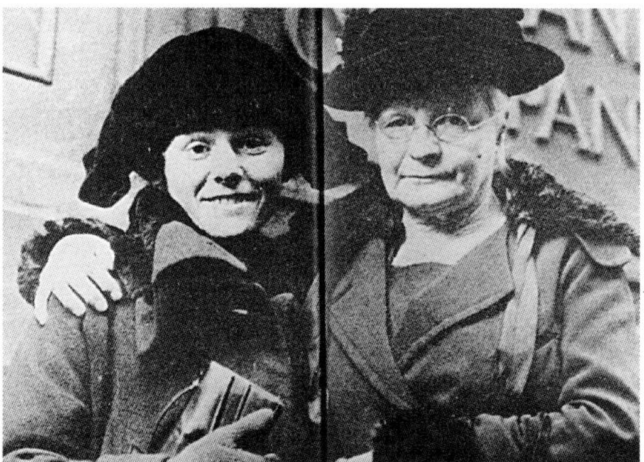

makes an even stronger contrast to the older, matronly Evans, who replete with neck wrinkles and brown complexion, frowns more here than in the photograph. The heightened contrasts between old and young underscore Evans's nurturing, maternal role; indeed, Sacco not only likened her to his own mother but called her "dear mother of the human oppressed."[48]

Mrs. Sacco is given a more secondary but still significant role in *In the Cage in the Court Room*, where the men appear in the prisoners' dock, looking tense and unusually angry **(fig. 9)**. Formally, the picture is the most abstract of the series, as Shahn relied on a United Press International photograph not only for its documentary information but also for its surrealism **(fig. 10)**.[49] Admiring the work of Eugène Atget and Henri Cartier-Bresson, Shahn embraced the particular ways that photographs can distort form and reveal unexpected truths, illuminating what he referred to as "the extraordinary aspect of the ordinary."[50] From this UPI source, Shahn took the strange space created by the metal bars of the cage and turned it into a spare, abstract design in the painting, removing some of its regularity and paring down the scroll-patterned border to thin lines without depth. Shahn exploited the disembodied quality of the figures found in the photograph; floating here, their bodies are nonexistent beyond the collars of their jackets. Rosina Sacco appears as a featureless silhouette in a blue coat, more upright in her stance (she leans forward in the source and is closer to Sacco), her pale blank face keeping her in her own space, disconnected from Sacco and Vanzetti. The faces of the two men are altered as well; Vanzetti looks more angry than anxious, with his one visible, demonlike eye focused in the direction of Rosina and his face inflamed with a fiery orange color. Sacco's expression is transformed from passive, inward reflection or worry to a more active look of scheming; his right eye even appears to wink at Vanzetti, as if in cahoots.

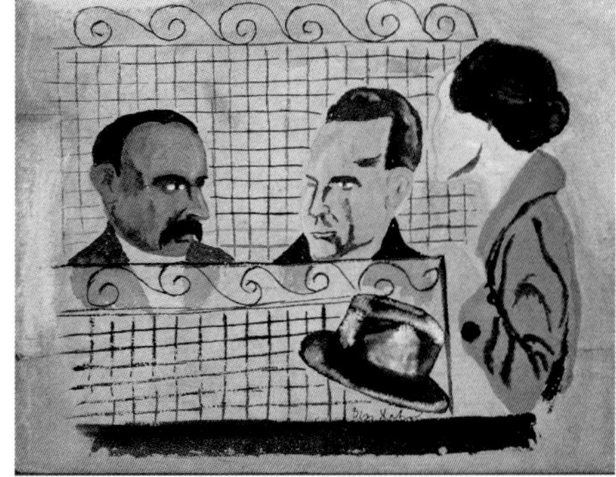

fig. 9

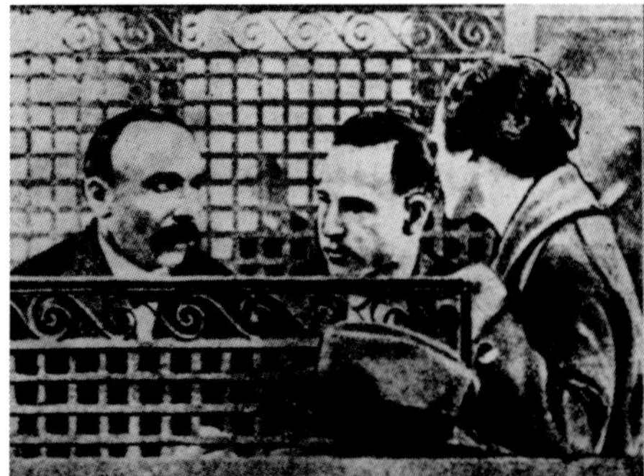

fig. 10

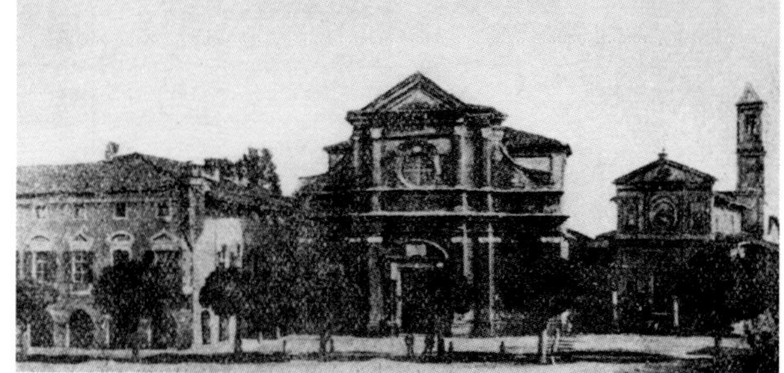

fig. 11

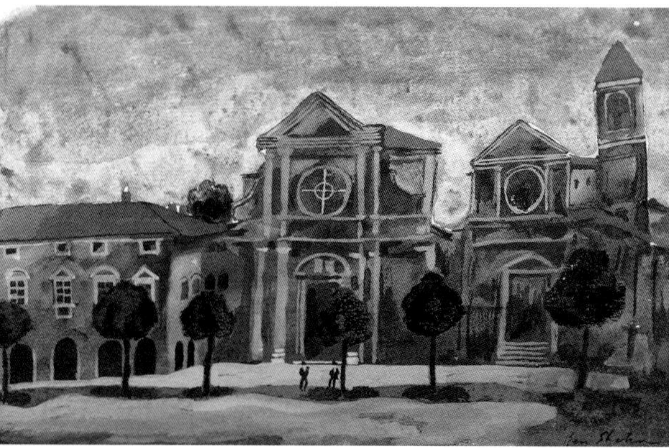

fig. 12

the courtroom as an observer, visitor or juror, and recalls the placement of his name on the empty picture frame shape in the background of *Nicola Sacco and Bartolomeo Vanzetti*. It is as if the artist were bearing witness to these momentous events, which he likened to a modern-day crucifixion, thus affirming his picture's authenticity.

Shahn was sensitive to what he perceived as the inhumane treatment of Sacco and Vanzetti, as symbolized by the cage structure (still commonly used in courtrooms at the time) and the emotional state to which such treatment could drive human beings.[51] By reducing the courtroom to just the bare outlines of the cage, Shahn increased the viewers' sense of the men's restricted physical environment. The whimsical designs of the railing at once contrast with the seriousness of the subject, and emphasize the men's haunting apparitions. Shahn's sympathy for the men is literally inscribed into the picture, as he placed his signature under the hat (reduced from two to one here), which hovers slightly above a precarious ledge. This gesture puts Shahn in

Vanzetti's family support is suggested in *Villa felletto, Vanzetti's Home Town*, and is expressed more directly in *Demonstration In Paris*. For *Villa felletto*, Shahn stayed close to the structures in the source photograph of this northern Italian town, where Vanzetti's father owned a farm **(figs. 11 & 12)**.[52] Shahn reduced the number of trees across the foreground, made the buildings less regular, and pulled out details such as windows, doors and columns, whose arched shapes he took delight in rhyming with the trees. He pushed the buildings closer together, which along with their warm, rusty colored rooftops, enhances their quaintness. This in turn implies a humble background for Vanzetti, who actually had grown up in the comfort of a middle-class home headed by a "substantial farmer."[53] Shahn also amplified the cross in the circular window of the central edifice and increased the size of the structure to its right, including the church tower. This alludes to Vanzetti's strict, devout Catholic upbringing and the looming presence of religion in his hometown community. The emphasis is ironic in light of the fact that as anarchists Sacco and Vanzetti abhorred organized religion for—in Vanzetti's words—"historical, economical, moral reasons." Suggesting piety (or pious backgrounds) was thus another way Shahn underscored the men's innocence, and aligned himself with supporters who anointed the men as saintly, Christlike martyrs. Shahn spoke of the event as a modern-day crucifixion, and of "recreating the religious drama." Even Sacco and Vanzetti themselves evoked Christianity in their own letters.[54]

Shahn altered the photographic source more dramatically when constructing *Demonstration in Paris*, which depicts Vanzetti's sister Luigia leading a Sacco and Vanzetti parade in Paris—and, for the initiated, recalls Shahn's own stint in Paris as a "lost generation" art student during the expatriate twenties **(figs. 13 &14)**.[55] By using only the central part of the news photograph, and by blowing it up, Shahn heightened the drama of the event. By singling out individuals in a crowd, he allowed a few to speak for the many. Such pictorial strategies also helped him to distinguish character, age, class and nationality. The range of men's hats from fedora to cap speaks to the bourgeois and worker presence in the demonstration, while the contrast between Luigia's Italian hat and the French beret and orange fringe scarf of the man escorting her reflects the different cultures involved in the event. Zooming in on the middle

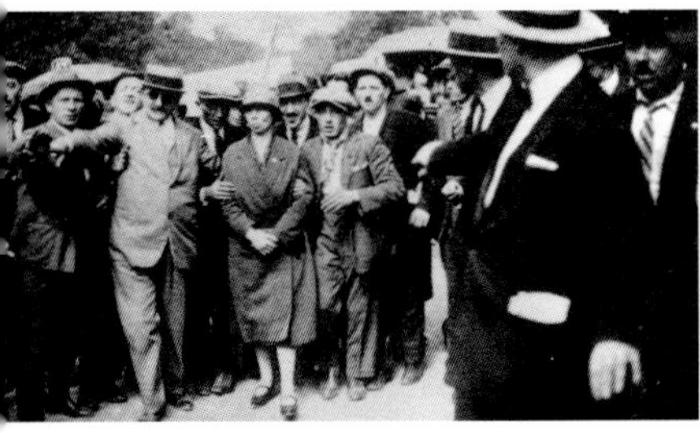

fig. 13

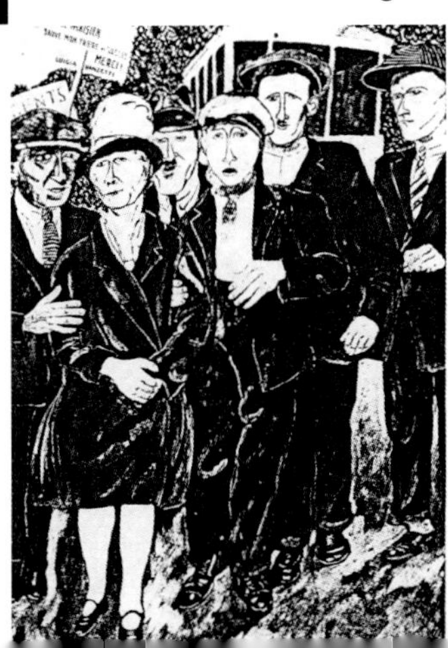

fig. 14

section of the photograph for his imagery also enabled Shahn to emphasize the hands of his subjects, figuratively linked here in international solidarity over the Sacco and Vanzetti cause.

Pushed closer to the viewers' space and given expressive facial detail, the figures in *Demonstration in Paris* confront us as specific individuals. They symbolize the great efforts and loyal support of Vanzetti's sister, who traveled to the United States via France on her brother's behalf. By 1927, Vanzetti had been apart from his sister for nineteen years; he desired to see her before he died.[56] Such family devotion would no doubt have been endearing to viewers, as is the support Luigia receives from the men leading her through the demonstration. In the painting, her worry—defined by droopy eyes, pursed lips, clasped hands, and overall distressed body language—is more palpable than in the source photograph. While she is protected in both, in the photograph she seems more vulnerable, surrounded by men in a larger crowd, some of whom clear the way for her safe passage, which suggests a stronger sense of pending doom.

The painting eliminates the chaos of the source, foregrounds Luigia's purpose, and renders the picture's content clearer. Such narrative clarity is strengthened by details that are sharpened and made readable here, such as the slogans on the signs appealing to the French people to save Luigia's brother and Sacco, and the foreshortened trolley-type object in the background. Enlarged and emphasized in the painting, Shahn gave the structure the same chartreuse shade he used for Luigia's hat and bow/collar, at once linking them and reminding us of her recent arrival. Shahn delighted in using painting's ability to achieve the kind of visual specificity more typically associated with documentary photography. He felt, in this respect, that he had more control in painting than in photography, which was one reason why he ultimately preferred the canvas to the camera in his own artistic practice.[57]

THE JUDICIARY AND PROSECUTION PICTURES

Shahn's paintings of the judiciary and prosecution side of the Sacco and Vanzetti case, although fewer in number than the defense pictures, are equally dependent on news photographs. Shahn used photographs to undermine the dignity and authority of the legal figures who officiated over the trial, and in the tradition of Honoré Daumier, Kathe Kollwitz, and George Grosz, employed the devices of political caricature to depict the "villains" in the case. Indeed, as one critic noted, Shahn "managed a magnificent assault on the seigneurs of the exalted Massachusetts judiciary."[58] In *The Four Prosecutors*, for example, Shahn exploited the matter-of-fact quality of the men's stances and expressions found in the source photograph, placing them against an architectural background of obsessively rendered bricks, which hardens their beings while providing formal grounding and urban context **(figs. 15 & 16)**.[59] Architecture, as in much of Shahn's work, functions here in Soby's words "as both psychological foil to human figures and as expressive abstract pattern."[60]

In the painting, Shahn distorted the lawyers' physiques by dropping their shoulders, elongating their necks, and tilting their heads more dramatically, making them disproportionate to their bodies. With his incisive graphic line, Shahn imitated and exaggerated the cutout quality of the figures in the photograph, which appear even stiffer against the painted architecture. The men also look older in the painting, with less flattering, even smirky expressions. This is seen, for example, in the figure of Frederick G. Katzmann (second from left), district attorney and head prosecutor of Sacco and Vanzetti at the Dedham trial, who was detested by them for his alleged lies and other unethical behavior.[61] Shahn emphasized Katzmann's head and

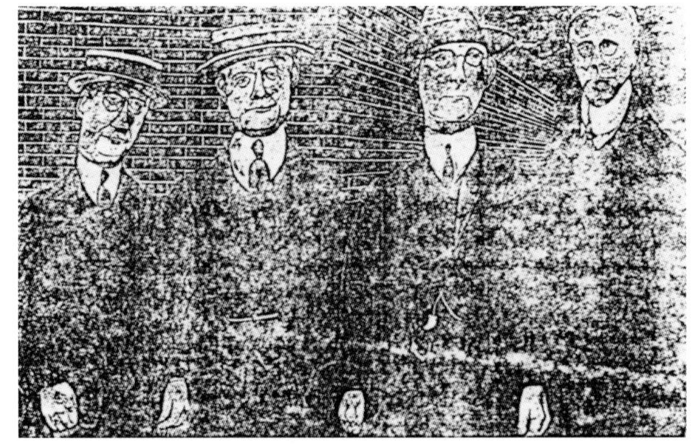

fig. 15

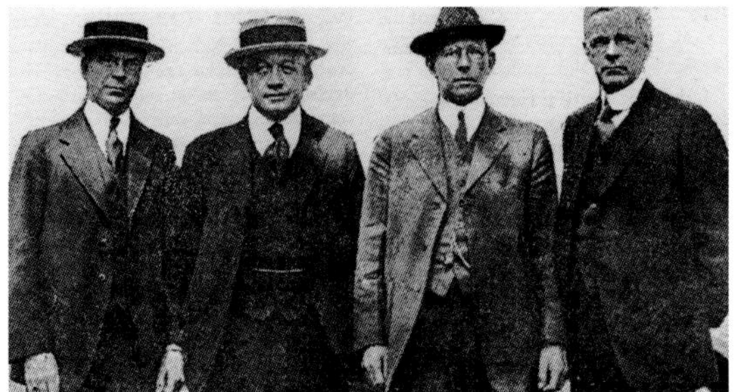

fig. 16

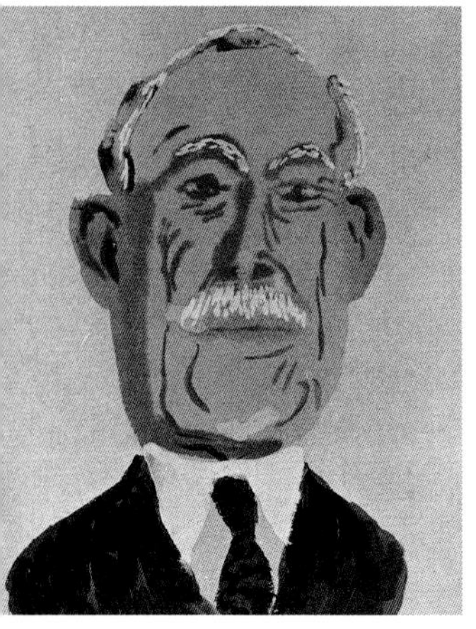

fig. 17

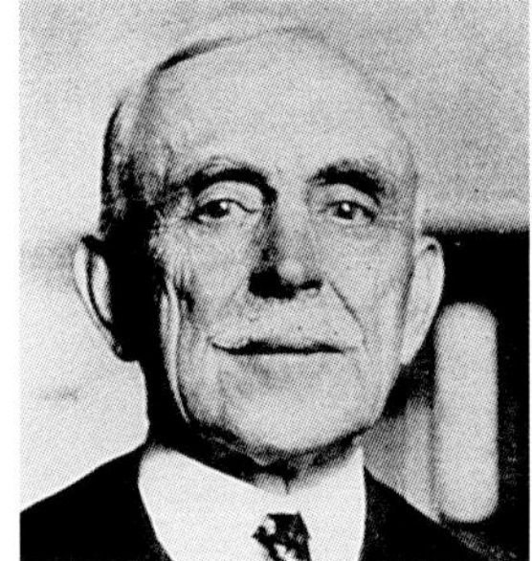

fig. 18

fig. 19

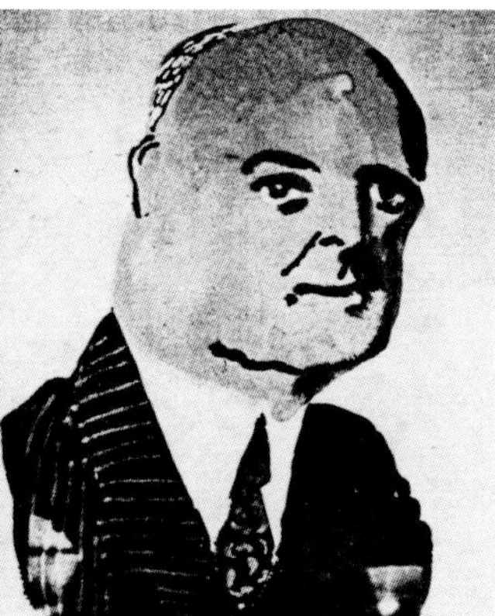

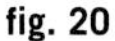

fig. 20

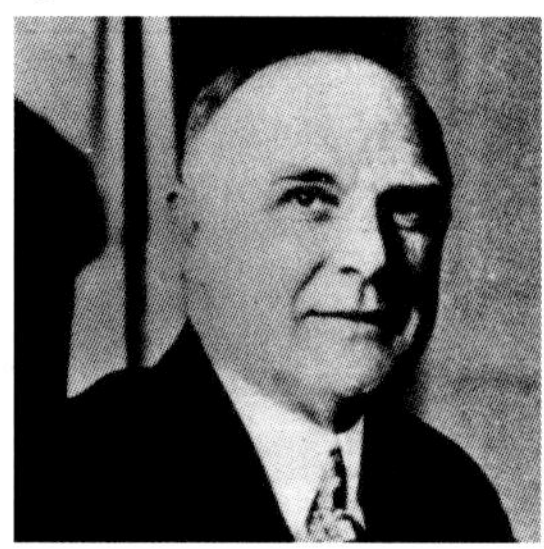

neck here, which like those of his fellow prosecutors (whose hands are also intensified) renders his form puppetlike. His colleague William F. Kane looks the silliest, as the rabbit's foot he dons suggests superstitions that further undermine the rational legal system that he—and his cohorts—were supposed to represent.

Subtle satirical mocking also characterizes *Judge Webster Thayer*, a portrait of the Boston blue-blood judge who found Sacco and Vanzetti guilty of first-degree murder on grounds of "consciousness of guilt" and pronounced the death penalty **(fig. 17)**. Thayer too appears older and less distinguished here than in the source photograph **(fig. 18)**.[62] By elongating and loosening the lines of his "square, stony New England face," Shahn softened some of the hardness of Thayer's straight, thin-lipped mouth and cold, penetrating eyes.[63] But the looser lines do not temper the judge's severity; rather they exaggerate his facial wrinkles, which in turn age him. Shahn used a white, rice-shaped brushstroke to convey the brittleness of Thayer's eyebrows, mustache, and hair and a royal blue applied more loosely for his formal attire and to highlight his enlarged ears. He brought the judge's eyes closer together and rendered them beadier and shifty; as they do not meet the viewer's eyes, Thayer's character and soul remain remote, impenetrable, and hence, questionable. Indeed, Thayer was the most reviled by Sacco and Vanzetti of the trial personalities; he had been accused of judicial indiscretion, blatantly expressing in public his deeply felt prejudices and hostility towards Italian immigrants of Sacco and Vanzetti's "ilk."[64]

The Massachusetts governor was portrayed more positively than Thayer in *Governor Alvan T. Fuller*, as Shahn drew on a more flattering, less frontal photograph to begin with **(figs.19 & 20)**.[65] A self-made millionaire, described by recent historians as "a successful car dealer, amateur politician, and White House aspirant," Fuller in 1927 appointed a blue-ribbon advisory panel (the Lowell Committee) to assess the fairness of the trial.[66] Lighter in mood than the Thayer picture, and retaining the full face, thick neck, and some of the pleasant smile found in its source photograph, the Fuller portrait expresses Shahn's probable awareness of the fact that certain Sacco and Vanzetti supporters had more faith in Fuller than Sacco and Vanzetti did. According to Vanzetti, "Fuller boasts himself, making the liberals believe, to be a liberal...some liberals know Fuller as an independent man, willing to do the right thing as he sees it...that he will do justice." Even though the governor turned down a petition for clemency right before the execution, he did grant an extension at the last minute to allow more appeals. Still, Sacco and Vanzetti thought Fuller was as evil as the rest of the trial officials; Vanzetti even referred to Fuller's article "Why I believe in Capital Punishment" to support his strong distrust of the governor.[67]

The Apotheosis Pictures

The most haunting painting in Shahn's series is the last one, *That Agony is Our Triumph*, which features Sacco and Vanzetti in their coffins being paid respects by a group of mourners. Since this picture is currently unlocated and no visual record of it is known to this author, its relationship to its photographic sources can best be gleaned from examining a work that it inspired, *The Passion of Sacco and Vanzetti* **(fig. 21)**.[68] Painted soon after the series was completed for an exhibition on mural painting sponsored by the Museum of Modern Art in 1932, this monumental panel retains Sacco and Vanzetti in their biers, but replaces the mourners with the Lowell Committee, the investigative group appointed by Governor Fuller that included President A. Lawrence Lowell of Harvard University, retired Judge Robert Grant, and President Samuel Stratton of the Massachusetts Institute of Technology.[69] A portrait of *Judge Thayer* (based on Judge Webster Thayer from the series) hangs in the columned courthouse background. The picture addresses the end of the Sacco and Vanzetti ordeal, focusing with sharp wit on the relationship between the accusers and the accused. It relates to another painting, *The*

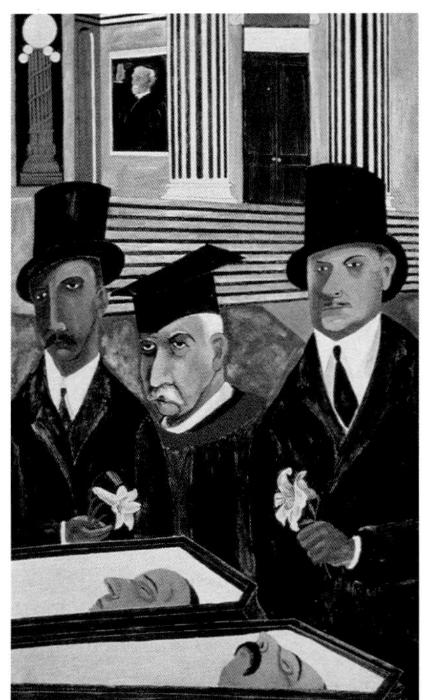

fig. 21

Lowell Committee, which Soby called "a scalding satirical image" in a series whose impact "comes from its laconic dignity." Matthew Josephson felt that Shahn "let himself go rippingly on the subject of Judge Thayer, the Lowell Committee, the Four Prosecutors and their colleagues. Here is fishy, green-eyed, bony-faced, lantern-jawed Thayer, painted for all posterity in his hollow robes of justice. Here are the three silk-hatted, degenerate-looking Yankees of the Lowell Committee, against a classical, papier-mache court-house."[70] *The Passion of Sacco and Vanzetti*'s complexity comes in large part from its photographic inspiration. The picture is unusual compared to those in the series in that it draws on elements from a number of photographic sources.[71] The process of using several photographs (or several photo-based paintings) to make one painting was akin to the detail-gathering of social scientists in the 1930s who similarly immersed themselves in the "facts" in order to responsibly make larger generalizations about their chosen subjects via case-study research and writing. From an article entitled "'Amnesty!' on Sacco-Vanzetti Day!," in the August 1931 issue of *The Labor Defender*, Shahn appropriated Sacco and Vanzetti's open caskets, but presented only part of them in his painting in order to give more attention to the men's faces **(fig. 22)**.[73] He exaggerated the disembodied, floating heads in the caskets, leaving more white space around Sacco. Most dramatically, Shahn substituted the original funeral mourners seen in the photograph—a crowd of workers who "came in thousands"—with the three Lowell Committee members derived from Keystone, Wide World, and Harris and Ewing news photographs **(fig.23)**.[74] This shifts the focus from the relationship of Sacco and Vanzetti and their loyal

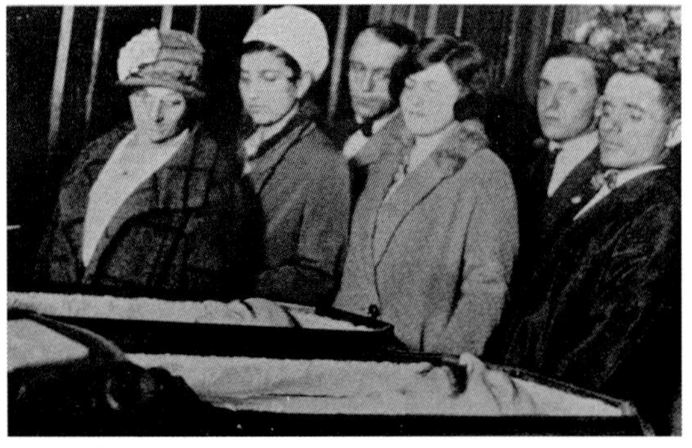

fig. 22

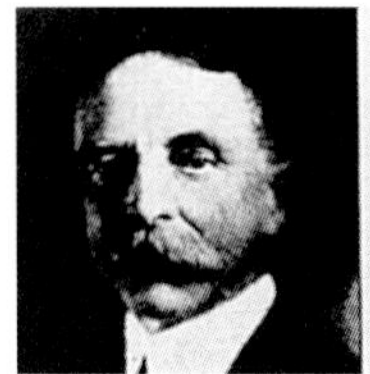
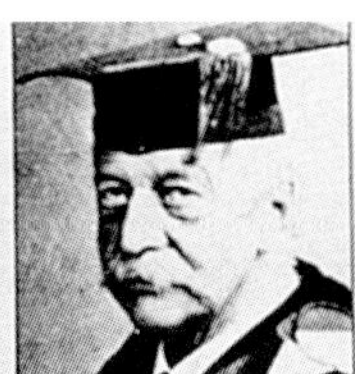
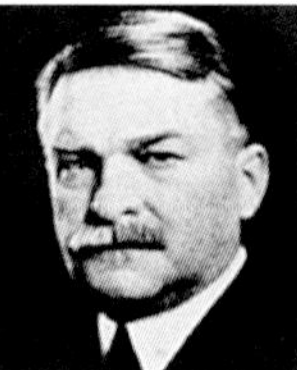

fig. 23

sympathizers (which he retained in *That Agony is Our Triumph*) to a more disturbing and provocative one between the men and their accusers. It also underscores tensions between social classes, affirming John Dos Passos's conclusion in *U.S.A.* (1938) that "we are two nations," as well as what historians James West Davidson and Mark Hamilton Lytle have cited as the "tensions besetting American society and particularly the sense among liberals and radicals that the ruling class had betrayed the nation."[75]

In the painting, Shahn distorted bodily and facial features, thinning out Grant and Stratton, dramatically sloping their shoulders, elongating their noses, narrowing their eyes, and thus tempering the dignified intensity of their photographic depictions. He added more of their bodies here than found in the source photographs, allowing them to uncomfortably hold single white lilies, which along with their wearing of stiff top hats (also added), emerge as pathetic, hollow and obligatory gestures of remorse. Their impassive expressions speak to the ineffectiveness of the men—icons of the social and educational elite of Massachusetts—on the Lowell Committee. According to historians Louis Joughin and Edmund Morgan, both Stratton and Grant were bad choices for the Committee. They claimed that Stratton "had no reputation in public affairs, and in the sittings of the Committee remained almost completely silent," while the elderly Grant, though well-read and traveled, "was defectively innocent of any realistic knowledge of the world in which he lived and he had no important reputation as a legal scholar." Lowell's smaller physical stature, sad eyes, white hair, and academic robes make him slightly more endearing than his cohorts, yet he by no means stands as the man of exceptional moral character for which he was known—"rich, revered and powerful throughout New England, and possessed of an intellect of the first order."[76] Shahn's ironic treatment, in fact, questions the sincerity of all three men, each of whom looks out of the picture instead of down at the dead bodies of Sacco and Vanzetti, the subjects of their visit. Even though the committee's expressions are somewhat opaque and implacable in the painting, when compared to their photographic sources, Shahn's unflattering caricatures become all the more evident.

Shahn extracted the background of the painting from a news photograph of the Dedham courthouse that he cut from a Sacco and Vanzetti Defense Committee pamphlet for his clipping files **(fig. 24)**.[77] The courthouse, according to Marion Frankfurter and Gardner Jackson "furnished a striking contrast to the background and antecedents of the prisoners. Dedham is a quiet residential suburb, inhabited by well-to-do Bostonians with a

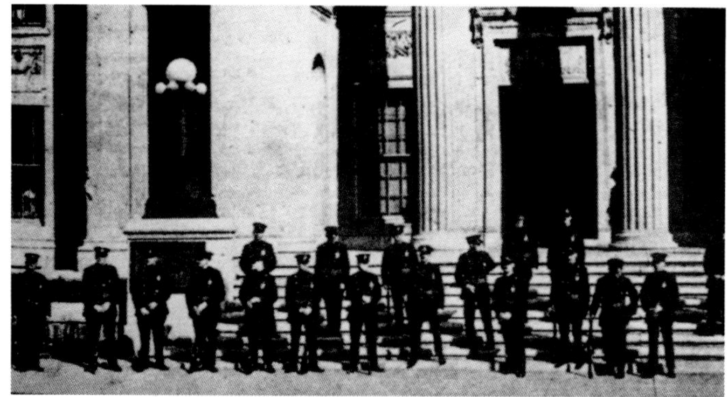

fig. 24

surviving element of New England small farmers."[78] From the source image, Shahn drew on the simplified, handsome granite architecture, the Doric columns, the stairs and lampposts, eliminating the police and the windows, and much of the architectural detail. Yet he retained essential features, such as the fluting on the lamppost and on the monumental columns, and the moldings flanking the central doorway, which along with the serious portrait of Thayer with his hand raised in an oath of truth telling, convey the weight of tradition and history. Such gravity is lightened only by the dynamism of the painting, which Shahn achieved by slanting and splaying the stairs, and by collapsing the pictorial space.

Time is equally collapsed in Shahn's picture, as the process of bringing together elements from several photographs (and paintings) combines different moments into a composite whole. The Dedham courthouse was where Sacco and Vanzetti's fate was sealed; Thayer was involved in the case from the beginning (and had been the judge in Vanzetti's earlier Plymouth trial); the Lowell Committee was the men's last hope to escape execution; and the funeral setting signifies the end of their lives and of the case, at least literally. The montaging of photographic images representing key moments in the ordeal endows the picture with an even more dramatic and culminating role than *That Agony is Our Triumph*, which was itself described by critics as "a most dignified last testament," that brought "the theme to a focal point" in an otherwise unclimactic and only loosely chronological series.[79]

NEWSPAPERS, PHOTOGRAPHS AND THE RHETORIC OF OBJECTIVITY[80]

It is almost impossible to be objective. You read your paper, notice its editorials, get praised for some stories and criticized for others. You "sense policy" and are psychologically driven to slant your stories accordingly.—**Leo Rosten, 1937** [81]

The most successful newspaper men and women of the future will be those with…the ability to avoid emotionalism and to remain objective, descriptive styles, the power of observation, and, above all, the ability to comprehend the meaning of immediate news events in relation to broader social, economic, and political trends.—**Curtis MacDougall, 1938** [82]

What does the [press] photograph transmit? By definition, the scene itself, the literal reality. From the object to its image there is of course a reduction—in proportion, perspective, colour—but at no time is this reduction a transformation*….Certainly the image is not the reality but at least it is its perfect* analogon *and it is exactly this analogical perfection which, to common sense, defines the photograph.*—**Roland Barthes, 1961** [83]

Shahn's use of photographs to construct the Sacco and Vanzetti series established a working process in which the artist would engage for several decades. This process became increasingly more complicated over the course of the 1930s and 1940s, as he drew on multiple newspaper and other documentary photographs that he and others took while working for government agencies such as RA/FSA and the Office of War Information (OWI). Employing photography enabled Shahn to feel engaged in the real world (and with his own photography, to speak about his subjects from firsthand experience). At the same time, the process allowed him to achieve an appearance of objectivity in his painting, which would in turn lend his work the weight of socially responsible documentation. Indeed, it was the "surgical" objectivity, the restraint and the seeming nonpartisanship of the Sacco and Vanzetti series upon which many of Shahn's reviewers commented.[84] This objectivity, however, as I have demonstrated, is thrown into question after close analysis of the photographic sources, for Shahn's changes from photograph to painting reveal decidedly leftist biases.[85]

The objectivity often associated with Shahn's series comes in part from his use of newspaper photographs and captions and the way he emulated the look of deadpan reportage in his gouaches. While the connection between newspapers and at least the intention of objectivity seems logical today, this was not always the case. According to sociologist Michael Schudson, objectivity in American newspapers was not an issue before the 1830s. The notion of an impartial news emerged in the Jacksonian period, and was a product of what Schudson calls "the democratization of politics, the expansion of a market economy, and the growing authority of an entrepreneurial, urban middle class." Impartial journalism involved the naive empiricist belief in "just the facts," which were understood as already existing in the world, as opposed to being constructed by human beings. Schudson claims that this was not objectivity, and in fact,

> *[n]ot until after World War I...did the ideal of objectivity as consensually validated statements about the world, predicated on a radical separation of facts and values, arise...when the worth of the democratic market society was itself radically questioned and its internal logic laid bare, did leaders in journalism and other fields, like the social sciences, fully experience the doubting and skepticism democracy and the market encouraged.*[87]

In other words, objectivity became a concern only when disillusionment with the institutions of capitalism and democracy emerged. "Even at the height of prosperity in the twenties," Schudson argues, "and even, or especially, among liberal intellectuals, there was deep pessimism about political democracy."[88] Pessimism increased in the 1930s with the rise of Nazism and Fascism in Europe, and with the American government's struggle to cope with the effects of the stock market crash.[89] Journalists and reporters became suspicious of "the facts" with the development of public relations, which was thought to have "managed or manipulated public opinion in the name of public service," and with the spread of World War I propaganda. One response by the press in the 1920s and 1930s to the "subjectivization of facts," says Schudson, was an embrace of subjectivity (through the use of by-lines), specialization, and interpretive journalism. The other response, he notes, was the call for professionalization in journalism, "to replace a simple faith in facts with an allegiance to rules and procedures created for a world in which even facts were in question. This was 'objectivity.'"[90]

Given that the concept of objectivity gained new currency, even urgency, in the 1930s (by middle of the decade, the term "objectivity" was commonly used in the press, as it connoted a respected professional value in journalism), it is tempting to think of Shahn's use of news photographs as an embrace of the ideal of objectivity for his painting. But just as objectivity, in Schudson's words "became an ideal in journalism...when the impossibility of overcoming subjectivity in presenting the news was widely accepted," Shahn's use of news photographs acknowledges the subjectivity of camera vision as much as it emulates its look of objectivity.[91] As mentioned earlier, Shahn valued newspaper photographs as much for their surrealism, and their distortions of the seen world, as for their realism. He enjoyed the ways he could achieve greater clarity and blow up details in his paintings that were blurry in many of the news photographs and photoengravings he gathered at the time. According to photo-historian Van Deren Coke, in Shahn's Sacco and Vanzetti series: "[f]rom photographs he took gestures, details, and situations which sometimes retain the visual energy of the prototype but more often mock the factuality of the camera."[92] Using newspaper photographs as sources was thus a way for Shahn to comment on the nature of those very sources, enabling him to engage in a kind of metacommentary not often associated with his seemingly straightforward illustration, didactic propaganda, and/or allegorical social realist practice.

Shahn's use of newspaper photographs as symbols of "objectivity" is further complicated by the fact that newspapers were commonly held in suspicion throughout the 1930s. Many were conservative, Republican, probusiness, and antilabor, leading Stott to claim that "in no other decade was the American press so out of step with its audience."[93] According to Robertson,

> *While news photographs might seem to have a superior claim [to truthfulness compared] to any other visual medium, in fact their power was compromised by the fact that they were seen, paradoxically, in newspapers. During this period, as newspapers consistently underreported the devastation of the Depression and (for the most part) railed against Roosevelt, their objectivity was held in dangerously low regard; the idea of "reportage," the complex investigation and rendering of an important trend or event, was developed in magazines and other media.*[94]

Shahn's awareness of this phenomenon is evident in what newspapers he preferred to read, which can be gleaned from his clipping and source files. While Shahn cut from a variety of major New York and Washington, D.C. newspapers, the *New York Times*, reputed for its mainstream objective reporting, and which radicals read with fervent seriousness, is predominant.[95] His attraction to news photographs, as mentioned earlier, can be seen as a response to what Robertson has called newspapers' "new emphasis on photography," which "given the low esteem newspapers were then held in...may have exploited the general sense of photography's truthfulness."[96]

Finally, employing newspapers for the Sacco and Vanzetti series may also have been a way for Shahn to speak to ordinary people. Newspapers signify the everyday world, both in the current events they report to broad audiences and in what they are physically: disposable material to be read and thrown away soon after. Even though Shahn later said to Dorsky that he intended his series for "Park Avenue, rather than fourteenth street," working class Italians and anarchists—not a typical gallery crowd—were among those who came to see the exhibition at the Downtown Gallery. (Ironically, they found the works ugly and did not purchase them despite Halpert's low prices).[97] Shahn made his own wooden frames for the pictures, which increased their humble folk quality, and his choice of gouache can be seen as a rejection of the preciousness and "high art" connotations of oil painting. His titles, which he apparently painted on the paintings initially, presumably to make them more accessible, simulate direct, matter-of-fact newspaper captions.[98]

PAINTING AND PHOTOGRAPHY: AN UNEASY ALLIANCE[99]

Art can be far more powerful than the camera, for where the photograph is limited to story-telling art can soar to interpretation of theme.

—William Vaughan, 1932[100]

You do have a chance, in comparing Shahn's photographs and paintings on the same subject, to study some of the essential and profound differences between photography and painting. The painter has opportunities for emphasis which we shall never have in photography, and we photographers have a convincingness (even when we are lying) that the public will always accept. Those painter fellows, maybe they put in what they wanted to, and made those people look mean, or dumb, or nice, when they really weren't. But the humble, honest photographer couldn't possibly do that with his camera.

—Mabel Scacheri, 1947[101]

Shahn's newspaper-inspired captions, his close formal reliance on news photographs, as well as his open requests to find photographic material from various Sacco and Vanzetti agencies and research institutions, suggest that he was not hiding his use of photographs in the painting process. But Shahn's attitudes towards using photography and publicly displaying the relationship between the two media in his work were inconsistent and fraught with ambivalence. This ambivalence was informed by prevailing prejudices about such artistic practice, about long-standing perceptions of the respective natures of painting and photography, and about the still tenuous status of photography as a fine art at that time. Shahn could be quite open about revealing the connections between his paintings and his own photographs, as evident in his 1940 response to Ann Henry of *PM Weekly*, who wanted to include examples of Shahn's work in both media in a two-page spread on painters who take photographs. He scribbled on her letter that he was "anxious to cooperate" and in a more formal response explained that he always took photographs for his own use, not for photography's sake, and that his point of view in both media was the same.[102] Six years later, Shahn was apparently displeased with the *U.S. Camera* article "Photos For Art," which juxtaposed his photographs and paintings more extensively than ever before. This was noted by Soby, who was organizing a Shahn retrospective for the Museum of Modern Art in 1947. Soby, who also did not like the article, thought it linked the two media in Shahn's work too closely and failed to acknowledge "how different the paintings are [from the photographs] in conception and spirit." Shahn was in fact reluctant to include his photography in the MoMA exhibition.[103] According to the art historian Frances Pohl, it was at this time that Shahn and Soby tried "to distance [his] paintings from his photographs, giving primacy to the former."[104] Both likely believed that exhibiting paintings and photographs together could encourage viewers to make simplistic connections between the two media, overlooking the nuances of the working process as well as the aesthetic independence and individual integrity of the paintings. Such juxtapositions could also make Shahn vulnerable to critics who might judge one medium superior to the other or attack his originality.[105]

From early on, Shahn openly acknowledged (and even boasted about) his photo-source files to interested critics and scholars, thereby naturalizing an artist's use of photographs as common studio paraphernalia and tools of the trade. He said in a 1964 interview that photographs formed the basis of much of his art from the late 1930s to the mid-1940s.[106] Later, after noting fourteenth- and fifteenth-century Italian painters' employment of detailed engravings and etchings as "the first use of 'photography' by artists," Shahn expressed annoyance at the endless debates on the relationship between painting and photography and hoped they would come to an end. He said to photography critic Arthur Goldsmith that

> *[t]he battle of art versus photography is an old, cold war and I wish everyone concerned would call a halt to it. If you have a good eye you can be either a good photographer or a good painter.... Both mediums have enriched each other over the years. Cezanne's "The Bather" was based on a photograph. Degas often used photographs, and the camera stimulated him to new compositional ideas—the abrupt portions of foreground objects, for instance, the use of high angles, and so forth.*[107]

Given these attitudes, it is curious that when retrospectively discussing his own paintings in writings, lectures, or interviews, Shahn typically did not mention specific photographs used or credit the photographers or newspapers from which the sources came. He implied instead that his experiences and memories, as they were recorded by preparatory drawings, were the seeds of his ideas.[108] These omissions can be explained partly by failed memory, by his own awareness of the biases against using camera images, and by the ubiquitous nature of photographs in our society. So thoroughly do photographs—especially newspaper images—saturate our culture, that they are considered authorless public property, fair game to be freely used, altered, manipulated, and reproduced.[109] This casual attitude was summed up succinctly in 1953 by the conservative art historian Kenneth Clark, who remarked:

> *we do not often cut out such [press] photographs for prolonged contemplation; on the other hand if you go to an artist's studio, it is ten to one you will find torn out press photographs pinned up on the walls.... The photograph is a piece of raw material. The artist likes it precisely because he can re-shape it, because it is still in a state to receive the imprint of his mind. And for the same reason we throw it aside after a single interested glance.*[110]

Shahn did in fact save many of his Sacco and Vanzetti photographic sources, and, despite his casual attitudes, in 1950 he told Dorsky "that at the time [of the series] he felt very insecure and guilty about his use of photos." Indeed, even though many painters of Shahn's generation had embraced the ease and convenience of the 35mm cameras as sketchpads to make notes for their painting, many others, like Moses Soyer, disapproved of the practice.[111] In 1934, photo-historian Beaumont Newhall noted that "[t]here is hardly an artist practicing today who does not consider the photograph a mechanical debasement of his art—anti-art—void of all creativeness."[112] Shahn was fully aware of the stigmas attached to a painter's use of photography, which might be thought of as compromising creative imagination and artistic integrity, taking short cuts towards noble ends, and hence, a form of cheating. For some, it was an indication that an artist couldn't draw. Shahn himself warned against artists working from photographs before they mastered drawing. He believed that "photography is no substitute for [drawing]—then use photographs to reinforce and stimulate your mind's eye."[113] Yet Shahn could also be irreverent and audacious about his use of photography and according to Dorsky he "delighted in the hostility of the artists in his milieu, who looked down upon photography used this way as artifice and unprofessional."[114]

Shahn's dealer, Edith Halpert, was not interested in displaying the results of such practice in her Downtown Gallery. In fact, she refused to exhibit Charles Sheeler's paintings and photographs together at the time, deliberately stifling public exposure of his photography. Halpert apparently feared that Sheeler's photographs would eclipse his paintings and thereby reorient his reputation as a painter that she had helped construct. In her view, the close relationship between the two might inspire critics and patrons to judge his paintings as "merely photographic," an additional hindrance to sales during the Great Depression.[115] These attitudes persisted. In reviewing Shahn's 1947 MoMA exhibition, photo-historian Nancy Newhall wrote: "[t]his vast and exciting field is still shunned by all but one or two art historians and art critics. The insult still contained in the word 'photographic' when hurled at a painter implies the same kind of creative impotence and superficial imitations as the word 'pictorial.'"[116] If a painter relied too closely on photographs (especially documentary or news photographs) to make their socially conscious paintings, there was also the danger that their pictures might be criticized for being too topical, or propagandistic, which could diminish their ability to transcend their time, transcendence being a quality so often expected of "high art."[117]

These are among the reasons why critics in Shahn's day may have overlooked or avoided close analysis of the photographic basis of his Sacco and Vanzetti series (and why perhaps Shahn himself did not go out of his way to advertise it). Either news photographs were considered too banal for serious attention, or examination of Shahn's reliance on photographic sources left him open to charges of slavish copying and imitation, which could in turn affect his artistic reputation. But the value of examining Shahn's dependence on photographs was not lost on all the reviewers of his work. In fact some, like Jean Charlot, a pioneer of true fresco mural painting in Mexico, with whom Shahn later studied in New York, offered perceptive commentary with far-reaching implications. Even though Charlot was writing about Shahn's Tom Mooney series (1932–1933), since that work is so stylistically close to the Sacco and Vanzetti project, involving similar working processes, his critique applies to the earlier paintings as well. Charlot wrote:

> *Much of Shahn's plastic [style] is explainable by his aims. Being a storyteller, his source material consists mainly of newspaper reports, his models being the photographs of rotogravure sections and tabloid sheets. Degas also used photographs, but depurated, stylized, lifted to the plane of his art. Shahn, on the contrary, delights in what is peculiarly accidental, cynical, and ungentlemanly in camera work. The gymnastics of inhibition by which we immediately substitute for any given spectacle a more anthropomorphic version in which hands and heads will be given the leading role, do not fool the camera, nor Shahn. For them a man, however intellectually eminent, will exist mainly through the bunch of folds and creases which are his clothes, his buttons, his shoe-laces.... Such an ousting of our lawful vision is a slap to the highly orderly and satisfying implications that this vision symbolizes. Yet the more one grows accustomed to this new version of the world, the more is one able to perceive in it a new order. The overgrown canine teeth of Governor Rolph, the bittersweet dimple at the corner of Mooney's mouth are enough to reassure one that this apparently mechanical vision is as heavily loaded with moral values as the more conservative and antiquated version.*[118]

In his interpretive description of Shahn's use of photography, Charlot hinted at ways for future critics to evaluate Shahn's photo-based work. For if Shahn's "mechanical vision is as heavily loaded with moral values as the more conservative and antiquated version," then the process of painting from photographs, Charlot implied, was no more truthful than painting from the imagination. This in turn suggests that we must be as critical of Shahn's photographic sources as of the paintings that they inspired, and as aware of the bias and manipulation involved in even the most seemingly objective of media. We must deconstruct the news photograph itself, and its presumed transparency, for its message, according to theorist Roland Barthes, "is formed by a source of emission, a channel of transmission and a point of reception," that is, by the newspaper staff who takes the picture; the text, title, caption and lay-out of the image in the newspaper; and by the public who reads the paper."[119] By examining the contexts of the news photographs that Shahn employed, and how their meanings change in different contexts—subjects that reach beyond the scope of this essay—we would not only gain further insight into the artist's process, but also deeper understanding of what it meant for Shahn, indeed, for the modern painter, in poet Louis Aragon's words, to "use the photographic eye as [he] has used the human eye."[120]

ACKNOWLEDGMENTS

For facilitating my research, I would like to thank Judy Throm and Annie Bayly, Archives of American Art, Smithsonian Institution; William Faucon and Roberta Zonghi, Department of Rare Books and Manuscripts, Boston Public Library; Brian Sullivan, Harvard University Archives, Pusey Library; Steven Smith and Mary Person, Art and Visual Materials, Special Collections Department, Harvard Law School Library; Abby Smith, Fine Arts Library, Harvard University Art Museums; Andrew Lee, Tamiment Institute Library, New York University; Patricia McDonnell and Laura Muessig, Frederick R. Weisman Art Museum, Minneapolis, Minn.: John d'Entremont and Diana Linden for their insightful comments on drafts of the manuscript, and Alejandro Anreus for his patience and support. I am grateful to Roia Ferrazares, Dolores Taller, and the late Dr. Stephen Lee Taller of the Stephen Lee Taller Ben Shahn Archive, now housed at the Fine Arts Library, Harvard University. Dr. Taller generously loaned me materials that were donated to his invaluable archive from Shahn's widow Bernarda Bryson Shahn and art historian Morris Dorsky.

My greatest intellectual debt goes to Deborah Martin Kao and Jenna Webster, Harvard University Art Museums, for their pioneering research on Shahn's art in the 1930s, especially on the artist's relationship to modern media. Our collaborative work for the book and traveling exhibition that we co-organized, *Ben Shahn's New York: The Photography of Modern Times* (New Haven, Conn.: Yale University Press, 2000), inspired many of the ideas presented in this essay.

List of endnotes on page 126

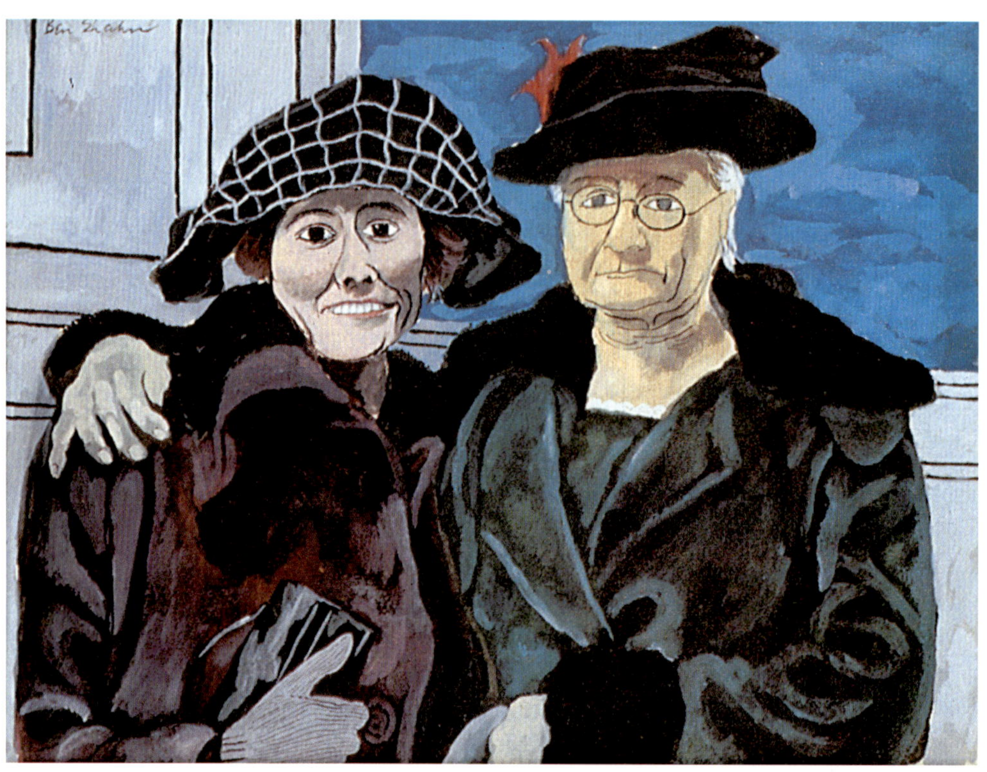

ABOVE
Ben Shahn
Mrs. Sacco and Elizabeth Glendower Evans, 1931–32.
Gouache on paper, 10 x 12 1/4 in.
Frederick R. Weisman Art Museum
Gift of Gertrude Lippincott.
University of Minnesota
Minneapolis, Minnesota

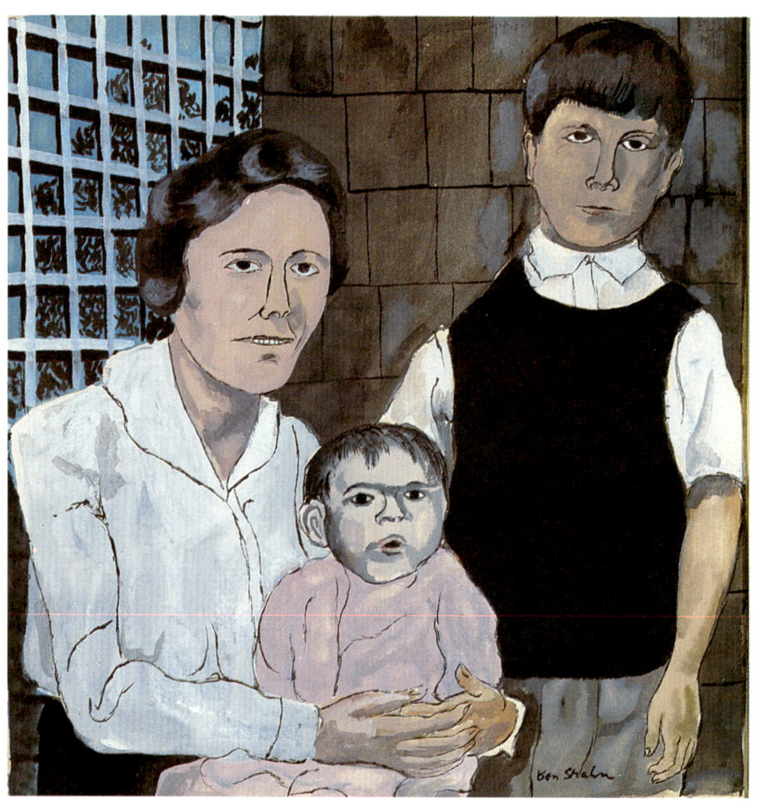

Ben Shahn
Sacco's Family After the Verdict
1931–32. Gouache on paper
10 x 10 in.
Collection of Mr. and Mrs.
Harry Spiro, New York

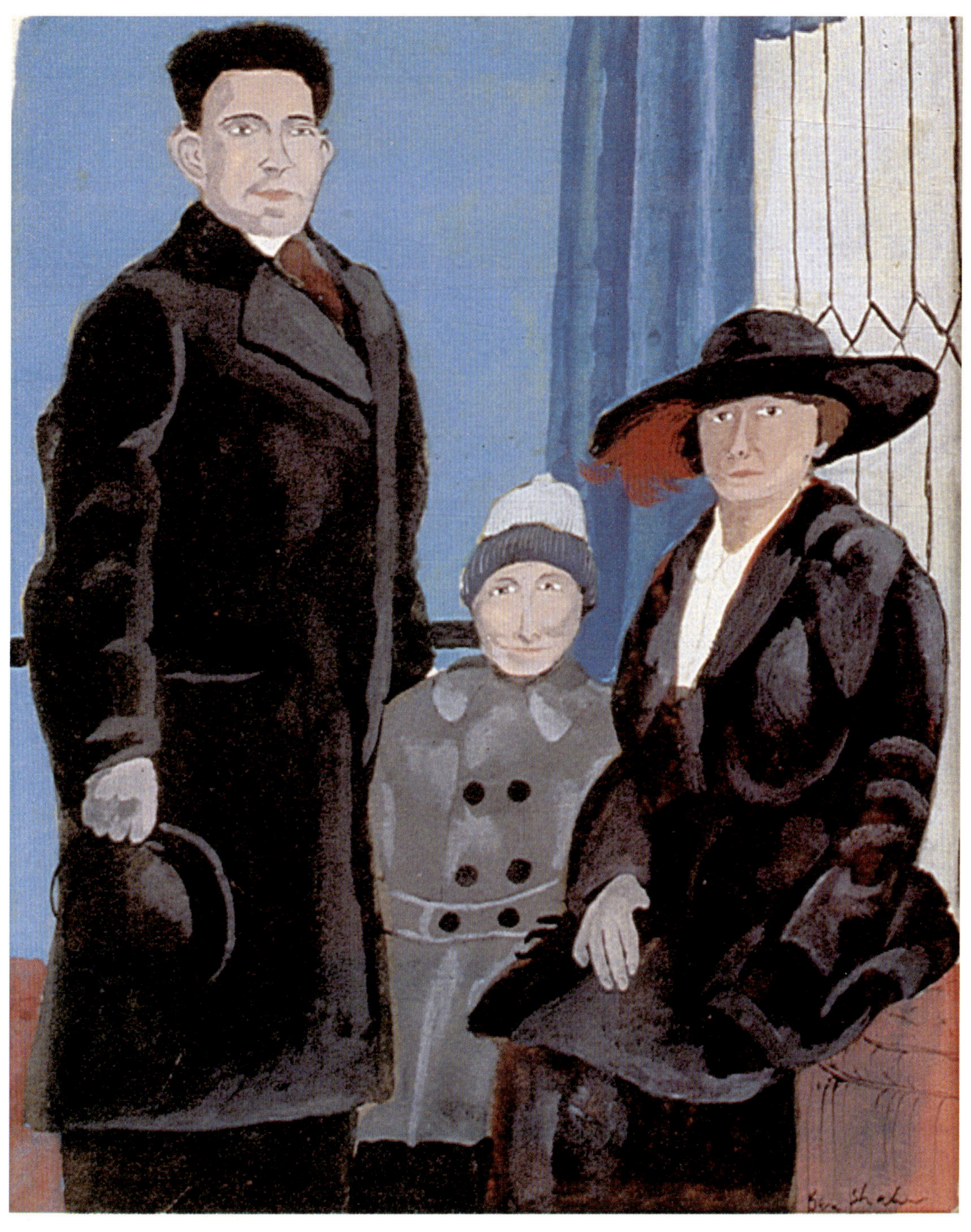

Ben Shahn
Nicola Sacco, His Wife and Their Son Dante, 1931–32.
Gouache on paper, 13 x 10 1/2 in.
Frederick R. Weisman Art Museum
Gift of Gertrude Lippincott.
University of Minnesota,
Minneapolis, Minnesota

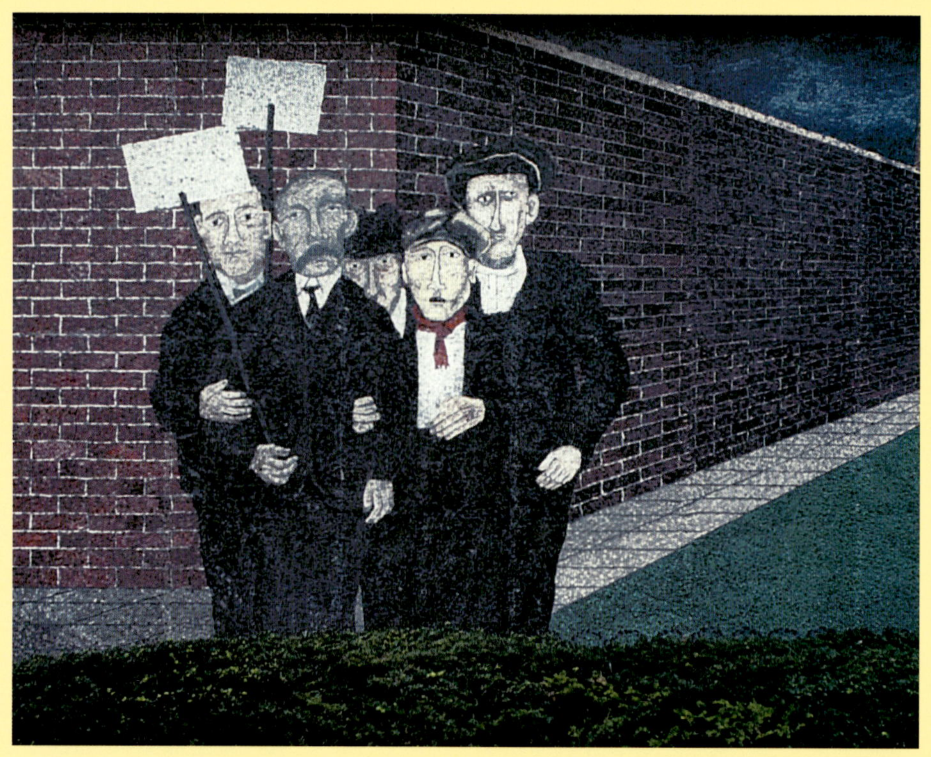

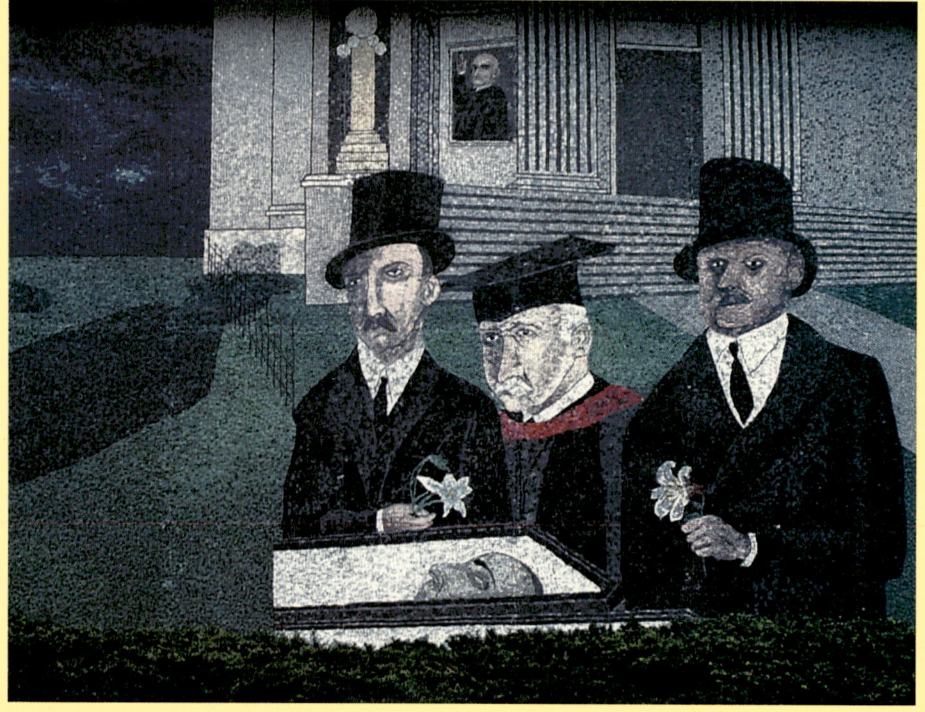

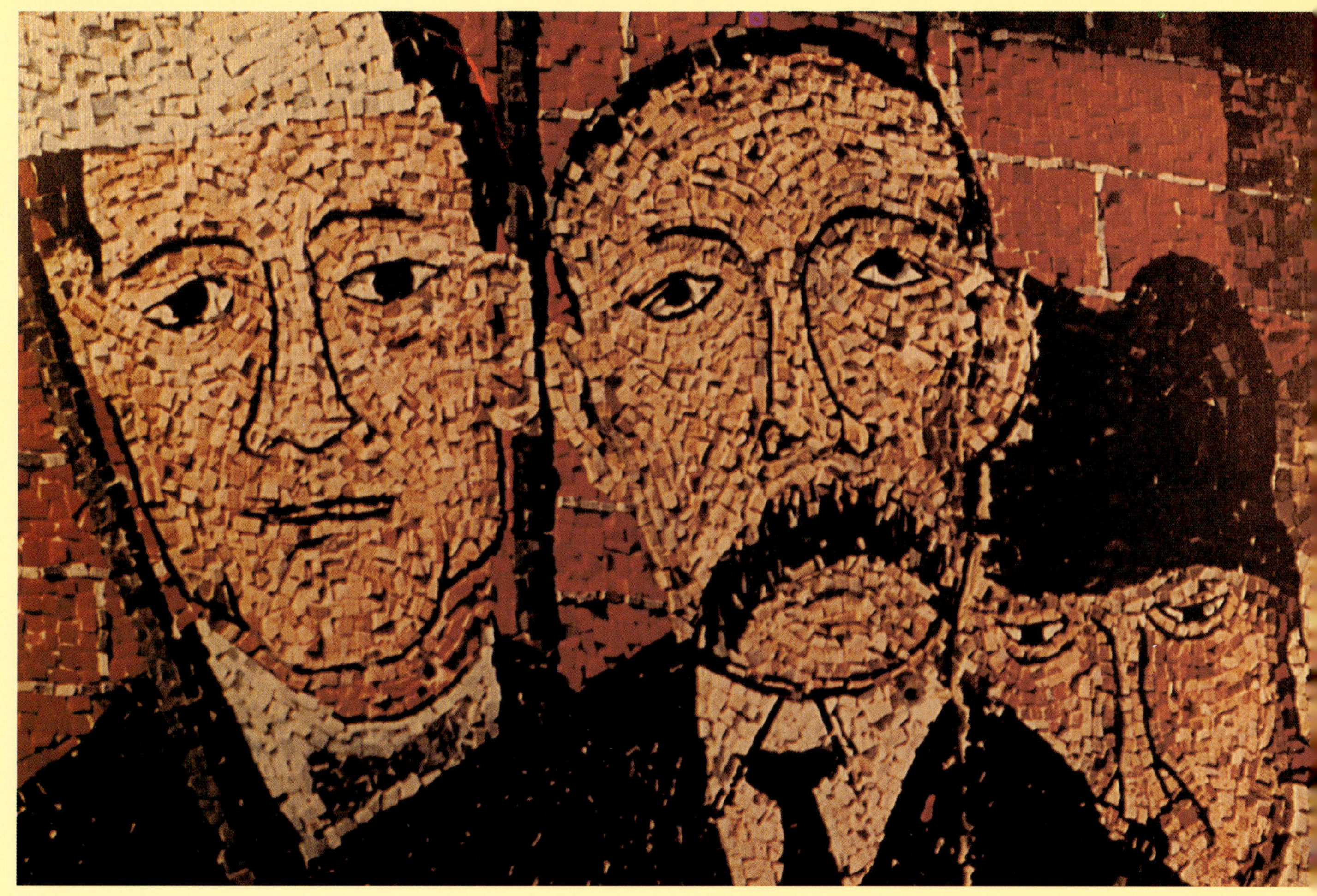

ABOVE
Ben Shahn
Detail of left panel of *The Passion of Sacco and Vanzetti*,1967. Mosaic. Syracuse University, Syracuse University, Syracuse, New York
Gift of Mr. and Mrs. Jacob Schulman, and Mr. and Mrs. Richard Evans, III

TOP LEFT
Ben Shahn
The Passion of Sacco and Vanzetti, 1967
Left panel. Mosaic.
Syracuse University, Syracuse, New York
Gift of Mr. and Mrs. Jacob Schulman, and Mr. and Mrs. Richard Evans, III

LEFT
Ben Shahn
The Passion of Sacco and Vanzetti, 1967
Right panel. Mosaic
Syracuse University, Syracuse, New York
Gift of Mr. and Mrs. Jacob Schulman, and Mr. and Mrs. Richard Evans, III

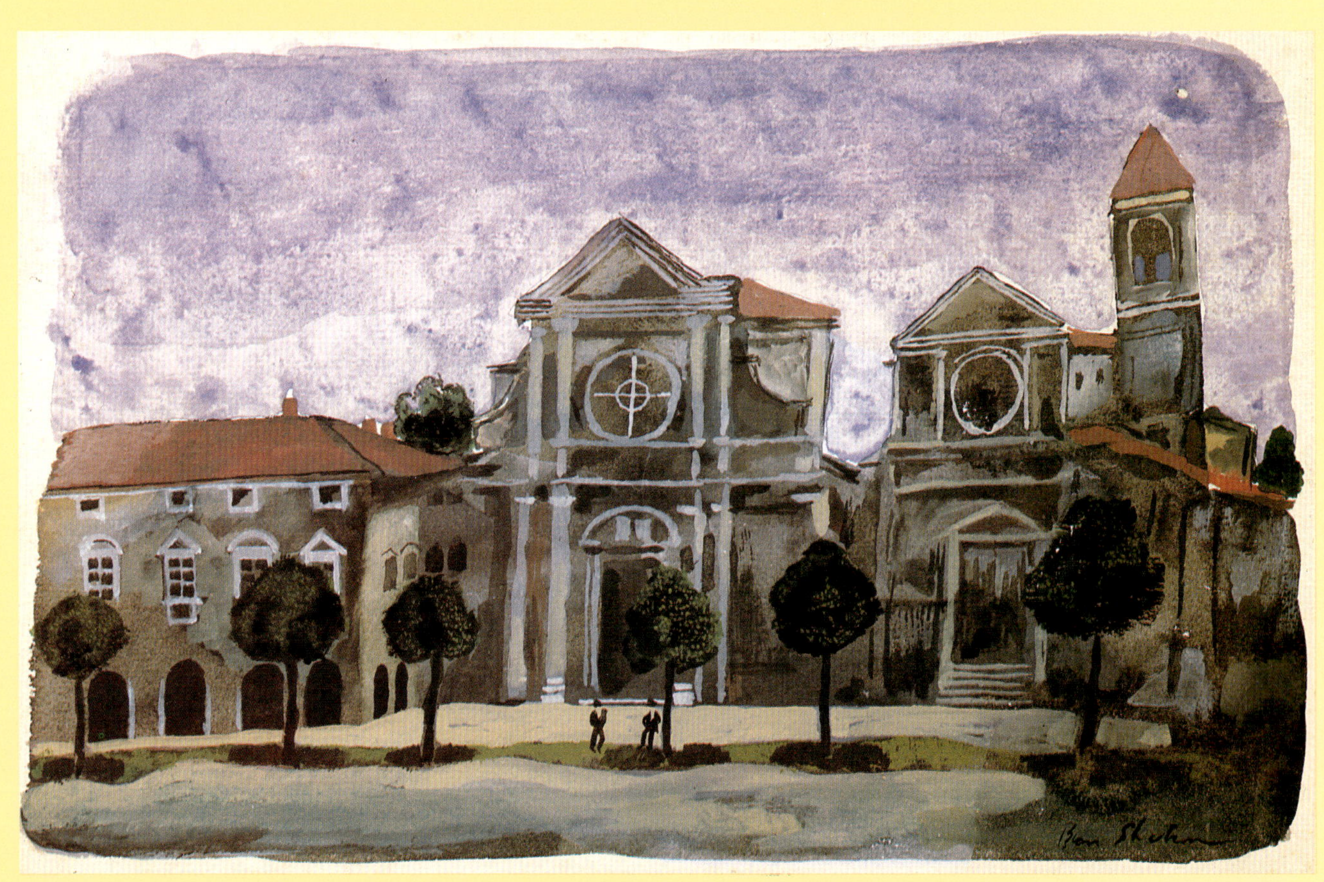

Ben Shahn
Villa Felleto, Vanzetti's Home Town
1931. Watercolor and gouache on paper, 9 x 13 in. Kennedy Galleries, New York, New York

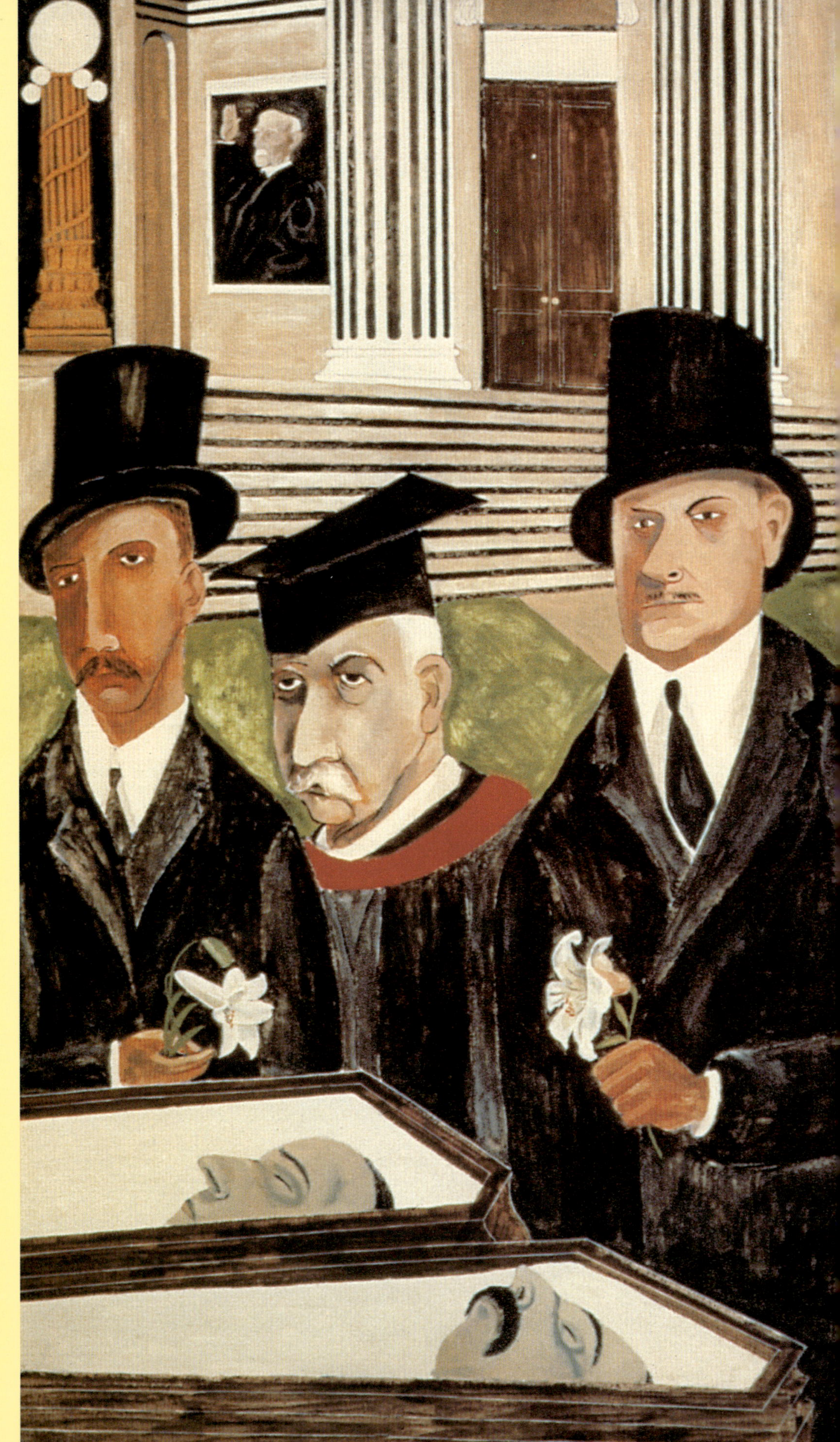

Ben Shahn
The Passion of Sacco and Vanzetti, 1931–32.
Tempera on canvas,
84 1/2 x 48 in. Whitney Museum of American Art, New York.
Gift of Edith and Milton Lowenthal in memory of Juliana Force

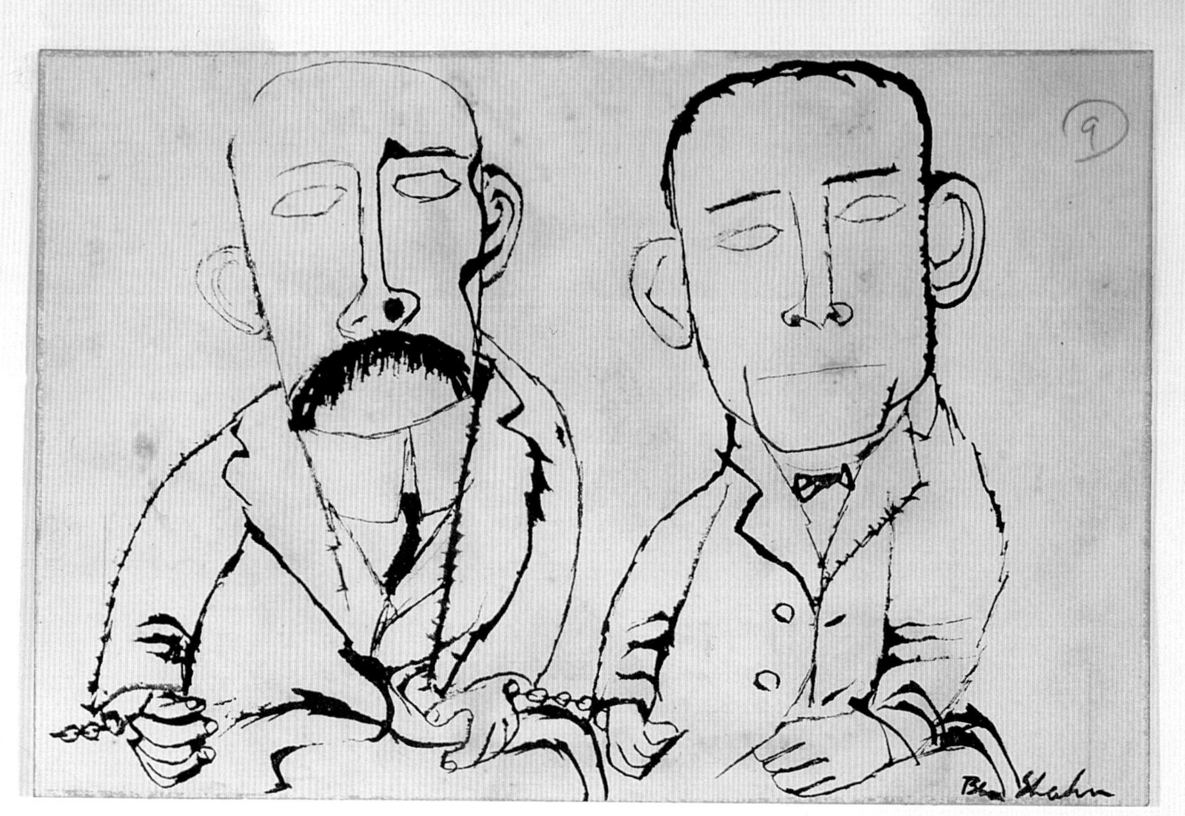

"If it had not been for these thing, I might have live out my life talking at street corners to scorning men. I might have die, unmarked, unknown, a failure. Now we are not a failure. This is our career and our triumph. Never in our full life could we hope to do such work for tolerance, for joostice, for man's onderstanding of man as now we do by accident. Our words—our lives—our pains nothing! The taking of our lives—lives of a good shoemaker and a poor fish peddler—all! That last moment belongs to us—that agony is our triumph." — Bartolomeo Vanzetti

Ben Shahn
Sacco and Vanzetti, 1952.
Black ink on cream wove paper, $5^{3}/_{4}$ x $8^{1}/_{2}$ in. Fogg Art Museum, Harvard University Museums
Gift of Meta and Paul J. Sachs

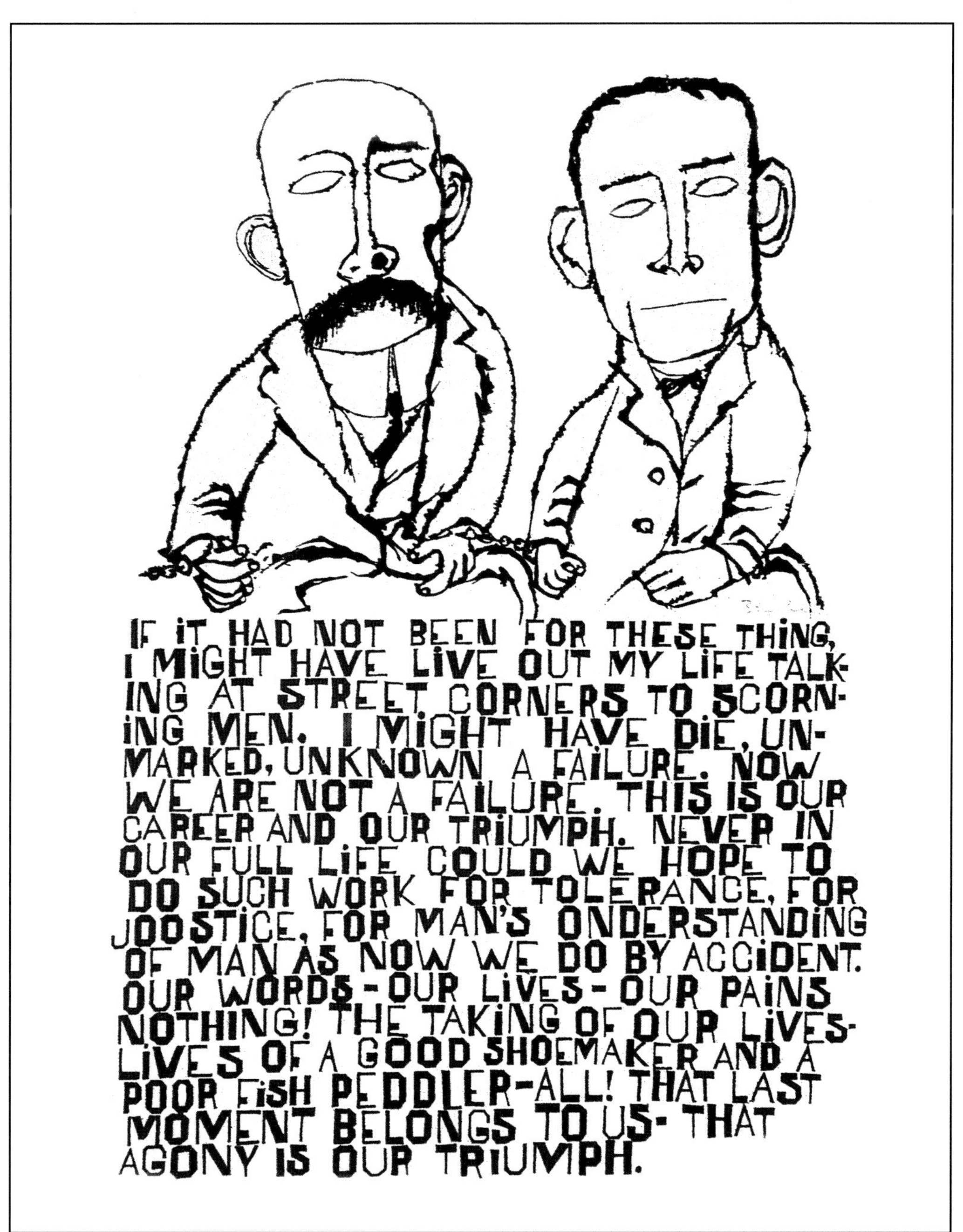

Ben Shahn
The Passion of Sacco and Vanzetti, 1958.
Serigraph, 25 3/4 x 17 1/2 in.
Gift of the Lessing and Edith Rosenwald Foundation.
New Jersey State Museum, Trenton, New Jersey

Diana Linden

What Becomes an Icon Most?: The Critical Reception of Ben Shahn's *The Passion of Sacco and Vanzetti*

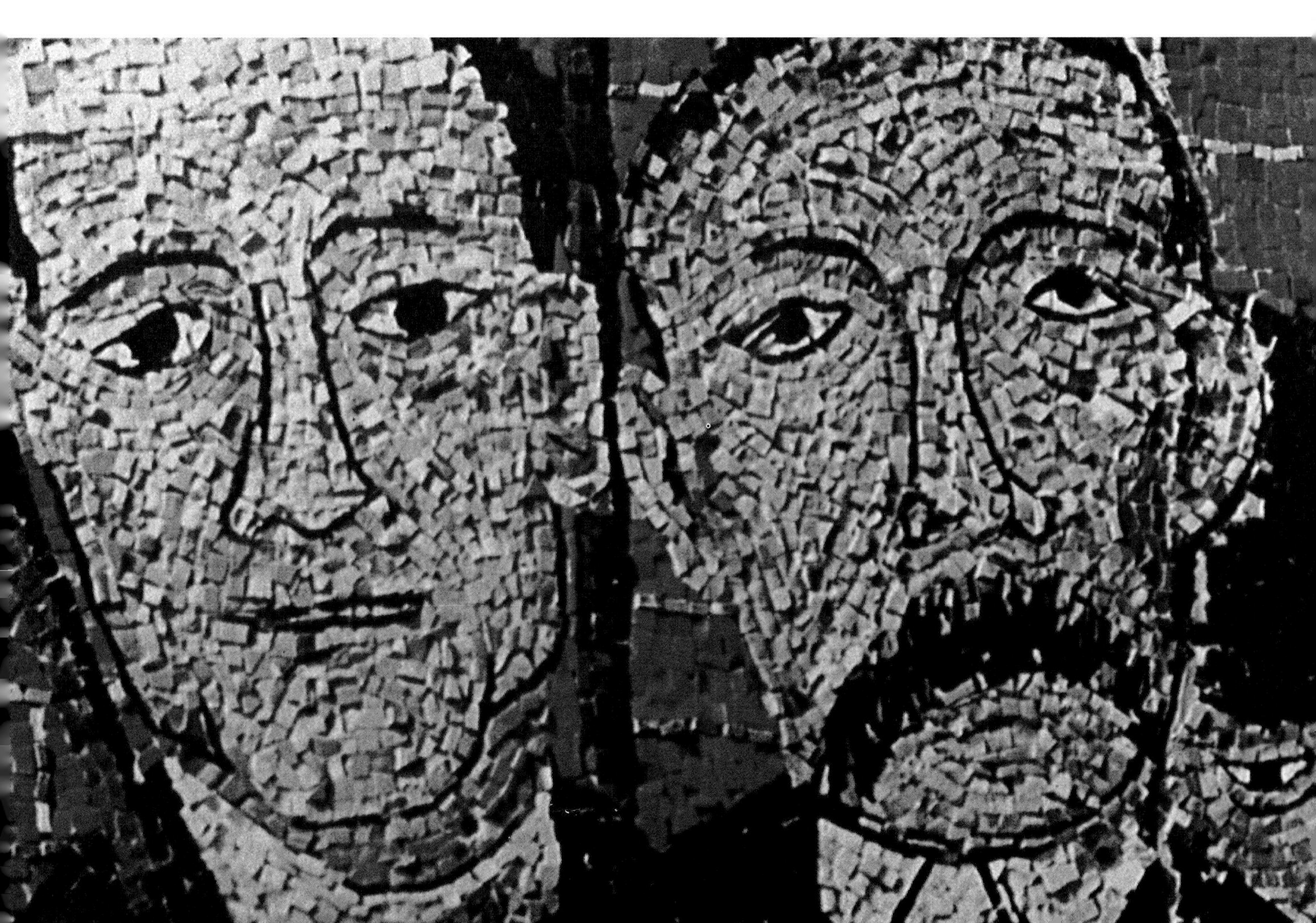

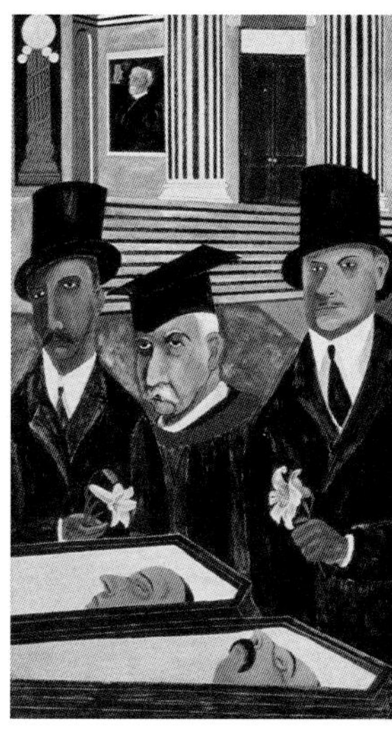

FIG. 21

Icon. By the end of the twentieth century, Ben Shahn's *The Passion of Sacco and Vanzetti*, (1931–32) had achieved the exalted status of cultural and artistic icon and was said to be among the "greatest achievements of twentieth-century art."[1] The Whitney Museum of Art which owns the only large-scale tempera from Shahn's series **(fig. 21)** rightly realized that to approach a work so well known and written about required not one, but several voices of appraisal. And so, the Whitney invited scholarly assessments of the paintings by the celebrated author and literary critic Alfred Kazin, art historian Frances K. Pohl (the leading authority on Shahn), and the lawyer Alan M. Dershowitz. This triumvirate of learned minds was necessary, one suspects, because Shahn's *Passion of Sacco and Vanzetti* is equally rooted in a specific cultural and historical milieu of radicalism and artistic agency, in the history of artistic realism and representation, and in legal and judicial matters.

Ben Shahn
Detail of left panel of *The Passion of Sacco and Vanzetti*,1967. Mosaic. Syracuse University, Syracuse, New York.Gift of Mr. and Mrs. Jacob Schulman, and Mr. and Mrs. Richard Evans, III

It has been more than seventy years since the state executed the "good shoemaker" and the "poor fish peddler," yet the controversy over Nicola Sacco and Bartolomeo Vanzetti's alleged actions and their execution has not ended, nor has a consensus as to their guilt or innocence been achieved. In the wake of the executions, Ben Shahn (1898–1969) commemorated Sacco and Vanzetti in a series of twenty-three gouaches that he entitled *The Passion of Sacco and Vanzetti*. The reception of Shahn's series was both strong and divided. Since the early 1930s, Shahn's paintings have been periodically reexamined and different conclusions drawn as to their merit and the artist's message. When the paintings were originally exhibited in 1932, critics were concerned with both Shahn's artistic style and his political message, in an era when artists created art specifically for progressive social change. Later, during the Cold War and McCarthy years, with the dominance of cultural and political conservatism and the rise of abstract expressionism, critics commented less often on Shahn's political message and its current relevancy, concentrating on style instead. In recent years, since the end of the Cold War, social art historians have resituated *The Passion of Sacco and Vanzetti* within the sociopolitical context of 1930s America, thus providing us with a richer sense of the artist, his vision, the era in which he worked, and the social change he hoped to impart.

This essay examines the critical reception of Shahn's *The Passion of Sacco and Vanzetti* over the past seven decades. While primarily concerned with Shahn's 1931–32 series, note will also be made of his later quotations and reinterpretations of the series in print, mosaic, and mural which date as late as 1967. The majority of the primary writings on the gouaches date from 1932, which was the last time that the series was seen in its entirety. Subsequent exhibitions, until this current one organized by the Jersey City Museum, have shown but a few examples from the series, as was the case with the 1947 Shahn retrospective at the Museum of Modern Art (MoMA) in New York City. This new exhibition breaks ground in that it resituates Shahn's gouaches and temperas on Sacco and Vanzetti in relation to their source photographs from the 1920s and to cultural ephemera and invites both art historians and historians to comment on the images and their legacy. In so doing, Jersey City Museum Curator Alejandro Anreus invites today's audiences to approach Shahn and Sacco and Vanzetti within a contextual and social framework and to see the reciprocal relationship between artmaking and political realities.

Reconstructing, tracing, and then evaluating the critical reception to key works within an artist's oeuvre offers many opportunities. Shahn has had a checkered reputation over the years, both praised as an artist with conviction and original vision, but also dismissed as being little more than a sly propagandist or pandering populist. By concentrating on his *Passion of Sacco and Vanzetti*, the images with which Shahn is most closely identified and are his most frequently reproduced works, we can examine how critics and writers have approached the broader issue of social commentary within art, as well as one of the most controversial legal cases of the twentieth century. One artist, one style, one subject, yet over time, these paintings were constantly seen anew. Accepting the claim at century's end that Shahn's images constituted an iconic achievement, how and when did they achieve this status? What is the power of these images? Why have writers and viewers continually returned to them—what do they offer? And finally, can we realistically step aside from the issue of Sacco and Vanzetti's guilt or innocence?

Recently, I projected slides of Shahn's gouaches, watercolors, and temperas from *The Passion of Sacco and Vanzetti* to introduce my students at the University of Michigan to Shahn and to Sacco and Vanzetti.[2] They pondered the artistic merit of working in narrative and serial form, of an artist taking a stand on legal matters, of combining realism with the bite of satire to tell a story. The students were drawn into the images by Shahn's deft use of outline, his decision to portray the two anarchists as emotionally reserved, silent, and even weary in order to permit the viewer to get close to and examine the men behind the actions and the cause, and Shahn's attention to details—handcuffs, drooping walrus mustaches, protesters melded into a group through shared anger and belief in the collective right to protest. Moved by the images and how they were constructed, the students were also confused and angered—"But the trial was a fake!" "But the judge hated foreigners!" "I didn't know this could happen ... not in America."

This is the power and legacy of these works. *The Passion of Sacco and Vanzetti* is neither solely about art nor politics—but instead both. Through these images Shahn pulls us into a specific moment in America's history. The issue of innocence or guilt most likely will never be resolved. Yet the very fact that the two men were denied their right to a fair trial threatens central principles on which our democracy and system of justice are based and which students (and museumgoers, and art historians, and critics) don't always pause to consider—at least not at an art museum.

"WE ARE TWO NATIONS": EXHIBITIONS OF THE 1930S

When Shahn began his series, the electrocution of Sacco and Vanzetti, after seven years of international protests and legal maneuvering, still incited public outrage and even violent retaliation. In 1931, Osmond K. Fraenkel wrote *The Sacco-Vanzetti Case* arguing that the two men were innocent, that the judicial proceedings had been concerned more with condemning radical politics than establishing the truth, and that the executions were unwarranted. That same year, Shahn began to paint *The Passion of Sacco and Vanzetti*.[3]

The Great Depression did not fully shift attention away from the recent executions of Sacco and Vanzetti. Instead, the economic collapse reinvigorated leftist action and many in the avant-garde—including Shahn—embraced the executed pair and believed that American justice was jaundiced. The two executed men became icons, symbols of injustice and political agitation, proof that American society was unjust and openly biased against foreigners and workers. As Abe Bluestein wrote, "the symbol of Sacco and Vanzetti has become the symbol of the Class Struggle. Because they were victimized by a court that pretends to impartial justice, but that cannot hide its subservience to the master class, they have become the universal beacons in the world wide war of the classes."[4] In viewing Shahn's works, critics, and perhaps viewers as well, felt that Shahn's poignant and bold choice of subject matter upheld the two men, whose lives had become even more symbolically meaningful *because* of the Depression. Upon seeing the exhibition of Shahn's works, one viewer wrote, "From the perspective of the springtime of 1932, when poor and rich alike have the sacred right to sit on park benches, the lifelong rebellion of Bartolomeo Vanzetti seems always more prophetic."[5]

Shahn exhibited his Sacco and Vanzetti paintings on three occasions at three separate venues over the course of 1932. In April, he displayed the entire series at New York City's Downtown Gallery located within blocks of Union Square, the site of 1920s protests on behalf of Sacco and Vanzetti that Shahn attended (and which he represented in the series), and where protesters now rallied for labor and civil rights. In May, Shahn submitted two works to the Museum of Modern Art's exhibition *Murals by American Painters and Photographers*. The exhibition invited artists to propose murals based on postwar events and was organized by Lincoln Kirstein, who had been inspired by the Mexican mural movement. In October, Kirstein arranged for the Harvard Society for Contemporary Art to display Shahn's series along with examples from his earlier *The Dreyfus Affair* (1930), which likewise addressed the legal persecution of an ethnic outsider. By exhibiting his works at Harvard, Shahn entered the center of Boston Brahmin social and cultural hegemonic power, a university and a city where key figures in the case—such as Abbot Lawrence Lowell and Justice Webster Thayer—were the elite.[6]

The critics who reviewed all three exhibitions included those who wrote for the mainstream presses, the literary and arts presses, the politically liberal and left newspapers, as well as various ethnic language periodicals which each had a decisive political orientation as well. As a collective, these papers reached the varied political, cultural, and economic strata of New York City. Of the three venues for Shahn's series, it was the Downtown Gallery exhibition that received the most press coverage, despite the fact that Shahn was not that well-known an artist.[7]

The Downtown Gallery issued a press release to announce the exhibition's opening in April 1932. It is useful to refer to the press release at length since many critics responded to it in their reviews, while others who were unable to see the exhibition (mainly those outside New York) quoted from it verbatim.[8] Gallery owner Edith Halpert enticed people to come see how Shahn addressed:

> *an issue which held the public attention for a long period—the Sacco Vanzetti trial. What his sympathies were in this much discussed episode is not relevant—no more than Rivera's in his paintings of "A Day in Moscow." It is of significance, however, that he interpreted the*

major events with passion, deep understanding, and a careful study of the material on hand, giving us a contemporary picture of a historical topic in American life.... The accent of "art for art's sake" is slowly being lessened and many artists are turning to theme painting again. The painting lesson has been learned, and the artists are bearing this knowledge to "storytelling" pictures without fear of scorn.[9]

Halpert tried to create a tone of political neutrality, to stress the artist's passion (as with genius, a buzzword for artistic motivation and temperament) and the importance of both narrative and commentary in art. In Shahn's series, as Alejandro Anreus and Laura Katzman discuss in this catalogue, he presented the condemned pair as quiet and contemplative, eschewing scenes of open conflict, high drama, or violent action. By employing pictorial restraint Shahn sought to subdue the intense emotions that the case provoked. Yet, Halpert's claim that the artist's political sympathies were irrelevant was an overstatement, for Shahn's choice of subject was itself partisan, as was his use of photographs from leftist newspapers—perhaps familiar images to viewers—as the source material for the paintings.[10]

Examining the criticism of the images evokes the tensions between audience and aesthetics and between social classes. Behind the pointed comments lurk such questions as who is worthy of commemoration in art? Who is the appropriate audience for a gallery or museum? Should artists express opinions on matters beyond that of color and line? When reviewing the Downtown Gallery's exhibition, mainstream newspapers speculated on the aesthetic virtues of Shahn's works, while remarking on the case's troubled legacy. Rarely did critics discuss aesthetics apart from politics. *The New York World-Telegram* praised Shahn's choice of theme (wryly noting that prior to the opening, eight works had already been sold to capitalists), his facility with rendering individuals from the case such as family members and attention to details, his skill at conveying varied emotions (such as Shahn's "bitter" treatment of the Lowell Committee his warm and sympathetic depiction of Sacco's family in Italy), and his overall narrative strength.[11] *The New York Times* commended the artist's facile and meaningful use of line and his singular use of color; the reviewer also applauded Shahn for tempering his rhetoric by not bending to easy arguments, noting "here are no pictorial polemics—Sacco as saint, Judge Thayer as Lucifer, and the Boston and Paris rioters as legions of the beast." To this unnamed reviewer, the gouaches surpassed the writings of Felix Frankfurter, the fiction of Upton Sinclair, and the multi-volume trial transcripts (published with funds provided by the Rockefeller family) in providing the layman with a "graphic and memorable record" of the historical events.[12] In a later, briefer notice, the *New York Times* praised the painter's decisive characterizations, writing that "Shahn's artistic economy matches his political reticence."[13] *The New York Herald Tribune* applauded Shahn for having stepped aside from feelings

Luigia, sister of Bartolomeo Vanzetti, among the Sacco-Vanzetti Committee in Paris. (details), c. 1927, photograph, Bibliotheque Nationale, Paris.

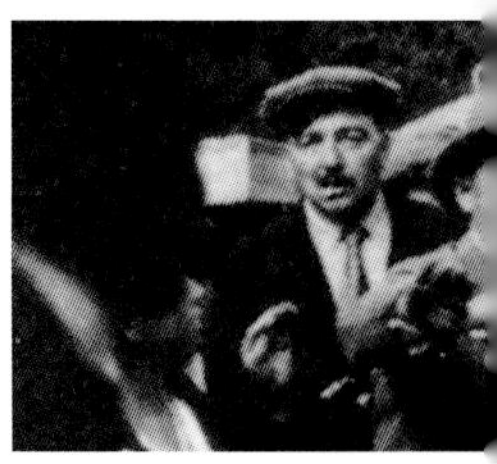

of malice and successfully kept a distance from the emotional tumult of the 1920s. The reviewer found his style "quaint" and akin to caricature while still maintaining an appropriately serious tone.[14] But what most held the attention of the critic for William Randolph Hearst's *New York Sun*—who felt it necessary to clarify that he was not a communist and believed that the trial *was* fair—was the audience who went to see Shahn's exhibition, rather than the works they were viewing. Commending Shahn for speaking directly to "the people," which the critic compared to Diego Rivera's popular appeal in Mexico, he went on to describe those in attendance as "unusual" people who expressed a somber reverence usually reserved for church.[15]

Shahn's Public. There has been a continued fascination with, and at times disdain for, those who constitute Shahn's audience in the criticism beginning in the early 1930s and continuing up to today. During the 1930s, both Shahn and Halpert were very concerned with reaching out to non-art-viewing publics. In turn, critics criticized Shahn for marketing his political views, rather than aesthetics, or chided him for not doing justice to "the people's" vision of Sacco and Vanzetti, or worried that the images were incendiary. Such comments by the press reveal tensions as to who constituted the art-viewing public, but also reveal desire (at points, delusion) that paintings could leapfrog over all the social, cultural, and political barriers that would separate a Ben Shahn from a Nicola Sacco.

In comparison to the more mainstream presses, the literary and art presses, far fewer in number, were less attentive to Shahn's works at the Downtown Gallery. However, these reviewers saw Shahn's work as having artistic precedents and precursors—that, in fact, Shahn was painting his way into a distinguished lineage of the artist as social critic. These scant reviews addressed Shahn's work in relation to European modernism and the tradition of artist as social conscience and satirist. Parallels were drawn between Shahn and the socially critical artists of the eighteenth and nineteenth centuries, and the critics praised how Shahn balanced bold imagery with equally bold political statements, and his nuanced sense of satire and caricature. *Gotham Life* judged Shahn's craftsmanship superb, displaying a veracity that called to mind the art of Daumier and Hogarth; the exhibition, simply put, was not to be missed.[16] *Creative Art* noted that the paintings were

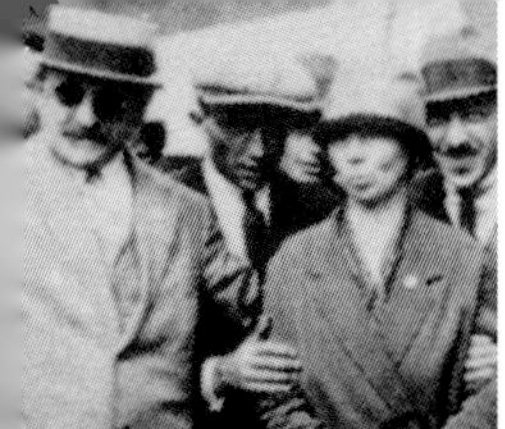

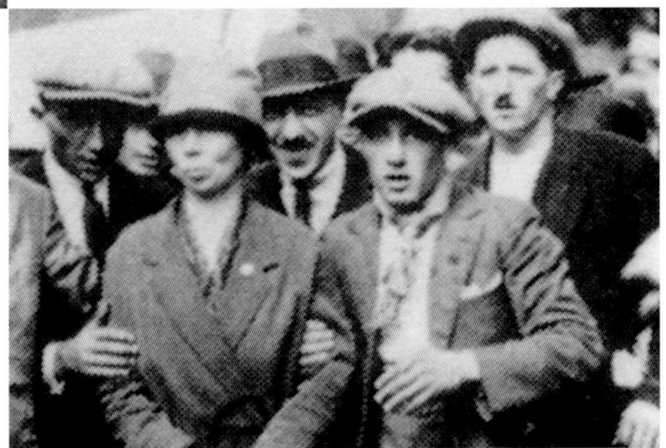

decidedly literary, with a naive style in the manner of Rousseau which might relate to "the simplicity of the people he is depicting."[17] Shahn, they concluded, worked with the zeal of the propagandist. *Art Digest* closely reiterated the Downtown Gallery's press release, while choosing to highlight the work's storytelling aspect.[18] Based on these "vital, pictorial documents," *Art News* concluded that Shahn was "henceforth someone to be reckoned with."[19] Diego Rivera reviewed the exhibition for V. F Calverton's *Modern Quarterly*[20] and praised it as being "as moving as anything of the kind I have ever seen. The Sacco and Vanzetti paintings are technically within the school of modernistic painting, but they possess the necessary qualities, accessibility, and power, to make them important to the proletariat."[21] However, other critics, journalists, and activists on the Left were not as supportive, nor even as interested as had been Rivera, for their concern was politics itself, rather than art at the service of political memory and justice. The 1932 exhibition predated the debut of the Artists' Union journal *Art Front* (1934–37) to which Shahn contributed and which would have been most supportive of Shahn's vision and message.

Prior to *Art Front,* readers went to one source for their news and another for gallery reviews; so mass media, separated its art and political commentary from each other. Most newspapers on the Left were singularly committed to criticism of, and agitation against, the state and capitalism and did not publicize the arts except as participatory people's events. Furthermore, these papers were directed at very specific segments of society, defined either by class (which attempted to bridge ethnic and linguistic barriers), various left political affiliations, or specific linguistic and cultural constituencies. New York in the 1930s was a multilayered society, polylinguistic, and culturally diverse, as it is today, yet with more newspapers to serve these audiences than currently exist. Bringing together the scant reviews from the left-liberal newspapers, as well as acknowledging those that bypassed the exhibition, recreates the cultural milieu which Shahn was part of and which he hoped to inform through his paintings.

For many people the anarchism was still viable and the memory of Sacco and Vanzetti still alive. Since the Italian anarchist weekly *L'Adunata dei Refrattari* was concerned only with political action, and in fact, was so insular and locked within the Italian-immigrant world, it is doubtful that the editors even knew of Shahn's exhibition at the Downtown Gallery. Neither the communist *Daily Worker*, nor the *New Masses*—both English-language—reviewed the exhibition; however, the latter did publish Hugo Gellert's article on MoMA's mural exhibition that Gellert reprinted two years later in *Art Front*, the Artists' Union's newspaper.[22] *Vanguard*, the bimonthly anarchist-communist youth publication, did not publicize the exhibition. Edited by the anarchist Carlo Tresca, who had helped arrange legal counsel for Sacco and Vanzetti, *Il Martello* did not mention Shahn's exhibition, and in fact, never covered the arts. Among the Yiddish papers, neither the anarchist *Frei Arbete Stimmer* which according to Paul Buhle was the most popular anarchist paper in America, the socialist *Jewish Daily Forward*—headquartered a short subway ride away from Halpert's Gallery on the Lower East Side", nor the communist *Morning Freiheit* printed reviews.[23] Again, this overall lack was due to the papers dedication to labor and civic issues rather than the visual arts.

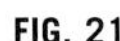

FIG. 21

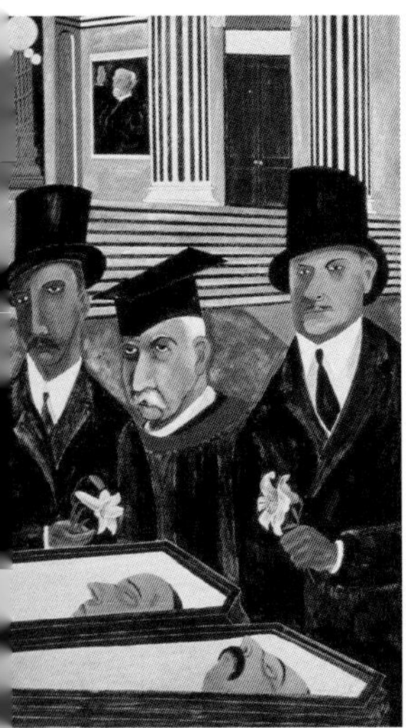

The anarchist, left and liberal presses, however, did not entirely overlook Shahn's work. The anarchist publication *The Road to Freedom* appreciated Shahn's "unusual talent," praised the relevance of his theme, saw his use of gouache as both simple and appropriate, his rendering almost "religious," and commented that the series provided both a record of the times and in a direct quote from the Downtown Gallery's press release, disproved the "old slogan of art for art's sake."[24] *The Nation's* Walter Gutman found Shahn's series "disappointing" and felt Shahn was simply not up to the task of representing the agonies, the ideology, and the emotions of the men, and the significance of their martyrdom.[25] Of an opposite opinion was The *New Republic's* Matthew Josephson, who praised Shahn for his vivacity, drama, and for bypassing gloom in favor of a noted "literary flair" for satire and character. Shahn's twenty-three gouaches, according to Josephson, were reminders of the power artists and poets held over human events.[26]

Such newspapers as *Il Martello* and *L'Adunata dei Refratti* paid annual tribute to Sacco and Vanzetti in their August editions to mark the anniversary of the 1927 execution. In August 1933, *Man: A Journal of the Anarchist Ideal and Movement*, a bimonthly publication, reprinted a black and white engraving based on Shahn's image of the Lowell Committee but misspelled the artist's name as Shahm.[27] This appropriation of Shahn's work, supposedly politically neutral, inserted it within an explicitly anarchist context. It is significant that the image chosen for reproduction, now in the collection of the Whitney Museum of American Art **(fig. 21)** mocks Lowell, Thayer, and the like in large figures, while presenting Sacco and Vanzetti (barely visible) as slain martyrs in their coffins, with just their noses peeking out to identify them. Shahn's other images from the series that showed Sacco and Vanzetti—in court, chained, weary, thoughtful—would not have been consistent with the chiseled, heroic, defiant portraits preferred by the anarchist presses when their own artists paid tribute to the men. Shahn's image served the anarchist cause precisely because Sacco and Vanzetti were not the prime visual focus. This same image had provoked ire because of the mocking stance towards the justices when Shahn exhibited it at the Museum of Modern Art in just the prior year.

A survey of New York's African-American newspapers, such as the *Amsterdam News* from the 1930s failed to locate any articles; it does not appear that Edith Halpert thought to send press releases to these papers. Many African-Americans were involved in the protests on behalf of Sacco and Vanzetti, and people such as the lawyer William Patterson were radicalized by the experience.[28] Yet with the arrest and conviction of the Scottsboro Nine in 1931, many within New York's African-American communities (located primarily in Harlem and in Brooklyn) shifted their focus to the Alabama case. Patterson, along with Benjamin Davis, both members of the Communist Party, led the Scottsboro campaign with the slogan that the men "shall not die!"—the same cry valiantly chanted on behalf of the two executed anarchists.

In the early 1930s, the cases of Sacco and Vanzetti and of the Scottsboro Nine became intertwined causes, at points shared, at other points pitted one against the other. As Mark Solomon notes, "had the executions (of the Scottsboro defendants) occurred, there is little doubt that the subsequent mourning and sense of defeat would have eclipsed what was felt for Sacco and Vanzetti."[28] The poet Countee Cullen in 1935 penned "Scottsboro, Too, Is Worth Its Song," wryly pointing out many poets' tributes to Sacco and Vanzetti but a general lack of artistic response to Scottsboro. Ironically, one artist who was planning to address the southern case was Ben Shahn, who soon after completing *The Passion of Sacco and Vanzetti* began plans for a series of narrative images. It is not known why he did not continue with the project.

CONTROVERSY AT THE MUSEUM OF MODERN ART

In May 1932, MoMA exhibited *Murals by American Painters and Photographers*, to which Shahn had submitted two paintings on the theme of Sacco and Vanzetti: a montage culled from images from the series and the same iconic image of the Lowell Committee now owned by the Whitney Museum of American Art.[30] Museum trustees sought to remove Shahn's works, along with those by William Gropper and Hugo Gellert, due to the works' strong socially critical edge and their derisive portrayal of social notables like J. P. Morgan, the senior Rockefeller, and Henry Ford, all keeping company with Al Capone. Shahn painted Sacco and Vanzetti laid out in the coffins flanked by the stony-faced patricians of the Lowell committee, with trial judge Justice Webster Thayer in the background. After MoMA's trustees, who were business and political associates of the caricatured men, voiced their complaints about the suppressed works, the press covered the controversy and artists organized in protest; finally the works were returned to the exhibition.[31]

Many critics singled out Shahn, Gellert, and Gropper's works for special scrutiny in their reviews, to let the public know what all the noise had been about. *The New York Sun* article opened by discussing the three "communist contributors" who had allegedly been rejected based on "their unflattering depictions of certain persons in high finance"; these works, turned out to be "heavy-handed," lacked imagination, and made the artists come off "less well than the financiers."[32] Helen Appleton Reed of the *Brooklyn Daily Eagle* was disdainful of the three men's works.[33] The *Chicago Evening Post*'s Rose Mary Fisk found Shahn's entries without "mural coherence and significance," a great departure from the earlier Sacco and Vanzetti gouaches which, she found, "particularly moving and 'right' in scale and feeling."[34] Still, Shahn had his powerful and vocal supporters, including the influential Lincoln Kirstein, chair of MoMA's exhibition committee, who wrote an essay on the exhibit for *Horn and Hound*, the literary journal he had helped found. In assessing Shahn's tempera of the Lowell Committee, Kirstein wrote that Shahn's emotional and political restraint bettered served the plastic elements of the work, noting that "...with an appraising accuracy [Shahn] merely installed the actors of the tragedy in their proper places in a frame, and their arrangement is an inscription more surgical than any partisan approach."[35]

THE ARTIST AND THE ANARCHISTS GO TO HARVARD

In October 1932, Kirstein arranged for the Harvard Society for Contemporary Art to exhibit Shahn's series at the university, where A. Lawrence Lowell, former head of the Lowell Committee, served as president.[36] Bringing the works to Massachusetts meant that they were in closer proximity to South Braintree, where the payroll murder attributed to Sacco and Vanzetti had taken place and to Dedham where the trial was held, as well as to the world of Judge Thayer and President Lowell. Although in Shahn's iconic image, he set Thayer at a distance safely protected by the courthouse and legal system, in reality he was far from safe. Just that September, on the heels of the August anniversary of the state execution, Thayer's Massachusetts home was bombed, forcing his evacuation.[37] Just a few weeks later, on October 17, Shahn's Harvard exhibit went on view.

On order of the Harvard University police, posters with images of President Lowell advertising the exhibition were torn down from bulletin boards of college buildings and dormitories.[38] The police explained that they took this action because the Harvard Society for Contemporary Art had not applied for permits to plaster the signs, yet Capt. Charles R. Apted did hesitantly admit that there were further reasons for the actions, "which he did not care to discuss." Harvard University reported that objections had been made stating that the works were "a serious study of the principal of the case," and were concerned that the paintings would "renew agitation on behalf of the two convicted men."[39] Shahn is overshadowed in the reviews by the names of the defendants, the prosecution, and the controversy attached to the Harvard exhibition. Reviews protested that Shahn's works were mere satirical caricatures rather than "true" art, which criticism the members of the Society tried to counter by explaining that Shahn's work was art in the modernist vein.[40] Clearly, while Shahn's rhetoric was restrained, his subject matter was itself a touchstone—particularly in Massachusetts, where the protests over and retaliations for the crimes and executions continued.

In 1933, Herbert B. Ehrmann published his first book on the Sacco and Vanzetti trials, *The Untried Case*.[41] A few years later, in 1937 for the tenth anniversary of the execution, Gutzon Borglum, best known as the sculptor of Mount Rushmore, presented the state of

Massachusetts with a bronze plaque of Sacco and Vanzetti, showing the men in heroic Renaissance-inspired profile accompanied by Vanzetti's final words before being sent to the electric chair. The state refused the gift since it was, they felt, politically inappropriate; he would again offer the gift in 1947, only to be turned down once again.[42] In 1937-38, Shahn reinterpreted the case of Sacco and Vanzetti for the first time, in his mural on the theme of Jewish immigration and labor unions for the Community Center in the Jersey Homesteads, New Jersey, a workers' cooperative community. Shahn appropriated from his large tempera of the Lowell Committee the portraits of the Italian anarchists shown displayed in open caskets, to comment on the vulnerability of immigrants and activists in America, as well as to refer back to his own political and artistic awakening.[43] This quotation of Sacco and Vanzetti received little comment at the time.

THE COLD WAR ERA: THE MoMA RETROSPECTIVE

As art historian Frances K. Pohl has established, Shahn created *The Passion of Sacco and Vanzetti* when he was at the forefront of a movement to use figurative imagery to convey social and political messages.[44] By 1947, leading artists were now engaged with abstraction, and the political climate had shifted to the right. These combined political and artistic changes meant that the reception of Shahn's work began to change as well. MoMA organized Shahn's first retrospective in 1947.[45]

In arranging the exhibition, curator James Thrall Soby chose not to include examples of Shahn's youthful works, his stylistic experiments of the 1920s, his imitations of Parisian styles, his *Haggadah* (1930), nor his series on the Dreyfus affair (1930).[46] Instead Soby's exhibition began with selections from the Sacco and Vanzetti series to establish his curatorial vision of Shahn as a humanist and a social critic, which in effect suggested that Shahn arrived at his commitment to social realism, his mature style and subject without struggle or experimentation. To Soby, Shahn was the defender of social-content art and a man who worked outside the mainstream of modernism, an against-the-grain stance that evidenced his Americanness.[47]

By the late 1940s, abstract expressionism rather than social realism was being promoted by such influential critics as Clement Greenberg. Shahn opposed pure artistic abstraction, the rejection of social commentary and narrative in art, and the dismissal of the figurative which he and other artists felt was still a vital art form. Broadly speaking, reviewers of the 1947 retrospective fell into two camps—those nostalgic for the social art begun in the 1930s and those who viewed Shahn's work as outdated, even insignificant. MoMA displayed only two examples from *The Passion of Sacco and Vanzetti*; therefore, the comments specific to these works are brief and cursory.

In the 1947 reviews, critics perceived Shahn's satirical tone differently than they had in 1932 when his work was seen to have a sharp bite. Now, several critics responded with a bemused sense of humor or perceived the images as depressing rather than inflammatory. Most were not concerned whether Shahn was, or was not, politically partisan in his treatment of Sacco and Vanzetti. But one theme that remained consistent between the 1932 and the 1947 presentations of *The Passion of Sacco and Vanzetti*, was the critics' fascination with Shahn's audience, the implication being that both the artist and his audience were outside the norm and out of place in Manhattan's museums.

In his overview of Shahn's career and exhibition for the *New York Herald Tribune*, Carlyle Burrow conceived of Shahn as "an artist both factual and critical, whose paintings combine strong satirical content and humor."[48] Edward Alden Jewell wrote, "from the beginning Ben Shahn's work has had, for the most part, a strongly satirical cast and most of it falls with the 'social commentary' classification." This, according to Jewell, was especially true of works from 1931–35, "when appeared his passionately pointed brush remarks on the Sacco-Vanzetti case."[49] Betty Chamberlain provided *Art News* with a favorable review but zeroed in on Shahn's use of architectural elements in *The Passion of Sacco and Vanzetti* as expressive tools and abstract designs, rather than commenting on the characters, their actions, and the artist's message.[50] Ralph M. Pearson, in "A Modern Viewpoint: Ben Shahn at the Modern," particularized what he saw as the artist's desire to tell stories (Pearson made reference to Sacco and Vanzetti as examples of storytelling) and to provide social comment, rather than display concern with aesthetics which according to Pearson set Shahn apart from recent trends in American art.[51] While Pearson acknowledged Shahn's strength as a storyteller, he did not see any merit in either his style or form. *The New York Sun* critic was more skeptical, claiming Shahn to be a sly propagandist whose guile was achieved with a few salient facts and cunning gestures, by which "the trick is done."[52] The writer found Shahn's "far-reaching public" of interest, yet never clarified his romanticized, unsubstantiated speculation that Shahn's "audience is the common folk, who are interested in the next meal and not a whit in aesthetics...." As for *The Passion of Sacco and Vanzetti,* he continued, "Memory is so short, chances are that half the populace won't remember the furor attending that trial in the late 1920s, and those who do are probably too busily engaged in new fields to look back. In either case, with or without facts, there can be no misunderstanding Shahn's caustic comments on the participants in that affair. In these pictures, as is true of all the crusading series, the color is macabre and depressing, though, admittedly, it does accentuate the deadly characterizations." This review is a far change from 1932, when Bostonians feared that the paintings might spur further anarchist activities; or earlier reviews which found Shahn's color and line exemplary.[53]

Two critics with polar opposite views of the Shahn retrospective were Clement Greenberg writing in *The Nation*, and Joseph Solomon, who wrote for the *New Masses*. To Greenberg, Shahn was an artist whose minor gifts were "rarely effective beyond a surface felicity."[54] The MoMA show proves that Shahn's art is lacking "in density and in resonance." While Greenberg did not specifically discuss *The Passion of Sacco and Vanzetti*, he did state that Shahn first came to attention as a "socially conscious" painter, for which he had been "momentarily successful within the very narrow limits of this style." Isolating on the formal aspects of Shahn's art, Greenberg offers the backhanded compliment that Shahn's work has improved with time, becoming more "sensitive and painterly." Yet Greenberg concluded that, overall, Shahn's art "is not important, is essentially beside the point as far as ambitious present-day painting is concerned, and is much more derivative than it seems at first glance."

For Solomon, Shahn's "work reveals a politically mature mind with a poet's sympathy for humanity and his social commentary can be grim, tender, and satiric by turns."[55] Solomon wrote that Shahn's "famous Sacco and Vanzetti series of 1931–32 combine acute psychological observations of character with the most trenchant satire. The gouache of 'Sacco and Vanzetti and Their Guards' is a fine revelation of the martyred workers' monumental dignity and the studies of Boston's legal hypocrites are scalpel-sharp. The series may be compared to journalism at its finest, like Heywood Broun's protest against the same case before the *New York World* decided to oust him."[56] Whereas Solomon pulled Shahn's works back into their original political context in order to appreciate the artist's message and style, Greenberg judged Shahn solely on aesthetics as conceived of by the then current artistic vanguard, rather than consider the validity of Shahn's own formal choices. Shahn's next major exhibition would be in 1954, and once more the artistic advances of the decade coupled with the repressive political climate of the Cold War shaped how critics spoke about *The Passion of Sacco and Vanzetti.*[40]

THE COLD WAR ERA: SHAHN AT THE VENICE BIENNALE

During the 1950s, many still believed that Sacco and Vanzetti were innocent, yet, despite this belief and public pressure, the Commonwealth of Massachusetts declined to repudiate its proceedings. Writers for the left and liberal press continued to insist on the men's innocence. Concurrently, the mythologizing of Shahn, begun originally by James Thrall Soby, continued. For example, in 1951 Selden Rodman published his *Portrait of the Artist as an American*.[57] Shahn's Sacco and Vanzetti paintings would play an important role in the script both Soby and Rodman wrote of Shahn as an authentic and heroic American artist. In turn, legal scholars and supporters of Sacco and Vanzetti would use Shahn's *Passion of Sacco and Vanzetti* as emblems of the case to symbolize the men's legacy and the belief that justice had not been served.[58] In 1952, for the twenty-fifth anniversary of the execution, Shahn reworked his portrait of Sacco and Vanzetti for the cover of the *Nation*. Yet, although the artist, the anarchists, and the images were becoming more closely identified, during the 1950s many who wrote on Shahn's series would seek to depoliticize its meaning and its historical origins. One wonders if behind the commentary lurked the actual and symbolic images of Ethel and Julius Rosenberg executed in 1953 as spies.

Shahn, who had established himself as an outspoken critic of repressive forces in America, was selected along with the abstract painter Willem De Kooning to represent the United States at the 1954 Venice Biennial, organized by MoMA.[59] James Thrall Soby was largely responsible for selecting both Shahn and his works for the exhibition, including MoMA's own portrait of Sacco and Vanzetti (1932). In his exhibition essay, Soby stressed Shahn's love of Italy that dated back to his childhood memories of an Italian barbershop in Brooklyn, his later Italian travels of the 1920s, and his grief over the Italian war disasters.[60] Soby highlighted Shahn's series on Sacco and Vanzetti, and noted that the men were "significantly, both Italian-Americans"; he mentioned as well Shahn's dedication to workers and labor. Both of these statements, as well as his emphasis on craft, culture, and loss, were targeted by Soby to resonate with the Italian public to generate nationalistic and class-based sympathies towards the artist. But what he never mentioned was Shahn's political beliefs, his sense of anger and moral outrage, and that felt by Italian-Americans and Italians alike over the execution of Sacco and Vanzetti. Soby carefully selected his works in order to veil the political realities of the case, as well as to avoid focusing on America, on America's role in the case, rather than Italy.

Similarly, in the exhibition catalogue Alfred H. Barr, Jr., stripped Shahn's theme of Sacco and

Vanzetti of its political intentions and historical conditions of the case, by solely equating the theme of Sacco and Vanzetti with that of Christ.[61] Barr included Shahn's often-quoted statement on what attracted the artist to the theme of Sacco and Vanzetti: "Ever since I could remember I'd always wished I'd been lucky enough to be alive when something big was happening, like the Crucifixion. And suddenly I realized that I was living through another crucifixion. Here was something to paint!"[62] Clearly, Shahn's use of the term "The Passion," for the series title had direct religious implications, as did the use of the word crucifixion. Yet, Barr purposefully played up this aspect in order to appeal to the predominantly Catholic host country but ignored Shahn's other statements as to American injustices and the continued vulnerability of laborers, immigrants, and radicals.

After the Venice exhibition, Shahn would continue to explore the theme of Sacco and Vanzetti, and in 1958 he produced a serigraph of the two men. In 1959, an effort to persuade the Massachusetts legislature to grant the pair a posthumous pardon was a complete failure.[63]

THE 1960S: ONE FINAL IMAGE AND THE ARTIST'S CAREER RECONSIDERED

In the early 1960s, Robert Montgomery published the first book to argue for the pair's guilt.[64] On the basis of new ballistic tests, Francis Russell wrote *Tragedy in Dedham*, which proposed the split-guilt thesis, which found Sacco guilty but exonerated Vanzetti. In 1963, James Thrall Soby again wrote on Shahn's Sacco and Vanzetti series, noting that "the characterization of the prisoners is pungent and memorable; the tragic intensity of their faces contrasts subtly with the complacent righteousness of their guards...and we should remember, as an indication of his solitary and unrelenting faith in what he wants to say as a painter, that the Sacco-Vanzetti series was completed at precisely the moment when abstract art was enjoying one of its perennial returns to favor with the profession and the 'advanced' public."[65] In his strong support of Shahn, Soby painted a picture of the artist as a loner and renegade but skewed the historical record. For when Shahn turned to the theme of Sacco and Vanzetti, he was but one of many artists engaged with social content imagery, artists who worked together at the John Reed Club and other artists' organizations, and who would continue to do so in the 1930s. Furthermore, although Shahn's images of Sacco and Vanzetti are the best-known representations, other artists ranging in style and political temperament from George Grosz to Gutzom Borglum also commemorated the men. In fact, Soby's words, used to describe the artistic milieu of the early 1930s, are actually best suited to the period of 1947 to 1954, when he was most involved with Shahn's work as a curator and scholar.

In the mid-1960s, Syracuse University invited Shahn to create a large mosaic on a theme of his own choosing. Shahn decided to return to *The Passion of Sacco and Vanzetti,* noting that he was surprised by the theme's relevancy, exclaiming "My God! This is still a very controversial thing and becoming more so again because of the many books and articles that are coming out on the subject."[66] In 1967, during the Vietnam War and large-scale social unrest, Shahn recognized the continued vulnerability of those, such as Sacco and Vanzetti, who sought to question the government. Yet the mural received little national commentary, little praise or protest, and it seems that Shahn did not in any way impact on then-current campus protests. Perhaps, the image was a bit out of step with the times. The Syracuse mosaic would be his final interpretation of Sacco and Vanzetti; the publication which followed the mosaic's completion discussed Shahn's involvement with the case as a young man and his subsequent 1932 interpretation. The artist died in 1969.

Throughout the 1970s, there were scattered references to *The Passion of Sacco and Vanzetti* in the art-historical literature, but a scholarly reappraisal of Shahn had yet to occur. Recalling the 1932 exhibitions, the artist and author Bernarda Bryson Shahn recalled that except for a "bitter attack" by the communist press, as well as disdain by conservative presses, the series was otherwise well received, and drew a non-art public to galleries.[68] Art historian Morris Dorsky provided the first critical reappraisal of the series' 1932 reception, writing that the response was spectacular and almost uniformly enthusiastic, except for Gutman's negative review in the Nation.[69] Yet the actual reception to the 1932 exhibitions was more complex and camps were not so easily divided as Bryson Shahn and Dorsky present. In 1976, the Jewish Museum hosted a Shahn retrospective, which once more invited his detractors—prominent among them Hilton Kramer and Harold Rosenberg—to write on the limits of social realism (not a style so much as a mood and moral outlook, according to Rosenberg) and on Shahn's audience. In fact, Kramer opens his article with the following: "Almost more interesting than the Ben Shahn retrospective that is now at the Jewish Museum is the public that comes to see it."[70]

CONTEXTUAL STUDIES OF BEN SHAHN: THE 1980S AND 1990S

During the 1980s, the scholarship on Ben Shahn and that of Sacco and Vanzetti would be reinvigorated by new voices and social art-historical theorists. Art historian Frances K. Pohl's series of articles and books reawakened interest in Shahn and demonstrated the importance of situating the artist within his social historical context. Her studies of the 1947 MoMA and 1954 Venice exhibitions discuss *The Passion of Sacco and Vanzetti*, quoting at length from Barr's and Soby's catalogue essays. In her dissertation, books, and articles, Pohl established that both Barr and Soby failed to mention the American government's negative attitude toward Italian immigrants and the position of organized labor as the stronghold of the Italian Communist Party in Italy, in order to craft a particular image of Shahn and "The Passion of Sacco and Vanzetti."[71]

Several new studies on Sacco and Vanzetti were written during the 1980s, including one by William Young and David E. Kaiser who concluded that the men were framed.[72] Francis Russell also published his second book, now arguing that both Vanzetti and Sacco were guilty.[73] Although the shifting perception of the legal case had little direct impact on how Shahn's series was valued, the writings helped keep the images current. Perhaps, we do best to follow historian Paul Avrich's argument that we should examine the historical circumstances which gave rise to anarchist activities and how the justice system failed to work, rather than scrutinize the pair's culpability, for we may never be able to prove guilt or innocence. In a similar vein, through Shahn's images, we gain access to social concerns and unrest of the 1920s and 1930s, an artist's search to find the plastic means to chronicle the immigrant, the outsider, and the political activist volatile in action and vulnerable to reprisal.

CONCLUSION

Despite earlier debates over the validity of realism and of art of social content, Shahn's *The Passion of Sacco and Vanzetti* has achieved canonical status. In surveys of American, western, and modern art, when Shahn is included it most likely is through his image of the Lowell Committee. Many changes have occurred over the past seven decades within American intellectual and cultural history serving to position Shahn's work so prominently. Among both scholars and the public there is a greater appreciation for American art, so often dismissed in years prior. Within the academy, the prominence of social art historians and the fields of American studies and cultural studies have reinvigorated the contextual treatment of Shahn's works.

Further, with distancing from the Cold War, scholars now attempt to understand the 1930s as giving rise to a unique mix of art and politics, rather than condemn or pass judgment on individuals' political beliefs. Shahn's *Passion of Sacco and Vanzetti* has the ability to bring us to specific moments in America's history—the 1920s with anti-immigrant backlash, with artists, activists, and intellectuals rallying behind Sacco and Vanzetti, as well as the 1930s, when artists saw themselves as moral guides. The visual power of the gouaches, the judicial and ethical questions that they pose, the history of immigration, radicalism, and social unrest that they draw us into, all these elements render the works iconic and uniquely about America.

The Jersey City Museum's exhibition of Shahn's *The Passion of Sacco and Vanzetti*, the first viewing of the majority of the series since its 1932 exhibitions, offers an extraordinary opportunity to form new thoughts on the gouaches, the artist's formal control, and the potency of his message. Will Shahn's series, instead of the few frequently reproduced images which have become icons of American art, prove the overall strength or weakness of Shahn's presentation? With regards to our current complex sociopolitical climate, with cancellation of funding for exhibitions with overt political messages, repugnant anti-immigrant backlash, and increasing employment of the death penalty, will Shahn's work function as merely a sentimental reminder of past injustices or an angry revelation of a continued lineage of social injustices? And just as critics from the 1930s onwards displayed an open fascination with Shahn's "unusual" audience, how will Shahn's current audience be viewed? New critical responses to Shahn's *The Passion of Sacco and Vanzetti* are to be welcomed so that we may all judge its legacy and the interrelated dynamic of twentieth-century art and social commentary.

ACKNOWLEDGMENTS I would like to thank Eric Rosenberg, Laura Katzman and most especially Kristen Hass for their insightful criticisms on earlier versions of this essay. Paul Avrich, Tom McGrath, Nunzio Pernicone, the late Stephen L. Taller, and David Vallilee all offered assistance with research and translation. A special thank you to Alejandro Anreus, Debbi Blehart, and Peter W. Ross for supporting my work on Shahn.

List of endnotes on page 136

George Biddle
Our senses will applaud this world again,
But who can clap life with murdered men?
(detail). 1930. Lithograph, 24 x 18 in.
Private Collection, New Jersey

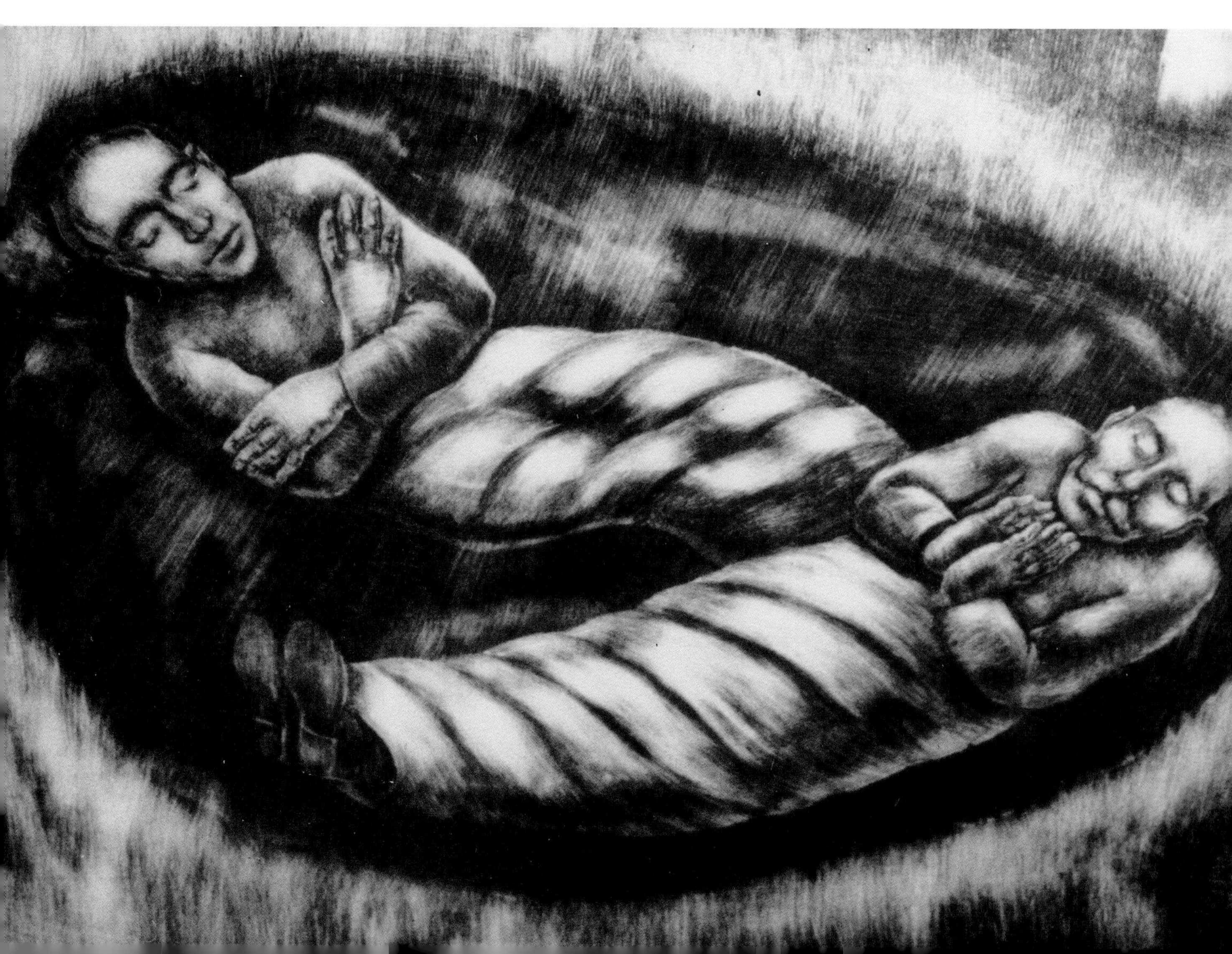

Alejandro Anreus

Ben Shahn and The Passion of Sacco and Vanzetti

On April 15, 1920, four, possibly five armed men shot and killed a paymaster and guard during a robbery of a shoe factory in South Braintree, Massachusetts. The stolen money, almost $ 16,000, was never recovered. Within a few weeks, the police had arrested two men they believed responsible for the crime: Nicola Sacco, a shoemaker, and Bartolomeo Vanzetti, a fish peddler. The arrest set in motion an international cause célèbre, which pitted civil libertarians, labor, the intelligentsia and other progressive elements against the New England Protestant establishment and national anti-immigrant elements, making for one of the most controversial prosecutions in twentieth-century America. Sacco and Vanzetti were only two out of hundreds of thousands of poor Italian immigrant workers. What made their case unique was that they were outspoken, militant anarchists who participated in strikes and demonstrations and had resisted the draft during World War I.

Their background as Italian immigrants (at a time when xenophobia was at an all time high) and their political radicalism, far more than any evidence adduced against them in the case, was the basis for the prosecution against them. After two trials before the same judge and the report of a blue-ribbon investigative committee appointed by the governor of Massachusetts—the guilty verdict stood. Sacco and Vanzetti were electrocuted at midnight in the Commonwealth of Massachusetts on August 23, 1927. The case continues to be "the case that will not die" as historian Nunzio Pernicone, in his essay in this catalogue, has written. Without a doubt, this is because it continues to raise questions about the kind of justice that the poor and adherents of radical and unpopular causes can expect in the United States.

THE REACTIONS OF ARTISTS

More than a year after the executions, the well-known literary critic Edmund Wilson summed up the case:

It revealed the whole anatomy of American life, with all its classes, professions and points of view and all their relations, and it raised almost every fundamental question of our political and social system. It did this, furthermore, in an unexpectedly dramatic fashion. As Dos Passos said, it was, during the last days before the executions, as if, by some fairy-tale spell, all the different kinds of Americans, eminent and obscure, had suddenly, in a short burst of intensified life, been compelled to reveal their true characters in a heightened exaggerated form.[1]

During the height of the uproar over the case, from 1920 to 1927, writers such as H.L.Mencken, Heywood Broun, Edna St. Vincent Millay, Upton Sinclair, John Dos Passos, and e.e. cummings, in addition to Wilson, as well as public figures like Congressman Fiorello La Guardia, Harvard law professor Felix Frankfurter and the physicist Albert Einstein spoke out against the conviction as a travesty of U.S. democratic ideals. The well-known American poet Edna St. Vincent Millay, attended pro-Sacco and Vanzetti demonstrations in Boston, and became so haunted by the case that she wrote several poems about it. The best known of these is "Justice Denied in Massachusetts":

Let us abandon then our gardens and go home
And sit in the sitting-room.
Shall the larkspur blossom or the corn grow under this cloud?
Sour to the fruitful seed
Is the cold earth under this cloud,
Fostering quack and weed, we have marched upon but cannot conquer;
We have bent the blades of our hoes against the stalks of them.
Let us go home, and sit in the sitting-room.
Not in our day
Shall the cloud go over and the sun rise as before,
Beneficent upon us
Out of the glittering bay,
And the warm winds be blown inward from the sea
Moving the blades of corn
With a peaceful sound.
Forlorn, forlorn,
Stands the blue hay-rack by the empty mow.

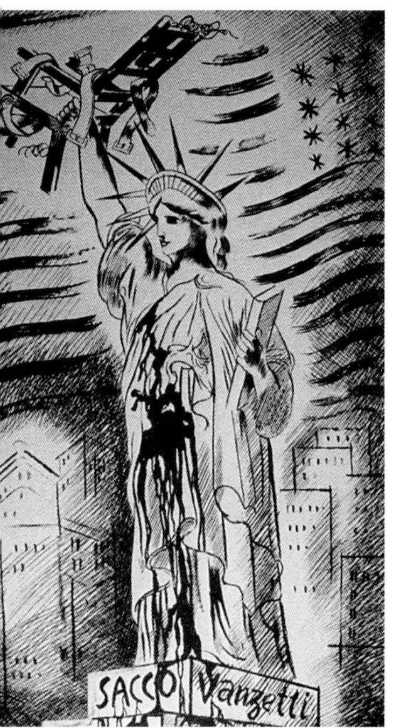

FIG. 25

And the petals drop to the ground,
Leaving the tree unfruited.
The sun that warmed our stooping backs and withered the weed uprooted—
We shall not feel it again.
We shall die in darkness, and be buried in the rain.
What from the splendid dead
We have inherited—Furrows sweet to the grain, and the weed subdued—
See now the slug and the mildew plunder.
Evil does overwhelm
The larkspur and the corn;
We have seen them go under.
Let us sit here, sit still,
Here in the sitting-room until we die;
At the step of Death on the walk, rise and go;
Leaving to our children's children this beautiful doorway,
And this elm,
And a blighted earth to till
With a broken hoe.[2]

The poem reflects a profound disillusion with the American justice system, which the Sacco-Vanzetti case would spread to many others in the intelligentsia. Other major literary responses would range from Upton Sinclair's *Boston*, a novelized version of the case, to Dos Passos's *The Big Money*, published in 1936, years after the executions.

As early as 1925, Julio Antonio Mella, the exiled Cuban communist and lover of the photographer Tina Modotti, called in the pages of the Mexican Communist Party newspaper *El Machete* for "Sacco and Vanzetti to be living subjects for the visual artist, so that by painting them in the midst of their ordeal, consciousness is raised, actions are taken and their freedom will eventually be won."[3] This was not to be; Sacco and Vanzetti would become subjects of visual art only after their execution. Between 1927 and 1933 several artists working in the United States produced works with Sacco and Vanzetti as the subject. George Grosz (at the time in Germany before his exile to the United States) did an ink drawing in September of 1927, shortly after Sacco and Vanzetti had been executed. Entitled simply *Sacco and Vanzetti* **(fig.25)**, it depicts in harsh, clear lines the Statue of Liberty, the symbol of immigration and American freedom, but instead of a torch, she holds up an empty electric chair. Blood

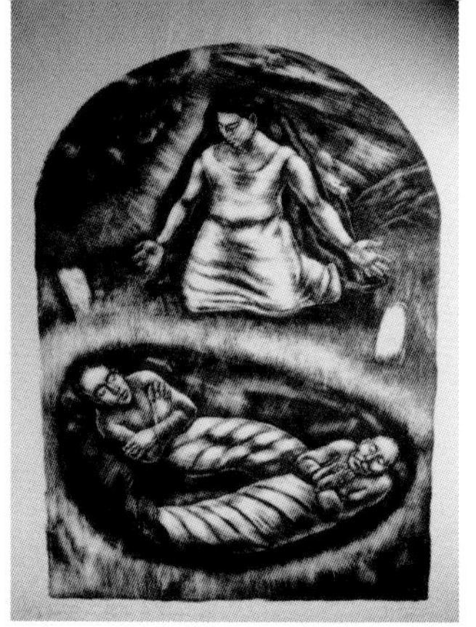

FIG. 26

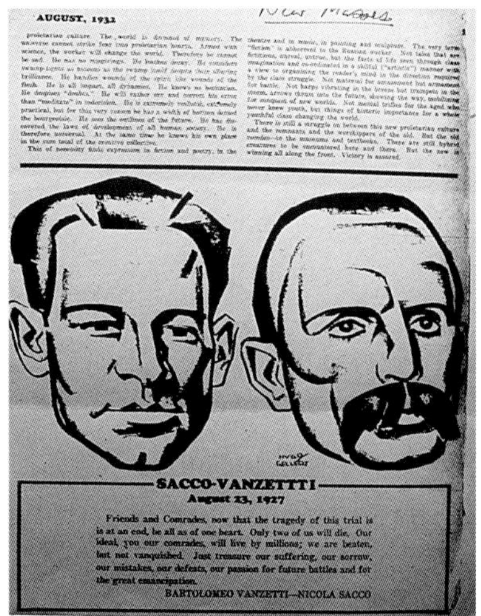

AUGUST, 1932

SACCO-VANZETTTI
August 23, 1927

Friends and Comrades, now that the tragedy of this trial is is at an end, be all as of one heart. Only two of us will die. Our ideal, you our comrades, will live by millions; we are beaten, but not vanquished. Just treasure our suffering, our sorrow, our mistakes, our defeats, our passion for future battles and for the great emancipation.

BARTOLOMEO VANZETTI—NICOLA SACCO

FIG. 27

drips from the chair to the statue's gown, staining a portion of it. On the base of the statue are written the names Sacco, Vanzetti. Behind the statue floats a large American flag, symbol of patriotism. Beneath the flag is the New York City skyline—its skyscrapers symbols of the prosperity of the "Roaring Twenties." In response to the case, Grosz drew a brutal allegory, one that made freedom, patriotism, and progress into backdrops of a conspiracy. Yet, the figures of Sacco and Vanzetti are absent; no hint is given of the individual identity of the martyrs.

The painter George Biddle, a New Deal liberal, created a lithograph in 1930, which he titled using a line from a poem by St. Vincent Millay: *Our senses will applaud this world again, But who can clap life with murdered men?* **(fig. 26)**. In this print, Biddle adopted Christian iconography—the lamentation and burial of Christ—and applied it to Sacco and Vanzetti. In a cemetery, a robust, sibyl-like woman weeps on her knees, her arms open. Behind her is a stormy sky. Below her in a hole in the ground are the corpses of Sacco and Vanzetti. Their arms are crossed, their bodies wrapped in shrouds. We recognize their masklike faces with their eyes closed. This graphic work reflects the direct influence of early Italian Renaissance painting, as well as Diego Rivera's Ministry of Public Education murals (1927), in particular the panel *The Blood of Martyrs Fertilizes the Soil*, which Biddle had seen during his visit to Mexico in the late 1920s. The overall emotional effect of the Biddle lithograph is mourning—within it Sacco and Vanzetti are not living, breathing individuals, but silenced martyrs.

In 1932, on the occasion of the fifth anniversary of the execution of Sacco and Vanzetti, the graphic artist (and Communist

Party member) Hugo Gellert produced a crayon drawing entitled *Sacco & Vanzetti* **(fig.27)**. The location of the original is not known, but it was reproduced in the August 1932 issue of *New Masses*. It consists of two simple, straightforward heads, drawn in a blocky, realistic style. They are powerful and heroic, reflecting the official Socialist Realist aesthetic that prevailed in the Soviet Union under Joseph Stalin. In Gellert's drawing, Sacco and Vanzetti are not depicted as human beings but as radical supermen, taking their martyrdom in stride.

ENTER BEN SHAHN

Typical for their times, the depictions of Sacco and Vanzetti by Grosz, Biddle, and Gellert were single, one-time representations that responded to the immediacy of the case, relied on no visual resources, and lacked a deep identification with the case itself. Allegorical, symbolic, or simply heroic—functioning principally as propaganda—they overlooked the individual humanity of Sacco and Vanzetti, as well as the specifics of the case itself.

By contrast, one artist would return several times in the course of a long career to the subject of Sacco and Vanzetti handling it with the complexity it merited. Starting in the early 1930s, then in the 1950s, and finally towards the end of his life in 1967, Ben Shahn produced 23 gouache/tempera paintings, an ink drawing, and three serigraphs, as well as a mosaic mural on the subject, not to mention a couple of uncompleted book projects.

As early as 1925, while living in Europe, Shahn took note of the ferment that the case had caused, not just among intellectuals but also in the working class. He was especially taken with the fact that children, boats, community centers, even ships were being named after the two anarchists.[4] While on a brief trip to the United States shortly before their execution, Shahn traveled twice to Boston to join in picketing on their behalf.

1930s

In the summer of 1931, during a stay in Truro on Cape Cod, Shahn began planning a series of small paintings on the theme of Sacco and Vanzetti. Earlier in the summer Shahn had completed a series of watercolors on the Alfred Dreyfus case—based on photos in a book Shahn had purchased during his last trip to France. Yet the Dreyfus case, even with its anti-Semitic element, was distant and in ways too French a story for Shahn; now, having moved back permanently to the U.S., he was interested in telling American stories. Shahn had become aware of the social and political implications of the Sacco and Vanzetti case seven years earlier, while living in Europe. Here was the opportunity to deal with a very American story.

In October of 1931, Shahn wrote to Gardner Jackson, secretary of the Sacco and Vanzetti Defense Committee and co-editor of *The Letters of Sacco and Vanzetti*, in order to obtain photographs of the case.[5] Jackson suggested that Shahn contact Aldino Felicani, another defense committee member, a friend of Vanzetti's, and the unofficial archivist of the case. Felicani made some materials available to him—mostly pamphlets. Shahn pursued his research at the New York Public Library Picture Collection, as well as at the library of the Rand School, a New York socialist organization. Shahn appropriated and transformed the photographs of the Sacco and Vanzetti case into twenty-three pictures, which were exhibited at Edith Halpert's Downtown Gallery in New York City, April 5–17, 1932.

Although the critical response to the exhibition was mixed, the series was not only a turning point for Shahn, signaling his artistic maturity, but a key early example in the development of social realism in the United States in the 1930s. The work of later social realist artists like Robert Gwathmey and Jacob Lawrence, both in terms of style and content, is inconceivable without the precedent of Shahn's treatment of Sacco and Vanzetti. The twenty-three Sacco and Vanzetti paintings defined Shahn's pictorial style with its flat areas of color and incisive calligraphy. Stylistically, Shahn had studied and absorbed the work of the Italian Primitives, as well as the modernism of Matisse, Rouault, and Dufy. He synthesized these various formal concerns into a highly personal visual vocabulary, where colors functioned as flat areas united by a linear structure.

It is interesting to note that Sacco and Vanzetti are represented in only six of the twenty-three pictures of the 1931-32 series. Although Shahn had access to photographic material from both the defense and prosecution in the case, he chose to make more paintings of the defense side. Most of the paintings in the series have

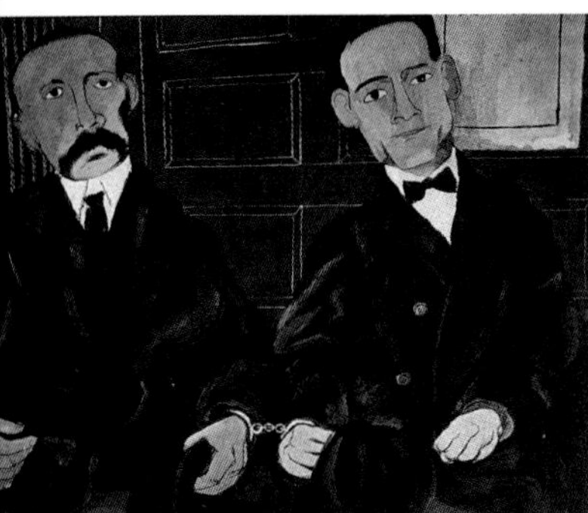

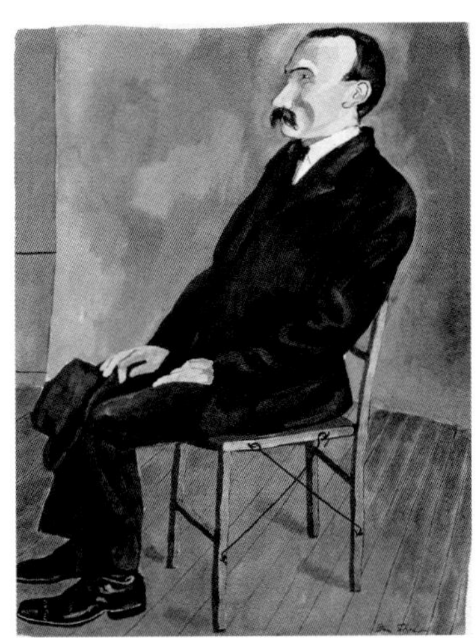

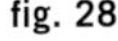

flat, impersonal backgrounds. Details, such as hats, buttons, Vanzetti's mustache, etc., have been exaggerated or emphasized, departing from and transforming the initial photographic image. In all the paintings in the series, Shahn increased the scale of the figures in relation to the background and pushed them closer to the picture plane, making the figures more intimate. In his depictions of Vanzetti and Sacco, Shahn tilted their heads, distorted their proportions (particularly the heads and hands), and exaggerated their features, to create a melancholic, wistful quality–making the two men more human and sympathetic.

In the hauntingly clear paintings *Bartolomeo Vanzetti and Nicola Sacco* **(fig. 2)** and *Bartolomeo Vanzetti* **(fig. 28)**, simple white lines over a dark brown-red background evoke the massive and claustrophobic quality of the courtroom. The suits and coats of Vanzetti and Sacco are rumpled, the shapes of their hats overemphasized. Delicate lines form the shapes of their hands with their knuckles, wrinkles, and fingernails. Again, small details, like the golden tacks on the red upholstered chairs, the handcuffs with their chains, the buttons on Sacco's overcoat, and the slightly disheveled tie on Vanzetti's neck, all make the image specific and concrete. The faces of the two men, with their pale tan background color, are drawn with a great economy of means. Two, at most three, lines give us an eye, the nose, lips, Vanzetti's thick mustache. The expressions are of a serene strength that does not belie vulnerability. The painting of Vanzetti in profile sitting on a rickety chair emphasizes fragile, worn-out elements: the thin wire that holds the chair's legs together, his scuffed boots, the worn floor boards, the fingers of his right hand, his long yet delicate nose. These details come together in a composition where the forms project a content of experience, of a life lived. The fragility of the chair, with its rickety legs and thin wire, is a metaphor for the peril Vanzetti faces.

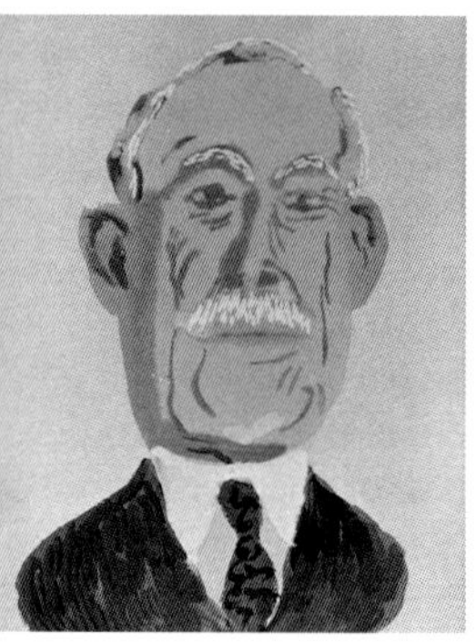

fig. 17

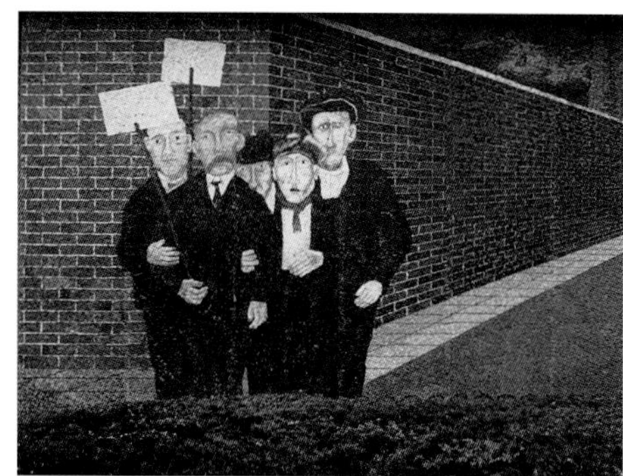

fig. 29

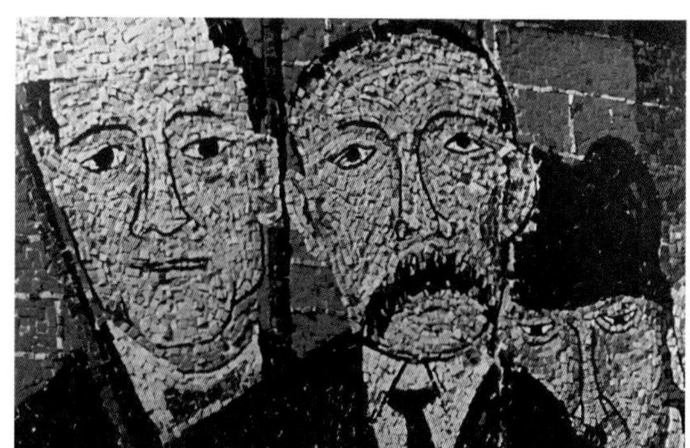

fig. 30

When Shahn depicts the characters on the judiciary and prosecutorial side, he employs the devices of political caricature. In *Judge Webster Thayer* **(fig. 17)** the head is made large and balloon-like, resting on a nonexistent neck and diminutive shoulders. The coloration of the judge's face ranges from pink to red. The features have been drawn using a wet-on-wet watercolor technique, so that the lines are not clear and precise, but spiderlike, stressing the facial wrinkles. Thayer's large, red ears may insinuate a nasty temper or a man flushed from drunkenness. By drawing the judge's eyes closer together, Shahn evokes a shifty personality. Thayer's large and grotesque head can represent several things; the official mask of the WASP establishment, judicial unfairness, and the face of xenophobia. Ultimately, Shahn has created an icon of illegitimate authority.

Soon after the completion and exhibition of the series, Shahn painted a mural maquette **(fig. 29)** and a monumental detail **(fig. 30)** for an exhibition of mural painting sponsored by The Museum of Modern Art in May 1932. The exhibition, which opened the museum's new quarters on 53 Street, was entitled *Murals by American Painters and Photographers.* Shahn's maquette was a panorama of the case, a kind of secular "stations of the cross" depicting the passion and death of Sacco and Vanzetti. Stylistically similar to the first series, flat areas of color are unified and held together into forms by Shahn's signature calligraphic line. From left to right, the viewer encounters a group of demonstrators with signs, in front of a brick factory building with a chimney. Vanzetti and Sacco are among the demonstrators. This portion of the maquette refers both to their rank-and- file status as militant radicals and to their spiritual presence among those who picketed for their freedom. The central area of the maquette represents Vanzetti and Sacco as giants—their figures almost completely cover the height of the painting. Their suits are rumpled, they are handcuffed to one another, and their facial expressions are calm and determined. On Vanzetti's right stands a miniature, or better yet, midget figure of Governor Alvan Fuller reading the findings of the Lowell Committee. The final, right-hand section of the maquette depicts the courthouse with Judge Thayer in the background, and the three members of the Lowell Committee holding funeral lilies immediately behind the open caskets containing the corpses of Vanzetti and Sacco. The monumental detail (84 1/2 x 48 inches, as opposed to the full maquette's 21 x 48 inches) is an enlarged version of the right section of the maquette.

Shahn places great emphasis on the figures of the Lowell Committee—Massachusetts Institute of Technology's president Samuel Stratton, President Lawrence Lowell of Harvard, and retired judge Robert Grant. Shahn's horrifying portrayal of Lowell is a visual equivalent of the poet e.e. cumming's assessment of Lowell and what he stood for in a 1927 conversation with Edmund Wilson:

> *Well, he was one of my father's greatest friends!—he goes around everywhere with a little poodle whose balls trail on the ground and make the letter H.—that's what he's like! I've known several of these young men who are being groomed—groomed is the word!—for big positions—First, their teeth go—then they wear glasses—then, you mightn't believe it, but it's really so!—they have to be seen at certain places on Fifth Avenue, at certain times, with a silk hat—and if they do that and are always on hand and make calls and suck pricks—after a while somebody dies, and they stand up and put on their silk hats and take out their pricks, and, if they've been good, they get the job. . . but Lowell wears a kind of thing (collar) that's just wrapped around his neck, and there's a kind of little black bow tie that they have to wear with it that gets way up on one side under their coat—so they wrap this old dried condom around their necks—and their Adam's apple falls out—you were speaking of old withered hollyhocks—well, Lowell has a neck like that—there's something indecent about it!*[6]

Shahn features these eminent members of both the educational and judicial establishments as pink-skinned, bony-faced effigies, whose facial expressions denote a mixture of boredom and ignorance. Stratton and Grant wear top hats, while Lowell wears his academic robe and hat. Grant and Stratton rigidly hold calla lilies, as a hypocritical offering towards the corpses of the victims in their caskets, whose pale faces convey a laconic dignity. In the background, through a courthouse window, we see Judge Thayer raising his right hand. Is he swearing in the dead defendants or blessing the committee that upheld his guilty verdict?

These two pieces by Shahn, together with Hugo Gellert's *Us Fellas Gotta Stick Together* and William Gropper's *Struggle in America Since the War*, also commissioned for the MoMA exhibit, created an uproar before the opening. Two of the Museum of Modern Art's trustees found the works "highly offensive and malicious in the representation of living persons who may be indirectly responsible for the future of the museum."[7] In his two mural proposals Shahn depicted two well-known academics and two judges as responsible for the execution of the two radicals on trumped-up charges. In his contribution, Gellert painted J.P. Morgan, John D. Rockefeller, and Henry Ford in the company of Al Capone, while Gropper depicted Morgan and Ford as strike busters. The museum's director, Alfred H. Barr, Jr., sent the following telegram to A. Conger Goodyear, then president of the museum's board:

> *We have had ten days of hell over these pictures stop The decision of Lewisohn [,] Clark and Nelson [Rockefeller] was made after the most careful consideration and after Mrs. Rock[efeller] before she left had agreed to leave them in stop DeBovoise and Lee are with them and they are acting principally on behalf of the persons caricatured stop They knew that you doubt strongly and had threatened to resign but they believe you would have been with them had you been here I implore you not to make a hasty decision but to talk with Mrs. Rock as well as Clark and Lewisohn Please keep this telegram confidential Devotedly—Alfred.*[8]

Goodyear sided with Mrs. Rockefeller and her son Nelson, and the paintings remained in the exhibition.

Shahn's paintings from the 1931–32 Sacco and Vanzetti series, synthesize the pictorial concerns of European Modernism; flat color and nervous calligraphic line, with a kind of home-grown American realism, one possessing the boldness and unpretentiousness of Folk Art. Unlike single depictions of the same theme by other artists, including even Diego Rivera's homage to the two anarchists in his 1933 *The New Freedoms* panel (for The New Workers School murals in New York City, where Shahn assisted him), Shahn on his own rejected allegory and symbolism, as well as heroic exaggerations. Rather, Shahn emphasized the humanity of Sacco and Vanzetti, their families and friends, by painting them as melancholic or serene, expressing solidarity with each other, even as frail individuals standing in the middle of a crucible. Judge Thayer and the Lowell Committee are the villains within Shahn's visual narrative—their villainy communicated through the devices of political caricature, which presents them as grotesque and remote.

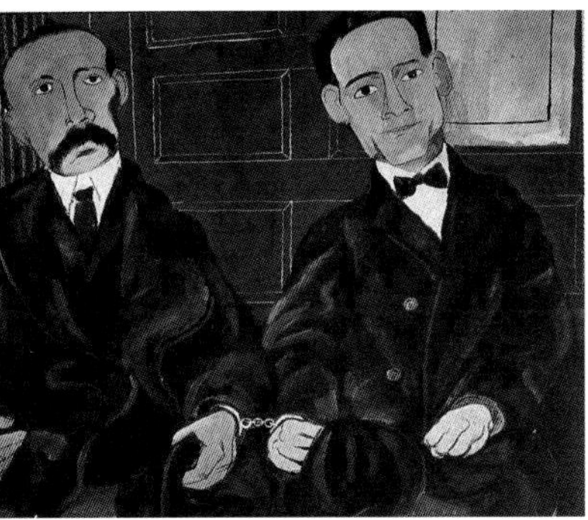

fig. 2

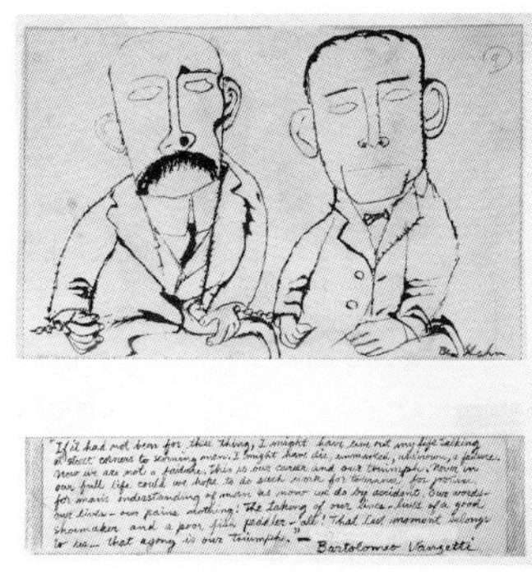

fig. 31

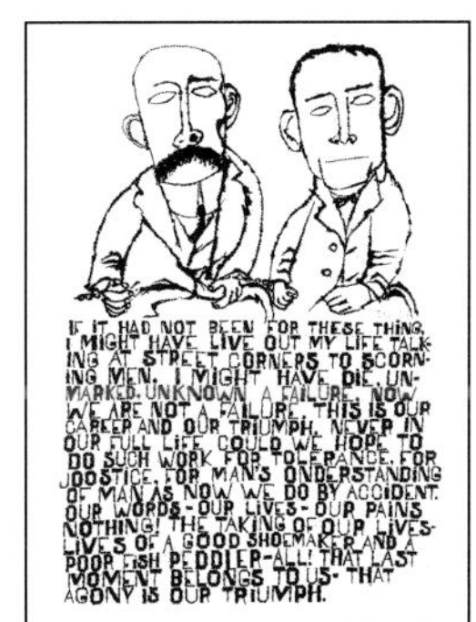

fig. 32

1950s

After two decades, Shahn returned to the theme of Sacco and Vanzetti in 1952. When he produced an ink drawing for the cover of the August 23 issue of *The Nation*, which was dedicated to "25 Years Since Sacco and Vanzetti." This work **(fig.31)** is a variation of the *Bartolomeo Vanzetti and Nicola Sacco* painting of 1931–32 **(fig. 2)**. The background is completely blank. A nervous series of ink lines, sometimes thin, other times rough like barbed wire, forms the two handcuffed men, rumpled coats and all. In the 1952 version, the faces have become masklike, with a minimum of features required to establish their physical resemblance. The eye sockets are empty, recalling ancient Greek theatrical masks. Below the figures Shahn has written out Vanzetti's last words. The image as a whole gives up the rumpled individuality of the earlier likenesses for a more formal visual language, presenting Sacco and Vanzetti as members of the pantheon of victims of American injustice.

Shahn was well aware of the hermetic and mythic visual vocabulary of abstract expressionism during the 1950s; this drawing and the prints that followed it later in the decade were an explicitly political response to the apoliticized formalism of the New York School. The drawing was produced at the height of the McCarthy period, when a communist witch hunt and blacklisting cast a pall over American society. Shahn, who was called to testify by the House Un-American Activities Committee (he was an unfriendly witness), made a very clear statement in the drawing by resurrecting the victims of an earlier Red Scare. In 1958, he transformed the 1952 drawing into three serigraphs. The first and largest of the three **(fig. 32)** is titled *The Passion of Sacco and Vanzetti* and it reproduces the figures from the drawing in a larger format. Starkly linear, the serigraph further simplifies the elements of the 1930s original. The heads are very large, just short of grotesque, emphasizing the indomitable quality of Sacco and Vanzetti's ideas by contrast to the frailty of their small bodies. Below the figures, Shahn's unique lettering reproduces Vanzetti's famous last words, typos and all:

> *If it had not been for these thing, I might have live out my life talking at street corners to scorning men. I might have die, unmarked, unknown a failure. Now we are not a failure. This is our career and our triumph. Never in our full life could we hope to do such work for tolerance, for joostice, for man's onderstanding of man as now we do by accident. Our word—our lives—our pains nothing! The taking of our lives—lives of a good shoemaker and a poor fish peddler—all! That last moment belongs to us—That agony is our triumph.*

This serigraph became in turn the basis of two smaller ones; one entitled *Immortal Words*, containing only Vanzetti's text in Shahn's lettering, the other *entitled Sacco and Vanzetti* containing just the figures. Both of these became very popular as posters throughout the politically turbulent 1960s and into the 1970s.

1967

In 1966 Shahn was approached by Syracuse University to execute an outdoor mural commissioned by Mr. and Mrs. Jacob Schulman (to memorialize their recently diseased son) and by Mr. and Mrs. Richard Evans, III. This occurred as the Vietnam War was causing a national crisis, on the scale of the Depression and the McCarthy era. Shahn at this time was producing some of his most abstract and symbolic work—dealing primarily with Judaic themes—but for the Syracuse mural he returned to the unrealized mural maquette of 1932 and adopted an earlier, less abstract style. Here again, we encounter a panorama **(fig. 33)** of the lives and deaths of the two immigrant anarchists. From left to right, we see Sacco and Vanzetti protesting in a crowd, then enlarged, as if inhabiting their martyrdom, their myth, the small and insignificant figure of Governor Fuller at their side. Finally, in the last section of the mural, they lay dead in their caskets, surrounded by their "executioners"—Judge Thayer and the Lowell Committee—who hypocritically mourn their deaths. Due to the nature of the mosaic medium, the outdoor mural lacks the details of the original 1932 maquette, yet the intense reds of the bricks against the deep blue sky throughout the composition push forth the darker figures of Sacco and Vanzetti. Clearly Shahn was drawing on two cherished icons to register his feelings about a new period of national, moral crisis—this time, the war in Vietnam.

Ben Shahn turned to the subject of Sacco and Vanzetti in his art during three distinct periods of social and political crisis in the United States: the Great Depression, McCarthyism, and the Vietnam War. Politically, Shahn evolved from a New Deal liberal in the 1930s to a progressive fellow traveler in the late 1940s and 1950s, to a liberal democrat who supported Eugene McCarthy against the Democratic Party establishment in 1968. Along the way, he returned to the theme of the "good shoemaker and the poor fish peddler" as icons of resistance questioning the status quo. Identifying with Sacco and Vanzetti as outsiders, as immigrants, and political radicals, Shahn made them into vehicles by which he could question American society whenever it failed to live up to its democratic ideals.

Many years after his death, Bernarda Bryson, the artist's widow, recounted the following:

> *When Ben was a child, one night there was a knock on the door of his house, his father or grandfather answered and allowed a man in, who was obviously on the run, and quickly hid him. Days later the man was taken elsewhere for continued hiding. The man was either a socialist or a Zionist, and the authorities were persecuting him. For Ben this episode was one of the many keys to his lifelong identification with the underdog, be it Sacco and Vanzetti, or Tom Mooney, or the fishermen of* The Lucky Dragon. *Once he said to me that if Sacco and Vanzetti had been Jewish and socialists they could have been members of his family.*[9]

Shahn's fascination with the Sacco and Vanzetti case began as a project by an artist demonstrating his solidarity with the American intelligentsia in a *cause célèbre*. But his involvement went deeper, tapping his own immigrant and working-class roots, as well as his family's socialist background. Issues of status and identity (being Italian or Jewish in a white, Anglo-Saxon Protestant society), as well as politics (being anarchist or socialist in a capitalist country) link Shahn and Sacco and Vanzetti.

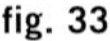

fig. 33

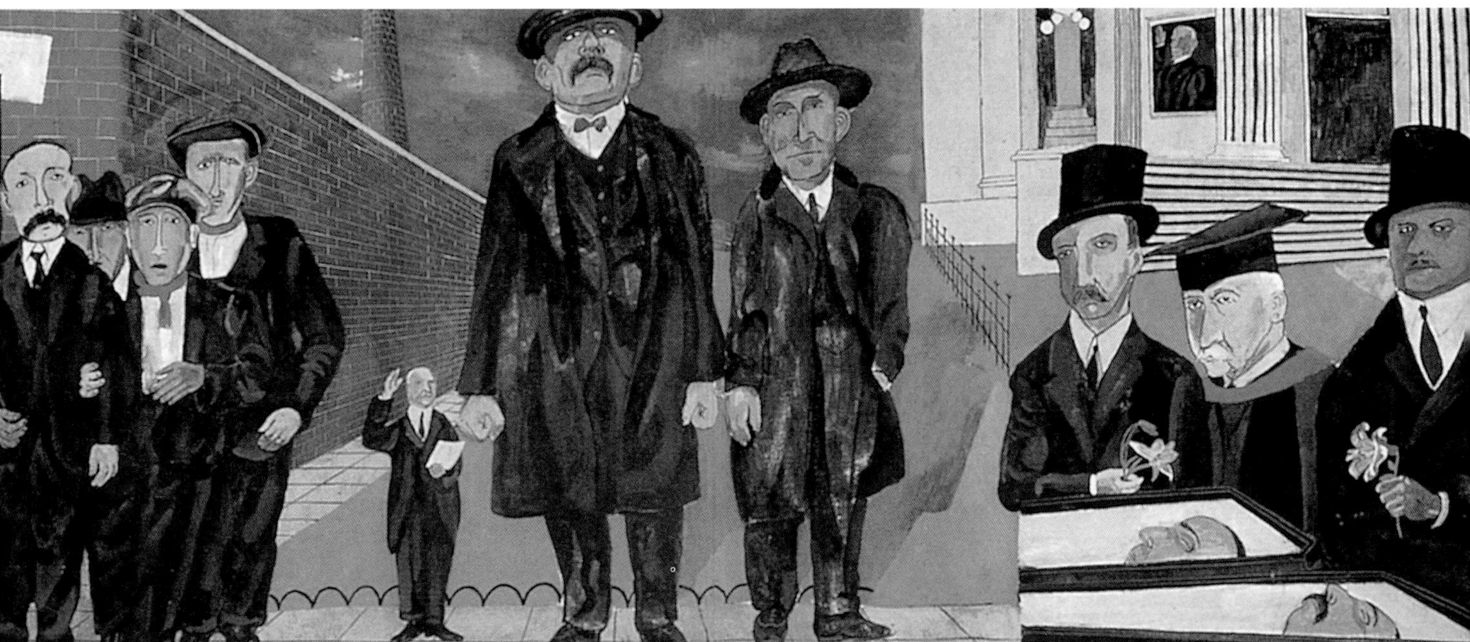

In a sense, Shahn's first Sacco and Vanzetti paintings, as well as his later variations on the theme were a more serene visual equivalent to John Dos Passos's evocation of the anarchists' cause in *The Big Money*:

> *they have clubbed us off the streets they are stronger they are rich they hire and fire politicians ...*
> *all right you have won you will kill the brave men our friends tonight*
> *the streets belong to the beaten nation all the way to the cemetery where the bodies of the immigrants are to be burned we line the curbs in the drizzling rain we crowd the wet sidewalks elbow to elbow silent pale looking with scared eyes at the coffins*
> *we stand defeated America* [10]

Perhaps the last word on Shahn's profound connection with the subject of Sacco and Vanzetti should be what he told an interviewer in 1944:

> *Then I got to thinking about the Sacco and Vanzetti case. They'd been electrocuted in 1927, and in Europe of course I'd seen all the demonstrations against the trial—a lot more than there were over here. Ever since I could remember I'd wished that I'd been lucky enough to be alive at a great time—when something big was going on, like the Crucifixion. And suddenly I realized I was! Here I was living through another crucifixion. Here was something to paint! I painted 23 pictures about the Sacco and Vanzetti case in seven months, and Edith Halpert exhibited them at the Downtown Gallery in 1932. A lot of people came and looked at them and bought most of them. I don't know where they are now. But from then on, I knew what I wanted to do, and I've been doing it ever since.*[11]

It was at the crossroads of immigration and political radicalism, at times of great social and political distress, that Shahn painted Bartolomeo Vanzetti and Nicola Sacco in their passion.

List of endnotes on page 138

Endnotes

Frances K. Pohl
Ben Shahn, Politics, and Art

1. Frances K. Pohl, *Ben Shahn: New Deal Artist in a Cold War Climate, 1947–1954* (Austin: University of Texas Press, 1989).
2. "Ben Shahn: Downtown Gallery," *Art News*, April 9, 1932, 10; Walter Gutman, "The Passion of Sacco-Vanzetti," *The Nation*, April 20, 1932, 475.
3. Quoted in Selden Rodman, *Portrait of the Artist as an American: Ben Shahn, A Biography with Pictures* (New York: Harper and Brothers, 1951), 63–64.
4. Walter Abell, "Art and Labor," *Magazine of Art* 39 (October 1946): 260.
5. Ann Leonard, "Around the Galleries: Ben Shahn, a People's Artist," *People's World*, December 1, 1948.
6. James Thrall Soby, *Ben Shahn* (New York: Museum of Modern Art, 1947), p. 5.
7. George Dondero, "Modern Art Shackled to Communism," *Congressional Record*, 81st Cong., 1st sess. (August 16, 1948): 11585–86.
8. Museum of Modern Art, New York, "Summary of European Press Reaction to the Exhibition 'Two Painters and Three Sculptors from the United States,' shown at the XXVII Biennale, Venice, June 19–October 17, 1954," October 1, 1956, 13.
9. Franco Catania, *Corriere de Sicilia*, August 24, 1954, as quoted in MoMA, "Press Reaction," p. 14. MoMA lists this paper as an "independent" daily.
10. Carlo Ragghianti, commentary accompanying Ben Shahn, "L'artista e il politicismo," *Sele Arte*, no. 9 (November/December 1953): 28, author's translation.
11. Ben Shahn, "The Artist and the Politicians," *Rights 1* (1953) : 4,8; *Art News* 52 (September 1953): 7.
12. Quoted in Rodman, *Portrait of the Artist*, 47.
13. Matthew Josephson, "The Passion of Sacco-Vanzetti," *The New Republic*, 20 (April 1932): p. 275

Nunzio Pernicone
The Sacco-Vanzetti Case: An Overview

1. Quoted in Eric Foner, "Sacco and Vanzetti: The Men and the Symbols," *The Nation* 225, No. 5 (August 20-27, 1977): 135.
2. Quoted in Paul Avrich, *Sacco and Vanzetti: The Anarchist Background* (Princeton, N.J.: Princeton University Press, 1991), 12.
3. Ibid., 19.
4. Ibid.
5. Quoted in Foner, "Sacco and Vanzetti," 139.
6. See Avrich, *Sacco and Vanzetti*; Robert D'Attilio, "La Salute è in Voi: The Anarchist Dimension," in Robert D'Attilio and Jane Manthorn, eds., *Sacco and Vanzetti: Developments and Reconsiderations*, 1979 (Boston: Boston Public Library, 1979), 75–89.
7. Quoted in Avrich, *Sacco and Vanzetti*, 26.
8. Ibid., 37.
9. *Boston Evening Transcript*, February 1, 1912.
10. Erik Amfitheatrof, *The Children of Columbus: An Informal History of the Italians in the New World* (Boston and Toronto: Little, Brown and Co., 1973), 169–170.
11. *New York Evening Journal*, July 31, 1900.
12. *New York Times*, July 31, 1900.
13. Quoted in Avrich, *Sacco and Vanzetti*, 130.
14. Quoted in Robert Justin Goldstein, *Political Repression in Modern America: From 1870 to the Present* (Cambridge, New York: Schenkman Publishing Co., 1978), 78.
15. Quoted in Avrich, *Sacco and Vanzetti*, 95.
16. Ehrmann, *The Case That Will Not Die* (Boston and Toronto: Little, Brown and Co., 1969), 46.

17. Vanzetti would later charge that Vahey had sold him out by urging him not to testify. Vahey insisted that the decision had been Vanzetti's. Suspicions regarding Vahey's commitment to his client arose four years later when he and Katzmann formed a partnership.
18. Bartolomeo Vanzetti, *Background of the Plymouth Trial* (Boston: Road to Freedom Group, 1926), 36.
19. Quoted in Francis Russell, *Tragedy in Dedham* (New York: McGraw Hill, 1962), 128.
20. Quoted in James West Davidson and Mark Hamilton Lytle, *After The Fact: The Art of Historical Selection*, vol. II (New York: McGraw Hill, 1992), 242.
21. Quoted in Ehrmann, *The Case That Will Not Die*, 462.
22. Quoted in Russell, *Tragedy in Dedham*, 133.
22. Quoted in Russell, *Tragedy in Dedham*, 133.
23. Quoted in Ehrmann, *The Case That Will Not Die*, 266.
24. Quoted in Felix Frankfurter, *The Case of Sacco and Vanzetti* (New York: Little Brown and Co., 1927), 43.
25. Quoted in *ibid.*, 64
26. Ibid., 59.
27. Quoted in ibid., 64.
28. Quoted in ibid., 67.
29. Quoted in Roberta Strauss Feuerlicht, *Justice Crucified: The Story of Sacco and Vanzetti* (New York: McGraw-Hill, 1977), 284.
30. Quoted in Ehrmann, *The Case That Will Not Die*, 198.
31. Quoted in ibid.
32. Quoted in Russell, *Tragedy in Dedham*, 265–266.
33. Technically, Moore had always been Sacco's lawyer, not Vanzetti's.
34. Quoted in Ehrmann, *The Case That Will Not Die*, 65.
35. Ibid., 322.
36. Quoted in Feuerlicht, *Justice Crucified*, 324.
37. Ibid., 329.
38. Frankfurter, *The Case of Sacco and Vanzetti*, 104.
39. Quoted in Ehrmann, *The Case That Will Not Die*, 451.
40. Ibid., 451–458.
41. Quoted in Russell, *Tragedy In Dedham*, 374.
42. Ehrmann, *The Case That Will Not Die*, 485.
43. Quoted in James West Davidson and Mark Hamilton Lytle, "Sacco and Vanzetti," *in After the Fact: The Art of Historical Detection*), vol. II (New York: McGraw Hill, 1992), 250.
44. Quoted in Russell, *Tragedy in Dedham*, 387-388; and Feuerlicht, *Justice Crucified*, 344.
45. William F. Buckley, Jr., "Sacco and Vanzetti, Again," *American Legion Magazine* 69 (October 1960): 50.
46. See Nunzio Pernicone, "Carlo Tresca and the Sacco-Vanzetti Case," *The Journal of American History* 66, No. 3 (December 1979): 535-547.
47. The proclamation and a report to the governor, compiled by his chief legal counsel, are reproduced in the appendix to the new edition of Upton Sinclair's *Boston: A Documentary Novel of the Sacco-Vanzetti Case* (Cambridge, Mass.; Robert Bentley, Inc., 1978), 757–799.
48. Carey McWilliams, "Massachusetts Pays Its Debt," *The Nation* 225, no. 5 (August 20–27, 1977): 133–135.
49. James E. Starrs, "Once More Unto the Breach: The Firearms Evidence in the Sacco and Vanzetti Case Revisited, " Parts 1, 2. *Journal of Forensic Sciences* 31, nos. 2 and 3 (1986): 630–654, 1050–1078.
50. Starrs, "Once More Unto the Breach," pt. 2: 1074.

Laura Katzman
"Mechanical Vision:" Photography and Mass Media Appropriation in Ben Shahn's Sacco and Vanzetti Series

1. Louis Aragon, "Painting and Reality," reprinted in *Art Front.* 2, no.12 (January 1937): 9.
2. Paul Strand, "Correspondence on Aragon," *Art Front.* 3, no.1 (February 1937): 18.
3. The literature on the Sacco and Vanzetti case is exhaustive. One of the best straightforward accounts remains Felix Frankfurter, *The Case of Sacco and Vanzetti: A Critical Analysis for Lawyers and Laymen* (Boston: Little, Brown, 1927).
4. These deportations were carried out by the United States Department of Justice. The Sacco and Vanzetti case continues to generate literature and public response, as the men's innocence is still being debated. In fact, Boston's Mayor Menino commissioned a sculpture in 2000 to commemorate Sacco and Vanzetti to be erected in Boston—the city that convicted the men in 1927. See Thomas Grillo, "Sculpture to remind of Sacco, Vanzetti," *The Boston Globe*, August 20, 1997, sec. B, p. 3.
5. "Probably not in the six-volume published records of the case, nor in the scholarly study of Felix Frankfurter, nor in Upton Sinclair's novel, will the layman find a more graphic and memorable record of the whole affair." K.G.S., "Sacco-Vanzetti Case in Art," *New York Times*, April 6, 1931, 23. Matthew Josephson referred to the series' "vivacity" and "dramatic intensity." Josephson, "The Passion of Sacco-Vanzetti," *The New Republic*, 70 (April 20, 1932): 275. Diego Rivera asserted that the paintings "are as moving as anything of the kind I have ever seen." Rivera, "The Revolutionary Spirit in Modern Art, " *The Modern Quarterly* 6, no.3 (autumn 1932): 56. Other visual artists of the period who took on the theme include William Gropper and Gutzon Borglum.
6. Diana Linden has insightfully noted that the reception of Shahn's work was more complex than has traditionally been acknowledged, as it varied according to the political orientation of the publication that reviewed the work. See Linden, "'What Becomes an Icon Most?': The Critical Reception to Ben Shahn's *The Passion of Sacco and Vanzetti*," in this catalogue. Frances Pohl wrote that "[t]he response to Shahn's exhibition at the Downtown Gallery was mixed," but that "[t]here were many within the art world, however, who were impressed with the work Shahn had produced." Pohl, *Ben Shahn* (San Francisco: Pomegranate Artbooks, 1993), 13–14.
7. Quote from Edith Halpert, "The Passion of Sacco and Vanzetti," exhibition press release, Downtown Gallery, March 30, 1932, James Thrall Soby Papers, Museum of Modern Art, I.35, 7B.
8. Shahn has typically been called a "fellow traveler" who was not a card-carrying member of the Communist Party, but evidence in Lincoln Kirstein's diaries recently uncovered by Deborah Martin Kao suggests that Shahn was in fact involved with Party activities in the early 1930s. See Kao, "Ben Shahn and the Public Use of Art," in Kao, Laura Katzman, and Jenna Webster, *Ben Shahn's New York: The Photography of Modern Times* (New Haven, Conn.: Yale University Press, 2000), 39; 126.
9. See correspondence between Shahn and Halpert, which reveals Shahn's awareness of the ironies of how controversy and scandal can bring attention to an artist's work. Both expressed their eagerness to see reviews of Shahn's Sacco and Vanzetti exhibition at Harvard's Society for Contemporary Art. Halpert wrote: "I am eager to see just how much excitement has been caused by your wicked collection." Edith Halpert to Ben Shahn, November 2, 1932; also October 26, 1932. See Ben Shahn to Edith Halpert, June 8, 1932; August 3, 1932; October 27, 1932; and November 5, 1932. Downtown Gallery Papers, unmicrofilmed, Archives of American Art, Smithsonian Institution, Washington, D.C., Artists File, Ben Shahn. This archive is henceforth referred to as AAA.
10. Morris Dorsky, "Ben Shahn's Passion of Sacco and Vanzetti: A Note on Its Reception," *American Imago*, 35, nos. 1–2 (1978): 146. Dorsky is one of the only art historians who have closely examined Shahn's use of newspaper photographs in his Sacco and Vanzetti series. Dorsky tracked down many photo sources, and with his largely formalist approach, laid the groundwork for my own, more contextual investigation. I have benefited enormously from Dorsky's findings, which he had donated to The Stephen Lee Taller Ben Shahn Archive before the latter was transferred to Harvard University. This archive is henceforth referred to as SLT/BSA. See Dorsky, *The Formative Years of Ben Shahn: The Origin and Development of His Style* (M.A. thesis, New York University, 1966).
11. For example, critic Carlyle Burrows wrote: "These studies, we are told, were based partly on personal observations of the artist and partly on photographs and other documents." Burrows, "Briefer Comment on Current Art Attractions in NY: Ben Shahn," *New York Herald Tribune*, April 10, 1932, sec. VII, p.10.
12. Dorsky, *The Formative Years of Ben Shahn*, 66. Frances Pohl has mentioned Shahn's use of photographs in the Sacco and Vanzetti series briefly yet significantly. "Several works...have been directly patterned after newspaper photographs of the trial. Shahn has not, however, slavishly copied the photographs in question. Instead, he has taken the arrangement of the figures and the settings and pared them down, producing works that are much more insistently two-dimensional, where the architectural details often appear as decorative forms and where the figures themselves take on an almost cartoonlike quality. Indeed, these images seem to reside somewhere between the newspaper photograph and the cartoon strip, their graphic quality enhanced by Shahn's use of sharp lines to articulate the edges of doors and buildings and the facial features of the men. Pohl, Ben Shahn, 13. Others, like Howard Greenfeld, who

wrote that a number of Shahn's paintings are "exact" copies of the photographs, have overlooked important nuances. Greenfeld, *Ben Shahn: An Artist's Life* (New York: Random House, 1998), 75.

Deborah Martin Kao, while not focusing exclusively on the Sacco and Vanzetti series, has brilliantly investigated the importance of Shahn's reportage aesthetic—his reliance upon newsphotos for his social and political realism of the 1930s. She has shown how leftist critics identified this aesthetic as a significant and defining feature in Shahn's work of this period. Although it is true that critics noted the phenomenon of the reportage aesthetic and Shahn's pioneering role in it, few described in depth the formal and stylistic relationship between the paintings and their photographic sources, one focus of my essay. Kao's work has been crucial for deepening my understanding of the importance of mass media to Shahn's social and artistic vision. See Kao, "Ben Shahn and the Public Use of Art," 52–58.

13. This view is exemplified by Beaumont Newhall, who in 1958 wrote to Shahn, asking him to include his work in a proposed article for *U.S. Camera Annual* on painters who photograph. Explaining his project, Newhall wrote: "Let me emphasize that this article will *not* concern itself with the use of photographs by painters. To my mind, this sort of comparison is beside the point. When a photograph is used for the information which it contains it seems to me that it is a substitute for nature, and if it has served the painter it has no further value." Beaumont Newhall to Ben Shahn, June 27, 1958, Ben Shahn Papers, AAA, Roll D146: 1352. These papers are henceforth referred to as BSP. My research on Shahn's photography has sought to reveal both the complexities of Shahn's use of photography and the nuances of the relationship between the two media in his work. See Katzman, *The Politics of Media: Ben Shahn and Photography* (Ph.D. diss., Yale University, 1997) and "The Politics of Media: Painting and Photography in the Art of Ben Shahn," *American Art* 7, no.1 (Winter 1993): 61–87, reprinted in revised form in Kao, Katzman, and Webster, *Ben Shahn's New York*, 97–117.

14. Portions of this section (revised here) are derived from my 1993 article "The Politics of Media" and my 1997 Ph.D. dissertation *The Politics of Media: Ben Shahn and Photography.*

15. Henry McBride, "Attractions in the Galleries," *New York Sun*, April 16, 1932, 10.

16. Van Deren Coke, *The Painter and the Photograph: From Delacroix to Warhol* (Albuquerque: University of New Mexico Press, 1972), 107.

17. The Dreyfus pictures were based on photographs from a book Shahn obtained in Paris. At least two pages that appear to be torn from that book are found in BSP. Shahn used photographs even earlier in lithography work. According to Dorsky, "In the first interview [Dec 4, 1950], in talking about the use of photos for *S & V*, Shahn said that he used photos in lithography. In making calendars, for example, he would be given a photo of a building and told to make it four times as big." Dorsky, *The Formative Years of Ben Shahn*, 112. By the time that Shahn took up photography himself around 1931–32, he had already been using the photographs of others as source and inspiration for his art in other media.

18. Bernarda Bryson Shahn donated Shahn's photographic source files to the Archives of American Art in the early 1990s. That these files have only recently surfaced in a public repository suggests Shahn's widow's concern over shaping and preserving her late husband's reputation as a painter, as well as an increased openness about photography as an aid in the artistic process. Mrs. Shahn subsequently donated a group of Shahn's Sacco and Vanzetti clippings and source material to the Stephen Lee Taller Ben Shahn Archive; this includes material that might have inadvertently been separated from the larger collection of source files that she gave to the AAA. According to the late Stephen Lee Taller, Mrs. Shahn found the former items in one of Shahn's masonite boxes that he made for files. One of the files in this box contained Sacco and Vanzetti material, including clippings about the case, exhibition information, etc. Apparently, Shahn cut up the June 1932 issue of *Creative Art* that featured his series and used it as a scrapbook for his clippings. On Shahn's photographic source files in the Archives of American Art, see Katzman, "The Uses of Photography II: Ben Shahn and the Archive," in *The Politics of Media: Ben Shahn and Photography*, 189–249.

Shahn's clipping files/source archive was inspired generally by the New York Public Library Picture Collection, which he and fellow artists used often in the 1930s for source material. Shahn kept his news photographs and clippings in alphabetized folders, and gave them headings of three types: famous people of the period; general "universal" categories; and mostly current events or pressing issues of the day. Many of the news photographs feature political figures and events, frequently with captions intact. This suggests that photography and politics are inextricably linked here and that Shahn often wanted to retain the documentary specificity of his sources. Given that Shahn gave Tom Mooney and the Scottsboro Boys their own files, one would assume his Sacco and Vanzetti file would have been a part of this larger archive as well. See Katzman, "The Uses of Photography II: Ben Shahn and the Archive," 189–249.

19. On Shahn's attitudes towards newspaper photographs see: Shahn, "Photos for Art," *U.S.Camera* 9, no. 4 (May 1946): 57; Shahn, "What is Modern Photography?," transcript of interview with Walter Rosenblum, 1950, BSP, Reel 5019:616-617; Richard Doud interview with Ben Shahn, April 14, 1964, AAA, pp.7–8; Arthur Goldsmith, "Ben Shahn: An Unfinished Interview," *Technical Photography* 1, no. 4 (July 1969): 33; in the latter interview Shahn mentioned arguments with Paul Strand. In 1947 Shahn said that when he was in New York: "I take in all the newsreels too, and I think they influence my work quite a bit. Movies are really the master medium." "Art: Angry Eye," *Time* 50, no.15 (October 13, 1947): 63. For a ground-breaking study of Shahn's involvement in film, see Jenna Webster, "Ben Shahn and the Master Medium," in Kao, Katzman and Webster, *Ben Shahn's New York*, 75–95.

20. John Morse, "Ben Shahn: An Interview," *Magazine of Art* 37, no.4 (April 1944): 138, 139; Goldsmith, "Ben Shahn: An Unfinished Interview," 29; Saul Benison and Sandra Otter interview with Ben Shahn, January 5, 1957, Oral History Research Office, Columbia University, pp.64–65, BSA.

21. William Stott, *Documentary Expression and Thirties America* (Chicago: University of Chicago Press, 1973, 1986), 128; Warren Susman, "The Culture of the Thirties," in *Culture as History: The Transformation of American Society in the Twentieth Century* (New York: Pantheon Books, 1973; 1984), 159. Susman wrote: "[T]he newly developed media and their special kinds of appeal helped reinforce a social order rapidly disintegrating under economic and social pressures that were too great to endure." "The Culture of the Thirties,"159. On the documentary aesthetic of the 1930s see, Stott, *Documentary Expression and Thirties America*; Miles Orvell, *The Real Thing: Imitation and Authenticity in American Culture, 1880–1949* (Chapel Hill: University of North Carolina Press, 1989), 140–299; and Alan Trachtenberg, *Reading American Photographs: Images as History, Mathew Brady to Walker Evans* (New York: Hill and Wang, 1989), 231–286.

22. Bruce Robertson, *Representing America: The Ken Trevey Collection of American Realist Prints* (Santa Barbara, Cal.: University Art Museum, 1995), 20. Robertson obtained his statistics from Henry M. Lester, "Evaluating Reader's Interest in Pictures," *19th Art Director's Annual of Advertising Art* (1941), 78; 82. See also Meyer Berger, *The Story of The New York Times*, 1851–1951 (New York: Simon and Schuster, 1951), 413, 422, 483; 560.

23. Susman, *Culture as History*, 159–160, 158, 157. Based on European models, *Life* magazine, specifically conceived of as a picture magazine in 1933, hit the newsstands in 1936. By 1936 rotogravure was outdated by wire photography and newsreels. Newsreel houses were a phenomenon of the times; in the late 1930s, in fact, movie theatres featuring exclusively newsreels and short subjects, mainly documentary, were opening up all over New York City. See Stott, *Documentary Expression and Thirties America*, 128.

24. This cultural phenomenon is best exemplified by the New Deal Arts Projects, which were responsible for an "outpouring of Americana"—in the amassing of "American stuff" such as maps and folklore for the Federal Writers' Project's state guides. See Jane de Hart Mathews, "Art and the People: The New Deal Quest for a Cultural Democracy," Journal of American History 62, no.2 (September 1975): 337.

25. Ben Shahn to Gardner Jackson, October 13, 1931, BSP, Reel 5006:718. Jackson also mentioned that "Horace Kallen gives you a very good send-off in his accompanying note." Kallen (1882–1974) was a German-Jewish philosopher, scholar, social and political activist, and a founding member of the New School for Social Research in 1919. He authored over thirty books on philosophy, education, and Zionism. Shahn knew Kallen and apparently sought his advice on the scandal caused by the Sacco and Vanzetti panels that the artist had submitted to the exhibition "Murals by American Painters and Photographers" held at the Museum of Modern Art in 1932. See Martin Bush, *Ben Shahn: The Passion of Sacco and Vanzetti* (Syracuse, N.Y.: Syracuse University Press, 1968), 20; Greenfeld, Ben Shahn, 84.

26. "In preparing for S & V, Shahn went to the New York Public Library, 42nd Street branch, for photos. He spent months looking through all newspapers, foreign and domestic. He wrote to the various defense organizations for pamphlets, which contained photos, and went to the library of the Socialist Rand School, known for its interest in accumulating material of this kind. This was at the height of the Depression, when, without a job, he could spend months preparing for and working out his project. He recalled from the beginning he knew it would turn out well." Dorsky, *The Formative Years of Ben Shahn*, 66. "Shahn had gone to the blurred photoengravings in the newspaper files at the New York Public Library for his documentation." Selden Rodman, *Portrait of the Artist as an American, Ben Shahn: A Biography with Pictures* (New York: Harper and Brothers, 1951), 120. On Shahn and the New York Public Library Picture Collection, see Katzman, "The Uses of Photography II: Ben Shahn and the Archive," 195–199. See also Anthony T. Troncale, "Worth Beyond Words: Romana Javitz and the New York Public Library's Picture Collection," *Biblion: The Bulletin of the New York Public Library* 4 (Fall 1995): 115–138. I am grateful to Jenna Webster for calling my attention to this article.

27. Morse, "Ben Shahn: An Interview," 37. According to Frances Pohl, Shahn "did not become fully aware of the political or social implications of the trial or the ferment it had caused until he went to Europe in 1925. In Paris, he witnessed massive demonstrations and the naming of all manner of things, from children to tugboats, after the two accused men. Upon his return to the United States at the end of 1925, he became actively involved in the growing defense efforts. He went twice to Boston to picket." Pohl, *Ben Shahn*, 11. Howard Greenfeld noted that as an art student in Paris, Shahn was exposed to the heated arguments about art and politics in the street cafes, the Sacco and Vanzetti case being one of the most fervently discussed topics. Greenfeld, Ben Shahn: *An Artist's Life*, 43. Although Shahn was aware of the Sacco and Vanzetti protests in France, according to some, his political activism did not begin until his return to America in 1929. At various times, Shahn noted his "exaggerated sense of injustice" (resulting from his Jewish background and the anticzarist, pogrom-plagued climate in Lithuania), the New Deal, the Sacco and Vanzetti case, the Great Depression, working with Diego Rivera, and Franklin Delano Roosevelt's 1936 presidential campaign as formative politicizing experiences. See Forrest Selvig interview with Ben Shahn, September 27, 1968, unmicrofilmed transcript, BSP, pp.3–6; Ben Shahn Autobiography, unpublished manuscript, c.1965, Part I; Part II, pp.13–14, BSA.

As a Jew whose family fled oppressive conditions in Eastern Europe, Shahn was clearly sensitive to the restrictive, anti-immigrant climate Sacco and Vanzetti faced in the conservative areas of Boston. The case held a lifelong interest for him. In 1932 Shahn submitted a mural panel and a tempera panel on the subject to a Museum of Modern Art exhibition; in 1932 and 1937 he was involved in two unrealized book projects for which he planned lithographs; in 1952 he made a drawing for *The Nation*; in 1958 he produced at least three serigraphs; and in 1967 he completed a mural at Syracuse University. In the Ben Shahn Papers, there is also evidence that Shahn collected later publications on the case. Despite his seriousness about the case, Dorsky wrote: "In the first interview, Shahn said that in the beginning the S & V series he was as flippant as with Dreyfus and that he became more serious as it evolved." Dorsky, *The Formative Years of Ben Shahn*, 124, 67; Dorsky, "Ben Shahn's Passion of Sacco and Vanzetti: A Note on Its Reception," 147. But in a 1957 interview Shahn spoke of the intensity with which he approached the project: "It wasn't until I came back in 1929 and after in 1930 having done those little Dreyfus pictures I thought this may be a thing I want to do. I began to re-read material, then actual research, finding out actual pamphlets, photographs to document myself and I sat down to do this. I made one picture after another. It was during a tough economic period. My father had a heart attack and he was in a hospital and I was the only one he wanted to see at the time and I'd go to see him from two to four...travel out to Newark and work, make drawings in a department store...work through until about two in the morning...go over to Brooklyn Heights where I lived and sleep for about four or five hours, get up and work on those Sacco-Vanzetti paintings. I did this for about six or eight months...I felt no great sacrifice. I was happy. I put in three or four hours a day on this thing, but I was full of it and one after another was coming out...Then I showed them to friends and they were excited and I showed them to people who had prestige in the art world, certain writers and they were excited about it." Benison and Otter interview, January 5, 1957, pp. 53–54.

28. "As with the *Dreyfus* pictures, the selection here was conditioned by what was available, not by choice, decision, planning—except from that imposed by the photos." Dorsky, *The Formative Years of Ben Shahn*, 67.

29. Dorsky, "Ben Shahn's Passion of Sacco and Vanzetti: A Note on Its Reception," 146, 147–148. Dorsky elaborated on this in his earlier thesis, "There is a pattern and order to the S & V series although a loose one, and one not originally intended by Shahn...In fact, in the bare outline, cohesive as well as chronological but by no means the usual narrative or concerned with key events. It has all the earmarks of a haphazard choice dependent on available photographs, and in this sense disdainful of the significance of the theme." Dorsky, *The Formative Years of Ben Shahn*, 67–68. "Shahn managed, through the use of photographs, to create what Kirstein suggested were paintings suggestive of postcards. This imposed a kind of objectivity or reality of the fact, as did the arbitrariness of his selection, as if one were, in fact, looking at a series of disconnected photos in a newspaper or pamphlet. The blandness of this incoherent, non-systematic shuffling of post cards, without dramatic cohesion and development; without highlight or dramatic incident leading towards a climax, added to the feeling of objectivity and detachment." Dorsky, *The Formative Years of Ben Shahn*, 99.

30. Moore was a Westerner, an "outsider," and a radical—a source of irritation regarding the relations between court and counsel. Marion Denman Frankfurter and Gardner Jackson, eds., *The Letters of Sacco and Vanzetti* (New York: Penguin Books, 1928, 1997), 334. Vanzetti felt that Moore had betrayed him and Sacco and that he did not defend them properly. Frankfurter and Jackson, eds., *The Letters of Sacco and Vanzetti*, 376. Problems with Moore also stemmed from his "serious doubts as to Sacco's innocence after angry exchanges with Sacco had led to his departure from the case." William Young and David Kaiser, *Postmortem: New Evidence in the Case of Sacco and Vanzetti* (Amherst: University of Massachusetts Press, 1985), 7. Significantly, Shahn did paint William Thompson, a prominent lawyer from Boston who became Vanzetti's counsel in 1924, and whom the two men respected and admired for his devotion to the case. The one prosecution witness whom Shahn painted, the policeman Benjamin Bowles, was problematic because he offered inconsistent testimony in the trial.

31. James West Davidson and Mark Hamilton Lytle have demonstrated how the raw materials of the past are used by historians and others to shape history, not unlike how Shahn used photographic sources for his paintings to construct a certain view of Sacco and Vanzetti. They use the Sacco and Vanzetti episode as one case study. See Davidson and Lytle, "Sacco and Vanzetti: The Case of History Versus Law," in *After the Fact: The Art of Historical Detection* (New York: Alfred A. Knopf, 1982), 263–295.

32. Lyons' book, which brought "to life the men and the society in which they lived," apparently sold 130,00 copies of its Russian edition. See Louis Joughin and Edmund Morgan, *The Legacy of Sacco and Vanzetti* (Princeton, N.J.: Princeton University Press, 1948; 1976), 377, 314.
In the material Bernarda Bryson Shahn donated to the Stephen Lee Taller Ben Shahn Archive, there are three pages of photographs that Shahn likely tore out of his own copy of Lyons's *The Life and Death of Sacco and Vanzetti* (New York: International Publishers, 1927). One of these is the source photograph for Shahn's *Bartolomeo Vanzetti and Nicola Sacco*. This is affirmed by Dorsky who wrote "[a]ll the photos for the three [paintings] in Shahn's possession come from the same source 'The Life and Death of S & V' which he probably owned and could work from." Dorsky, *The Formative Years of Ben Shahn*, 126.

33. "They saw each other daily during the trial, May 31 to July 14, 1921, and during the four brief periods when arguments were heard on motions for a new trial...After sentence was pronounced, April 9, 1927, they were together until the end." Frankfurter and Jackson, eds., *The Letters of Sacco and Vanzetti*, 6.

34. James Thrall Soby, *Ben Shahn* (New York: Museum of Modern Art, 1947), 7.
35. Soby, *Ben Shahn*, 8. While Davidson and Lytle do not discuss the painting and its source photograph, they note that "[Shahn] transformed the photograph in subtle yet effective ways," and that "the changes lend more force to the painting." Davidson and Lytle, *After the Fact*, 289.
36. I discovered the fuller version of this photograph in Harold Blumenfeld, *Sacco and Vanzetti: Their Story in Pictures* (New York: Scholastic Book Services, 1972), 17, with the "In 1927 the two men, handcuffed to a guard, willingly posed for news photographers. Nervous breakdowns had sent both men into the prison hospital, and each had gone on a fast." In a pamphlet that Shahn likely saw or owned, Elizabeth Glendower Evans, *Outstanding Features of the Sacco and Vanzetti Case* (Boston: New England Civil Liberties Committee, 1924), 8, the more familiar cropped version of the photograph appears with the caption "Vanzetti, And Sacco On His Twenty-Fifth Day Of Hunger Strike."
37. The paper may also allude to the notes that Vanzetti consulted when in court. See David Felix, *Protest: Sacco and Vanzetti and the Intellectuals* (Bloomington: Indiana University Press, 1966), 8.
38. Thompson was impressed with Vanzetti's calmness and self-control, which the former witnessed in his last meeting with the accused, and which he recorded on August 22, 1927, a few hours prior to Vanzetti's execution. Frankfurter and Jackson, eds., *The Letters of Sacco and Vanzetti*, 405. Sacco was in fact the more isolated of the two men, because unlike Vanzetti, he was unemployed during much of his seven years of imprisonment. Frankfurter and Jackson, eds., *The Letters of Sacco and Vanzetti*, p.1 viii.
39. Frankfurter and Jackson, eds., *The Letters of Sacco and Vanzetti*, x–xi; 404. See also lix. However, in David Felix's *Protest: Sacco and Vanzetti and the Intellectuals*, the author "holds that liberals and intellectuals were victims of first defense attorney Moore's success in turning attention away from the double murder of a paymaster and guard...and focusing it rather on the Italians national origins, draft dodging, and activism in the anarchist movement." See Robert Clements, "Knights-Errant In Error?," *New York Times Book Review*, January 30, 1966, 3.
40. Paul Avrich, Sacco and Vanzetti: *The Anarchist Background* (Princeton, N.J.: Princeton University Press, 1991), 56–57. For more on this subject see Nunzio Pernicone, "The Sacco and Vanzetti Case: An Overview," in this catalogue.
41. In comparing the painting with the source photograph, Dorsky wrote: "The faces while completely recognizable, have lost much of their distinctiveness. We have instead a more appealing, beseeching expression, in the place of adamance and strength. They appear here as victims, in the slouch of the shoulders, the twist of their heads, the softness of their eyes and in their sympathetic expressions. Both seem as one, with Vanzetti a bit more pathetic. This is not the way they appear in the photo, where their inherent strength though different is evident. Vanzetti seems more aggressive and Sacco less assertive. The characterological presence and distinctiveness of Sacco and Vanzetti as seen in the photo is nowhere to be found in the painting, which has an overtone of the plaintive and naïve." Dorsky, *The Formative Years of Ben Shahn*, 73–74.
42. Rodman, *Conversations with Artists* (New York: Capricorn Books, 1957; 1961), 224–225.
43. Pohl wrote that in the transformation from photograph to painting in several of the Sacco and Vanzetti paintings, Shahn "produced works...where the architectural details often appear as decorative forms and where the figures themselves take on an almost cartoon-like quality." She also noted that certain reviewers at the time identified a folk quality in Shahn's two-dimensional, simplified style, which to Shahn indicated "directness" and "unselfconsciousness." See Pohl, *Ben Shahn*, 13.
44. "Appendix I: The Story of the Case," in Frankfurter and Jackson, eds., *The Letters of Sacco and Vanzetti*, 336. According to Felix Frankfurter, "The alibi for Vanzetti was overwhelming. Thirty-one eyewitnesses testified positively that no one of the men that they saw in the murder car was Vanzetti. Thirteen witnesses either testified directly that Vanzetti was in Plymouth selling fish on the day of the murder, or furnished corroboration of such testimony." Frankfurter and Jackson, eds., *The Letters of Sacco and Vanzetti*, 336. The source photograph of Vanzetti's witnesses is reproduced in the pamphlet *Are They Doomed* (New York: Workers Defense Union, 1920), 27. The caption reads "Six Witnesses Who Bought Eels From Vanzetti in Plymouth, 28 Miles From Bridgewater, On The Day of The Hold-Up at The Latter Place."
45. This photograph appeared in the pamphlet *Are They Doomed*, p.5, with the caption "Nicola Sacco, His Wife, And Their Son Dante. This photograph was taken shortly before Sacco's arrest." It also appears in the pamphlet *The Story of the Sacco-Vanzetti Case: Including An Analysis of the Trial* (Boston: The Sacco-Vanzetti Defense Committee, 1921), 35 with the caption "Nicola Sacco, His Wife And Their Son Dante." This photograph, taken shortly before Sacco's arrest, is the one that was rejected at the Italian consulate as being too large for passport purposes. It bears the signature of Giuseppe Andrower, clerk, who saw it on the crime-date." See Frankfurter and Jackson, eds., *The Letters of Sacco and Vanzetti*, 335–336.
46. This photograph appeared in the pamphlet *Are They Doomed*, p.11 with the caption "Nicola Sacco's Father And Mother In His Boyhood Home At Torremaggiore. Italy; And His Nephews And Nieces. His brother has lately been elected mayor of that town. Until his arrest Sacco sent remittances regularly to his parents."
47. This photograph is reproduced in Blumenfeld, *Sacco and Vanzetti: Their Story in Pictures*, 26–27 with the caption "Most faithful and

most diligent of the Boston society women who helped the Sacco-Vanzetti cause was Mrs. Elizabeth Glendower Evans, the widow of a Harvard Law School classmate of Judge Louis Brandeis. She had been active in civil rights causes. When she saw Mrs. Sacco for the first time at a Boston protest meeting in 1923, she threw her arms around her and they posed for this excellent camera study of the young and old women of Boston."

48. Frankfurter and Jackson, eds., *The Letters of Sacco and Vanzetti*, 8.
49. Shahn obtained and mounted a photostat of this photograph for his own clipping and source files, BSP, Reel 5024:1282. The photograph is reproduced in Evans, *Outstanding Features of the Sacco-Vanzetti Case*, p.4 with the caption "Vanzetti Sacco In the Cage In Court Room." Shahn said: "If I were asked to pick the fifty best photographs taken during any year, I would look only at the work of newspaper photographers. Their pictures have everything—even surrealism if you look for it." Shahn, "Photos for Art," 57.
50. Shahn quoted in John D. Morse, "Henri Cartier-Bresson," *Magazine of Art* 40, no.5 (May 1947): 189.
51. "The prisoners were established some twenty feet forward of the judge's high bench in a cage used until recently in capital cases. Actually, 'cage' is a misnomer. It was a kind of pew with a latticework of metal strips. The prisoner could lean forward and rest his chin on the railing in front as he studied the other actors in the trial." Felix, *Protest: Sacco-Vanzetti and the Intellectuals*, 60.
52. This photograph is reproduced in Evans, *Outstanding Features of the Sacco-Vanzetti Case*, p.29 with the caption "Villa Felletto, Vanzetti's Home Town."
53. Frankfurter and Jackson, eds., *The Letters of Sacco and Vanzetti*, 77, 363. Sacco was "born into a modestly well-to-do family." Davidson and Lytle, *After the Fact*, 279.
54. Frankfurter and Jackson, eds., *The Letters of Sacco and Vanzetti*, xiv, 275. Shahn's title for the series evokes the martyrdom of Christ. He said: "Ever since I could remember I'd wished that I'd been lucky enough to be alive at a great time—when something big was going on, like The Crucifixion. And suddenly I realized I was. Here I was living through another crucifixion." Morse, "Ben Shahn: An Interview," 137. He later wrote "I...set about revealing the acts and the persons involved with as rigorous a simplicity as I could command. I was not unmindful of Giotto, and of the simplicity with which he had been able to treat of connected events—each complete in itself, yet all recreating the religious drama, so living a thing to him." Shahn, The Biography of a Painting, in Shahn, *The Shape of Content* (Cambridge, Mass.: Harvard University Press, 1957), 37–38.
55. This photograph is reproduced in Ronald Creagh, *Sacco et Vanzetti* (Paris: Editions La Découverte, 1984), figure b., between pp.152 and153. The photograph resides in the Bibliothèque Nationale, Paris. "As the day of execution approached, Vanzetti asked the defense committee to send a cable to his sister Luigia in his boyhood home in Villa Falletto, to ask her to come to the United States. En route she led a crowd of 5,000 in a Paris demonstration." Creagh, *Sacco et Vanzetti*, 56.
56. See previous endnote. Vanzetti had a chance to see his sister within the last-minute, twelve-day respite that he and Vanzetti were granted before the execution date. It was both consoling and sad for Vanzetti to see Luigia. See Frankfurter and Jackson, eds., *The Letters of Sacco and Vanzetti*, 293, 300, 319, 325.
57. Shahn said: "I felt I had more control over my own medium [painting] than I did over photography. Extraneous material entered into it that I couldn't control in photography except in very few instances where I felt there was a total picture, but in my own work I feel I have complete control." Doud interview, p.24. Shahn was also aware of the way photographs could get used and even abused towards different political ends, depending on whose hands they ended up in. Doud interview, pp.11–12; 17.
58. Pohl, *Ben Shahn*, 13; The critic is Michael L. Simmons, "Shahn's Way," *The Official Metropolitan Guide* (April 1932), 11.
59. This photograph appeared in *The Story of the Sacco and Vanzetti Case*, p.40 with the caption "The Four Prosecutors: District Attorney Frederick G. Katzmann is second in line from the left, his assistant, Harold D. Williams, is first; and his other assistants, William F. Kane, George E. Adams are third and fourth."
60. Soby, *Ben Shahn*, 7–8. Shahn told Morris Dorsky (with regard to a Mooney series painting) "I couldn't tolerate the vague painted in background. There had to be substance there...It sharpened the perspective and I thought there was an innate value in sharpened perspective alone." Dorsky, *The Formative Years of Ben Shahn*, 127.
61. Vanzetti wrote about how Katzmann ignored certain evidence and introduced questionable evidence into the court, and about the lengths to which Katzmann would go to discredit Sacco and Vanzetti and prejudice the jury against them. See Frankfurter and Jackson, eds., *The Letters of Sacco and Vanzetti*, 369, 372. "District Attorney Frederick G. Katzmann misled the jury by purportedly reading excerpts from the transcripts of Vanzetti's interrogation after his arrest; but the actual transcripts were not introduced into evidence, and Vanzetti was at times misquoted and thereby made to appear deceptive." Frankfurter and Jackson, eds., *The Letters of Sacco and Vanzetti*, x–xii.
62. The source photograph is reproduced in Lyons, *The Life and Death of Sacco and Vanzetti*. It is on one of the three pages that Shahn appears to have torn out of this book.
63. Felix, *Protest: Sacco and Vanzetti and the Intellectuals*, 5.
64. Thayer refused new evidence and new trials, and he waited a long time to respond to appeals. Sacco and Vanzetti thought he was

bigoted, cruel, and unjust. He was reported as saying to a Dartmouth College professor in 1924: "Did you see what I did with those anarchistic bastards the other day? I guess that will hold them for a while." Frankfurter and Jackson, eds., *The Letters of Sacco and Vanzetti*, 375, 117–118, xiii.

65. This photograph appeared on the same page as the Thayer photograph, the page that Shahn tore out of Lyons, *The Life and Death of Sacco and Vanzetti.*
66. Davidson and Lytle, *After the Fact*, 291.
67. Frankfurter and Jackson, eds., *The Letters of Sacco and Vanzetti*, pp.217, xiii, 259-261, 268-271, 311.
68. Mentions of *That Agony is Our Triumph* appear in Josephson, "The Passion of Sacco-Vanzetti," 275, and Simmons, "Shahn's Way," 11. I thank Alejandro Anreus who shared with me his documentation of the recollections around this painting from Jacob Lawrence (1991) and Bernarda Bryson Shahn (1993). Anreus to Author, January 11, 1999.
69. My analysis of this work is based on the large tempera panel entitled *The Passion of Sacco and Vanzetti* that Shahn submitted to the 1932 MoMA exhibition "Murals by American Painters and Photographers." The work is currently owned by the Whitney Museum of American Art, New York.
70. Soby, *Ben Shahn*, 7; Josephson, "The Passion of Sacco-Vanzetti," 275. Josephson stated that Shahn's treatment of the men was "similarly 'hardboiled,' by making his 'anarchist bastards' pathetically funny, sallow martyrs though reverent all the while."
71. Because *The Passion of Sacco and Vanzetti* was inspired by, and is a composite of aspects of *That Agony is Our Triumph*, *The Lowell Committee*, and *Judge Webster Thayer*, it is difficult to know whether Shahn worked directly from photographic sources, or from these earlier photo-based paintings in order to construct this mural panel. Since *That Agony is Our Triumph* is unlocated, and since Shahn used photographs similarly in the earlier paintings, I have taken the liberty to discuss *The Passion of Sacco and Vanzetti* as if he worked directly from the photographic sources. It would be equally illuminating to examine the mural panel with regard to Shahn's more mediated process of painting from photo-derived paintings.
72. On social science writing in the 1930s see Stott, *Documentary Expression and Thirties America*, 152–170.
73. The source photograph for Sacco and Vanzetti in their coffins is reproduced in *The Labor Defender* 6, no.8 (August 1931): 149 with the caption "And Workers Came In Thousands saying 'We will never forget—'." This page belongs to the materials Mrs. Shahn donated to BSA. It appears to have been separated from the entire issue of the journal, which exists in Shahn's source file on Tom Mooney, BSP, Reel 5022.
74. The source photographs for the Lowell Committee members are found in a photostat that Shahn obtained from the New York Public Library Picture Collection. It is now part of the materials Mrs. Shahn donated to STL/BSA.
75. See John Dos Passos, *The Big Money* in *U.S.A.* (New York: Harcourt, Brace, 1938); Davidson and Lytle, *After the Fact*, 294. Historian John d'Entremont has reminded me that class divisions between groups do not always indicate political divisions among them. At this time, many members of ethnic minorities were profoundly conservative politically and used an exaggerated antianarchist stance to signify their American patriotism.
76. Joughin and Morgan, *The Legacy of Sacco and Vanzetti*, 302–303. For Vanzetti's views on the Lowell Committee members see Frankfurter and Jackson, eds., *The Letters of Sacco and Vanzetti*, 301–303.
77. The architectural background for *The Passion of Sacco and Vanzetti* was derived from yet another photostat that Shahn clipped for his files, BSP, Reel 5024:1282. Shahn likely obtained this photograph from *The Story of the Sacco-Vanzetti Case*, p.45, with the caption "The Atmosphere At The Dedham Court House."
78. Frankfurter and Jackson, eds., *The Letters of Sacco and Vanzetti*, 333.
79. Josephson, "The Passion of Sacco-Vanzetti," 275; Simmons, "Shahn's Way," 11. According to Greenfeld, the paintings in the series are organized "more or less chronologically."" Greenfeld, *Ben Shahn*, 75.
80. Portions of this section draw on my 1993 article and 1997 dissertation.
81. Leo Rosten, *The Washington Correspondents* (New York: Harcourt, Brace, 1937), 351. This was a statement that Rosten asked reporters to respond to as part of his doctoral dissertation research.
82. Curtis MacDougall, *Interpretative Reporting* (New York: Macmillan, 1938), 251.
83. Roland Barthes, "The Photographic Message," *in Image, Music, Text* (New York: Hill and Wang, 1977), 17.
84. Lincoln Kirstein referred to Shahn's "surgical" approach when writing about the latter's mural panel for MoMA, *The Passion of Sacco and Vanzetti*, but his commentary applies to the entire series. "Shahn did not imagine the apotheosis of this affair as an anarchist or a communist sympathizer, as an Italian or as the member of an oppressed class. But with an appraising accuracy he has merely installed the actors of that tragedy in their proper places within a frame, and their arrangement is an inscription more surgical than any partisan approach." Kirstein, "Art Chronicle: Contemporary Mural Painting in the United States," *Hound and Horn* 5, no. 4 (July–September 1932): 660. On the restraint of the series see for example, "A Roster of Recently Opened Shows," *New York Times*, April 10, 1932, sec. VIII, p.10.

85. We must remember that there were some reviewers who saw the series as Shahn's "personal indictment of the Boston episode." They commented on the satire and the caricature of the series, "a social sermon stronger than the most impassioned polemic." Simmons, "Shahn's Way," 11. Halpert's press release for the Downtown Gallery exhibition noted [w]hat his sympathies were in this much discussed episode is not relevant...[I]t is of significance, however, that he interpreted the major events with passion."
86. Michael Schudson, *Discovering the News: A Social History of American Newspapers* (New York: Basic Books, Inc., 1978), 4, 6.
87. Schudson, *Discovering the News*, 122. In this quote, I reversed the order of sentences as they appear in Schudson's text.
88. Schudson, *Discovering the News*, 123. Schudson continued "Walter Lippmann, in *Public Opinion* (1922), had begun to knock the 'public' off the perch that the rhetoric of democracy had built for it. In *The Phantom Public* (1925), he was still more severe and critical of democratic ideals...The spirit of business in the twenties was buoyant, and there was a feeling of liberation in social science, the arts, and the social life of the urban Bohemians. But the liberation into a new culture marked the rapid disintegration of the old, and many serious thinkers began to fear that the new edifices of the arts and sciences were being raised without foundations." Schudson, *Discovering the News*, 123, 126. Schudson cited Roscoe Pound and John Dewey among other thinkers of the 1920s and 1930s to support his points.
89. Schudson, *Discovering the News*, 125.
90. Schudson, *Discovering the News*, 141, 144–159, 7. On interpretive journalism he claimed: "The Newspaper Editors advocated interpretation, and later observers explain its rise, as a response to a world grown very complex. The idea is that the war, the depression, and then the New Deal made political, economic, and social affairs so complicated that they forced journalism to emphasize 'the meaning' of the news and the context of events." Schudson, *Discovering the News*, 148.
See the writings of Walter Lippmann, such as *Public Opinion* (New York: The Free Press, 1922; 1965), as Lippmann was considered the most sage and compelling advocate of the ideal of objectivity in journalism at the time. On the press in the 1930s see Robert and Helen Lynd, "Getting Information: The Press," in Lynd, *Middletown in Transition: A Study in Cultural Conflicts* (New York: Harcourt, Brace Jovanovich, 1937; 1965), 373–387; Frank Luther Mott, American Journalism, A History: 1690–1960 (New York: The Macmillan Company, 1941; 1962), 674–737; and James Boylan, "Publicity for the Great Depression: Newspaper Default and Literary Reportage," in Catherine Covert and John Stevens, eds., *Mass Media Between the Wars: Perceptions of Cultural Tension*, 1918–1941 (Syracuse, NY: Syracuse University Press, 1984), 159–179.
91. Schudson, *Discovering the News*, 156–157.
92. Coke, *The Painter and the Photograph*, 109.
93. Stott, *Documentary Expression and Thirties America*, 78. On the conservative nature of newspapers in this period and newspaper publishing as a branch of big business in which power was concentrated in the hands of the few, see Frederick Lewis Allen, *Since Yesterday: The Nineteen-Thirties in America, 1929–1939* (New York: Harper and Brothers, 1940), 218.
94. Robertson, *Representing America*, 20–21; Stott, *Documentary Expression and Thirties America*, pp.78–79; Boylan, "Publicity for the Great Depression." Robertson continued: "Readers did not indiscriminately swallow the photographs printed by newspapers." He cited the research of Jack Willem, who in the late 1930s discovered that travel ("escape") news pictures were the most popular, followed by objects and places, science and technology, and "cheesecake." Robertson, *Representing America*, 21; Lester, "Evaluating Reader's Interest in Pictures," .84, 85.
95. Stott, *Documentary Expression and Thirties America*, 136. "The radicals prided themselves on being 'aware of every heartbeat of their time,' Murray Kempton said; 'they read and discussed every interior short paragraph of the *New York Times*.'" Stott, *Documentary Expression and Thirties America*, 136. Just a few years earlier, writing from Europe in 1929, Shahn expressed his contempt for the *New York Times*. See Greenfeld, *Ben Shahn*, 53. Other papers represented in Shahn's clipping and source files include: *New York Herald Tribune*; *Daily News*; *Washington Daily News*; *New York Evening Journal*; *Washington Herald*; *Evening Star*; *New York Post*; *New York World Telegram*; *New York Evening Graphic*; and *New York American*, among others. There is also evidence here that Shahn read *Editor and Publisher: A Newspaper for the Makers of Newspapers*. See BSP, between Reels 5006–5027.
96. Robertson, *Representing America*, 65.
97. Dorsky, *The Formative Years of Ben Shahn*, 102; Dorsky, "Ben Shahn's Passion of Sacco and Vanzetti: A Note on Its Reception," 148–149. Pohl wrote "Edith Halpert, the owner of the Downtown Gallery, had offered the [Sacco-Vanzetti Club in Little Italy] one of the paintings for ten dollars (the regular price was $100) but the club members refused, having found the paintings 'grotesque.' Perhaps they, like Gutman in *The Nation*, were looking for more heroic images. Shahn was undoubtedly disappointed by the club's refusal, but was probably pleased that its members, and many other people whom seldom, if ever, frequented art galleries, had come to the exhibition. Shahn was more concerned with engaging in a dialogue with a broad audience than in convincing those who made up this audience that he was right." Pohl, *Ben Shahn*, 13–14. See also Rodman, *Portrait of the Artist as an American*, 118–119; Greenfeld, *Ben Shahn: An Artist's Life*, 77–78.
Shahn's paintings, however, were also praised for their "high art" qualities. For example, Josephson wrote: "[y]et the painter is by no

means a man of narrow gifts; nor is it to be taken that he has in any great measure 'betrayed' Pure Art," and implied that Shahn's "theme-painting" has "observe[d] the traditional formal demands of good painting." Josephson, "The Passion of Sacco-Vanzetti," 275.

98. According to Dorsky, Halpert "objected to the titles which were painted on each of the paintings in the manner of the Dreyfus Case, in different lettering styles. Shahn cut them off. Her objection to the titles themselves, which she thought too naive, he ignored and insisted on keeping." Dorsky, *The Formative Years of Ben Shahn*, 94. On the long captions, see also Greenfeld, *Ben Shahn*, 74–75.

99. This section draws on my 1993 article and 1997 dissertation.

100. William Vaughan, "Young Shahn Turns from Ivory Tower," *New York American*, April 16, 1932, 32. Comments such as these were common, despite efforts made earlier in the century by Alfred Stieglitz and others to prove photography's aesthetic worth.

101. Mabel Scacheri, "Your Camera," *New York World Telegram*, October 2, 1947. This was a review of Shahn's MoMA retrospective.

102. Ann Henry to Ben Shahn, June 13, 1940; Ben Shahn to Ann Henry, June 17, 1940. BSP, Reel 5007F235-5007F236. Deborah Martin Kao and Jenna Webster researched this *PM* feature to no avail. While the proposed spread was never published, *PM* did print some of Shahn's photographs in an FSA feature story "The Small Town," *PM* (October 18, 1940). In 1944, *Minicam Photography* wanted to do a story on Shahn's technique of using the Leica to make sketches for paintings. See Frank Zachary to Ben Shahn, November 30, 1944, BSP, D146: 539. That same year, Shahn participated in a symposium Willard Morgan organized for the Museum of Modern Art entitled, "Photography and the Other Arts," on April 19, 1944. See correspondence in Willard Morgan Papers, Newhall Files, Department of Photography, Museum of Modern Art, New York.

103. James Thrall Soby to Ben Shahn, December 16, 1946, BSP, Reel D147: 1433; James Thrall Soby to Ben Shahn, September 18, 1947, BSP, Reel D147: 1450. With regard to the catalogue for the 1947 exhibition, Soby said that he wanted "to work out the photography business carefully and accurately." James Thrall Soby to *Ben Shahn*, December 16, 1946. In the catalogue text, Soby made a point to note the ways in which Shahn departed from his photographic sources in his paintings, making separate and distinct images, his results "quickened by the most exacting and imaginative painterly means," as Shahn "proceeds under the compulsion of a painter's inner vision." Soby, *Ben Shahn*, 12–13. Some of Shahn's photographs were in fact exhibited in the 1947 show, but on their own as a separate group, not integrated with the paintings to which they related. On Shahn's photography vis-a-vis MoMA see Katzman, "The Politics of Media"; and *The Politics of Media: Ben Shahn and Photography.*

104. Pohl, *New Deal Artist in a Cold War Climate: Ben Shahn*, 1947–1954 (Austin: University of Texas Press, 1989), p.57.

105. For example, Clement Greenberg claimed that Shahn was a better photographer than painter, while Nancy Newhall asserted just the opposite. See Clement Greenberg, "Art," Nation.165, no.18 (November 1, 1947): 481–482; Nancy Newhall, "Ben Shahn," Photo Notes, November 1947, 3. Other reasons why Shahn may not have wanted his photographs to be featured in his 1947 retrospective include his feeling that his camera work was a small accomplishment in terms of his larger oeuvre (even though he was quite proud of the RA/FSA project and believed in its goals), and that he "felt something of a poacher for having crossed the line" into the field of photography. See Goldsmith, "Ben Shahn: An Unfinished Interview," 29. See also Pete Sekaer to Ben Shahn, November 18, 1947, BSP, Reel 5007: 503–504. Sekaer wrote of Shahn's exhibition: "I was glad you included some of the photographs, I have told lots of people that you are the real, if illegitimate, father of American 'documentary' photography, and you should have credit (blame??) for it, even if you do think it is a piddling accomplishment."

106. Morse, "Ben Shahn: An Interview," p.139. Shahn's casual views about the practice of using photographs from his files can be gleaned from comments he made in this interview; Doud interview, p.13; Author's phone interview with Van Deren Coke, Santa Fe, New Mexico, 1990.

107. Goldsmith, "Ben Shahn: An Unfinished Interview," 29. An undated newspaper clipping from *Life* magazine that Mrs. Shahn donated to the BSA is further revealing of Shahn's attitudes towards the painters' use of photography. The clipping features the artist Walter Stuempfig's response to a letter that questioned whether he had actually traveled to a place he had painted because the painting was based on a National Geographic photograph of that same site. Stuempfig wrote: "Mr. Cross' son Dick was correct to have spotted the 'National Geographic' picture as a kind of pattern for my painting. There is nothing very unusual in the fact however. Artists may and do draw upon photographs of nature as well as upon nature itself. The quality of any painting is in the paint and also in the exercise of the artist's eternal prerogatives of selection, rejection or rearrangement of forms to suit his own esthetic ends. Artists have always used photographs and works of previous artists for their own uses." Shahn must have clipped this from the magazine because it reflected his own views.

108. See for example, Morse, ed., *Ben Shahn* (New York: Praeger, 1972), 41-58; Shahn, "The Biography of a Painting," 25–52.

109. Shahn may not have thought of his photographs as "sources" per se, but rather as vehicles for pictorializing ideas already formulated in his mind, or for documenting experiences that in themselves were the actual inspirations for his art in other media. He seemed to have no qualms about using RA/FSA photographs for his art, perhaps because these existed in the public domain, without copyright restrictions. And, newspaper photographs were commonly perceived as public property. News agencies in this period typically owned the copyright of photographs, and photojournalists often faced problems securing credit and authorship for their work.

110. Kenneth Clark, "The Relations of Photography and Painting" (1953), repr. in *Aperture* 3, no.1 (1995): 13.
111. Dorsky, *The Formative Years of Ben Shahn*, 124, 125, 130.
112. Beaumont Newhall, "Photography and the Artist," *Parnassus* 6, no.5 (October 1934): 24. Newhall went onto demonstrate that this was not the case for mid-nineteenth-century painters who embraced mechanical devices and the use of photographs." American realist artist John Sloan was critical of "[a] great many contemporary artists who are using photographs for documentary detail...drawing directly from the photograph—repeating all the visual distortions." John Sloan, *Gist of Art* (New York: American Artist's Group, Inc., 1939), 155. British artist Paul Nash faced problems when he wanted to exhibit his photographs with his paintings, feeling his process would be misunderstood as cheating. Marina Vaizey, *The Artist as Photographer* (New York: Holt, Rinehart and Winston, 1982), 77–78.
113. Goldsmith, "Ben Shahn: An Unfinished Interview," 29, 33. Shahn said: "However, I think it is dangerous for an artist to start out too soon to rely on photography. The function of an artist is to render three-dimensional objects in two dimensions. If you work too closely from photographs too soon you abdicate your responsibility as an artist." Goldsmith, "Ben Shahn: An Unfinished Interview," 29.
114. Dorsky, *The Formative Years of Ben Shahn*, 56. "[P]hotography was deeply attractive to him, that he began to use it as a 'joke,' found that it answered his needs and delighted in the hostility of the artists in his milieu, who looked down upon photography used this way as artifice and unprofessional...He would be working from 'copy' or a prepared program which was, like Evans' raw material, 'real' and, like Evans, he would make it Art, through selection, taste and his artistic sensitivity. It satisfied, too, his need for a work-oriented preparation, a series of things, prepared in advance and with continuity; again as was the case with the series of photos which was typical of Evans' work. The audacity of using photographs also appealed to him as did another crucial element in Evans' aesthetic." Dorsky, *The Formative Years of Ben Shahn*, 56, 61.
115. See Diane Tepfer, *Edith Gregor Halpert and the Downtown Gallery Downtown: 1926-1940: A Study in American Art Patronage* (Ph.D diss., University of Michigan, 1989), 98–101; Theodore Stebbins and Norman Keyes Jr., *Charles Sheeler: The Photographs* (Boston: Museum of Fine Arts, 1987), 40. According to Stebblins and Keyes, "[Halpert's] gallery did not deal in photography, and she was simply not interested in the medium. Moreover, Halpert urged Sheeler to do nothing but paint, and to keep his photographs out of gallery exhibitions (though she is not known to have discouraged their inclusion in museum retrospectives)." Stebbins and Keyes, *Charles Sheeler: The Photographs*, 40. See also pp.44; 47–48; 51-52.

Halpert did in fact show some of Shahn's New York photographs as they appeared in the November 1934 issue of *New Theatre*, in her Downtown Gallery exhibition "Practical Manifestations in American Art," December 13–31, 1934. Exhibition brochure, BSP. This exhibition displayed the alternative arts that painters produced for sustenance during the Depression, and when the first government art project (PWAP) was suspended. Later, Halpert was cooperative when Van Deren Coke wanted to include Shahn's work in his pioneering exhibition and catalogue *The Painter and the Photograph* (Albuquerque, NM: University of New Mexico Press, 1964). *The Painter and the Silver Icon* was Coke's original title. See Halpert to Coke, May 10, 1963, BSP, Reel 5010F82; Halpert to Shahn, September 14, 1963, BSP, Reel 5010F12; Halpert to Shahn, October 11, 1963, BSP. Reel 5010F611.
116. Newhall, "Ben Shahn," 3.
117. According to Patricia Hills, "The accusation against topicality often parallels the carping against 'propaganda' in art, a criticism always calculated to denigrate the artistic worth of paintings which are partisan." This was the case with Philip Evergood who was "[s]ometimes accused of dealing with topical subjects." Hills, "Philip Evergood's 'American Tragedy': The Poetics of Ugliness. The Politics of Anger," *Arts Magazine* 54, no.6 (February 1980): 141. See also Cecile Whiting, *Antifascism in American Art* (New Haven, Conn.: Yale University Press, 1989), 164–166. Whiting wrote: "The emergence of allegory during the war years when propaganda was coming increasingly under attack was yet one more means of claiming high-art legitimacy for antifascist imagery: any picture capable of making a timeless statement stood a better chance of escaping damnation as topical propaganda." Whiting, *Antifascism in American Art*, 165.
118. Jean Charlot, "Ben Shahn," *Hound and Horn*, 6, no.4 (July-September 1933): 633-634. Reprinted in slightly altered form in Charlot, *An Artist on Art, Collected Essays of Jean Charlot* (Honolulu: University Press of Hawaii, 1972), 186.
119. Barthes, "The Photographic Message," 15.
120. Aragon, "Painting and Reality," 9.

Diana Linden

What Becomes an Icon Most?: The Critical Reception of Ben Shahn's The Passion of Sacco and Vanzetti

1. Adam Weinberg, *Frames of Reference: Looking at American Art, 1900–1950, Works from the Whitney Museum of American Art* (New York: Whitney Museum of American Art, 2000): 11. Shahn's *The Passion of Sacco and Vanzetti*, 1931–32, owned by the Whitney Museum of American art is reproduced in several surveys of American, western and twentieth-century art. For example, Matthew Baigell calls the work "the first major monument of social realism." See his *A Concise History of American Painting and Sculpture* (New York: Harper Collins, 1996), 267.
2. I would like to thank the undergraduates in my seminar on Ben Shahn, fall 2000, University of Michigan-Ann Arbor, for their immediate and studied responses to Shahn's works. I would especially like to acknowledge the thoughtful work of Emily Baumgartner.
3. William Young and David E. Kaiser, *Postmortem: New Evidence in the Case of Sacco and Vanzetti* (Amherst: The University of Massachusetts Press, 1985), 7.
4. Abe Bluestein, "Editorial: Sacco and Vanzetti," *Il Martello* (August 28, 1934): 4.
5. Matthew Josephson, "The Passion of Sacco-Vanzetti," *New Republic* (April 20, 1932): 275.
6. However, unlike Sacco and Vanzetti, Dreyfus was not a radical, did not reside in the United States, and the case had less temporal immediacy.
7. Brief articles and notices on Shahn's exhibition at Halpert's Downtown Gallery, all 1932, which rely on the press release, appeared in the Kansas City (Missouri) Star, the Springfield (Massachusetts) *Republican*, the *Boston Evening Transcript*, and the *Chicago Post*.
8. Most of the original writings on the series, meaning articles that were not dependent on a press release circulated by the Downtown Gallery, were written for New York City newspapers.
9. Press Release, March 30, 1932, Edith Halpert Papers, Archives of American Art, Smithsonian Institution, Washington, D.C. (hereafter AAA).
10. See Laura Katzman's essay in this catalogue.
11. "Sacco and Vanzetti Story Told at Young Artist's Show," *New York World-Telegram* (April 6, 1932) clipping, Ben Shahn Papers, AAA.
12. K.G.S., "Sacco-Vanzetti Case in Art," *New York Times* (April 9 1932) clipping, Ben Shahn Papers, AAA. Publicity surrounding the case escalated with the March 1927 publication of an article "The Case of Sacco and Vanzetti," in the *Atlantic Monthly* written by the Harvard law professor and future U.S. Supreme Court justice Felix Frankfurter. The author argued for the pair's innocence and maintained that the judicial proceedings were unfair.
13. "The Week in New York: A Roster of Recently Opened Shows," *New York Times* (April 10, 1932): 10X.
14. Carlyle Burrows, "Briefer Comment on Current Art Attractions in New York: Ben Shahn," *New York Herald Tribune* (April 10, 1932): section VII, 10.
15. "Attractions in the Galleries," *New York Sun*, April 16 1932, Edith Halpert Papers, AAA.
16. Michael L. Simmons, "Shahn's Way," *Gotham Life* (April 10-16, 1932): 11.
17. *Creative Art*, June 1932, 396–97.
18. "Sacco-Vanzetti Series," *Art Digest* (April 15, 1932): clipping, Edith Halpert Papers, AAA.
19. "Ben Shahn: Downtown Gallery," *Art News* (April 9, 1932): clipping, Ben Shahn papers, AAA.
20. For information on Modern Quarterly, see Michael Denning, The Cultural Front: *The Laboring of American Culture in the Twentieth Century* (London and New York: Verso, 1996), 101. See also Mari Jo Buhle, Paul Buhle, and Dan Georgakas, eds., *Encyclopedia of the American Left* (Urbana and Chicago: University of Illinois Press, 1992), 482–83, and Alan M. Wald, *The New York Intellectuals: The Rise and Decline of the Anti-Stalinist Left from the 1930s* to the 1980s (Chapel Hill and London: University of North Carolina Press, 1987), 111–12.
21. Diego Rivera, "The Revolutionary Spirit in Modern Art," *Modern Quarterly* 6 (Autumn 1932): 56–57.
22. Hugo Gellert, "We Captured the Walls," *New Masses*, June 1932, 29, and *Art Front* 1, no. 1 (November 1934): 6. See Francine Tyler, "Artists Respond to the Great Depression and the threat of Fascism: The New York Artists' Union and its Magazine," *Art Front* (1934–1937) (Ph.D. diss., New York University, 1991).
23. I would like to thank the research staff at YIVO for their assistance.
24. H. Sachs, "The Passion of Sacco-Vanzetti," *The Road to Freedom: A Monthly Journal of Anarchist Thought and Interpretation* 7, no. 9 (May 1932): 5.
25. Walter Gutman, "Art: The Passion of Sacco-Vanzetti," *The Nation* (April 20, 1932): 475.
26. Josephson, "The Passion of Sacco-Vanzetti," 275.

27. *Man!: A Journal of the Anarchist Ideal and Movement 1*, nos. 8–9 (August–September, 1933): 1. The August editions of many anarchist papers commemorated the execution which had taken place on August 7, 1927.
28. Mark Naison, *Communists in Harlem During the Depression* (New York: Grove Press, Inc., 1983), 15.
29. Mark Solomon, *The Cry Was Unity: Communists and African Americans*, 1917–1936 (Jackson: University of Mississippi Press, 1998), 203.
30. See Martin H. Bush, *Ben Shahn: The Passion of Sacco and Vanzetti* [with an essay and commentary by Ben Shahn] (Syracuse, N.Y.: Syracuse University, 1968) for full discussion of attempts to both purchase and block Shahn's work from being included in the MoMA exhibition.
31. For coverage of the exhibition's planning, the controversy, and the resolution, see Frances K. Pohl, *New Deal Artist in a Cold War Climate*, 1947–1954 (Austin: University of Texas Press, 1989), 45; "Exhibit Accepts Murals Caricaturing Notables" (no reference); "Museum of Modern Art Plans Exhibit of Murals," *New York Herald Tribune* (February 1, 1932) "Insurgent Art Stirs Up Storm Among Society," *New York Herald Tribune* (May 2, 1932) clippings, Goodyear Papers, MoMA.
32. "Opening Exhibition of Murals at Museum of Modern Art Proves Disappointing," *New York Sun* (May 7, 1932) clipping, Goodyear Papers, MoMA.
33. Helen Appleton Reed, "American Murals," *Brooklyn Daily Eagle* (May 8, 1932) clipping, Goodyear Papers, MoMA.
34. Rose Mary Fisk, "Murals by Americans is Dull Show," *Chicago Evening Post* (May 10, 1932) clipping, Goodyear Papers, MoMA.
35. Lincoln Kirstein, "Contemporary Mural Painting in the United States," *Hound and Horn*, July/September 1932, 660.
36. *The Sacco-Vanzetti Case: Transcript of the Record of the Trial of Nicola Sacco and Bartolomeo Vanzetti in the Courts of Massachusetts and Subsequent Proceedings*, 1920–7, 6 vols. (New York: Henry Holt, 1928-1929), V. 53781, quoted in Paul Avrich, *Sacco and Vanzetti: The Anarchist Background* (Princeton: Princeton University Press, 1991), 4.
37. Avrich, *Sacco and Vanzetti*, 213.
38. "Sacco Posters Torn Down at Harvard Where 'Fan Dance' Placard Flourished," unidentified clipping, Edith Halpert Papers, AAA.
39. "Sacco-Vanzetti Paintings Shown," *Boston Herald*, October 17, 1932, no pagination, clipping in the Edith Halpert Papers, AAA.
40. "Sacco-Vanzetti Paintings Shown: Harvard Society Officials Deny Portraits Caricatures," *Boston Herald* (October 17 1932) clipping, Ben Shahn Papers, AAA. See also, "The Mail: Contemporary Art Society," *Harvard Crimson* (October, 1932); H.L.B., "Reviewer Discusses Ben Shahn's Portrait Work," *Harvard Crimson*, October 18, 1932; "This is Art–Not Caricature," *Boston Herald*, October 17, 1932; and "Sacco-Vanzetti Exhibit of Art Arouses Harvard," *New York Herald Tribune*, October 18, 1932, Stephen Lee Taller/Ben Shahn Archives, Berkeley, California.
41. Herbert B. Ehrmann, *The Untried Case: The Sacco and Vanzetti Case and the Morelli Gang* (New York: Vanguard, 1933), argued for the collusion of the Morelli gang of Providence, R.I., which specialized in stealing shoe shipments from manufacturers.
42. "Massachusetts Refuses a Plaque in Honor of Sacco and Vanzetti," *Life* (September 6, 1937) 24. In 1947, Borglum along with Eleanor Roosevelt and Albert Einstein again extended the offer, and again the state refused.
43. Shahn originally conceived of the two figures as Jewish pogrom victims, and then as African-Americans. Shahn's changes have been the subject of much scholarly debate and comment. For a variety of interpretations, see: Ziva Amishai-Maisels, "Ben Shahn and the Problem of Jewish Identity," *Jewish Art* (1986–87): 304–19; Diana L. Linden, "The New Deal Murals of Ben Shahn: The Intersection of Jewish Identity, Social Reform, and Government Patronage," (Ph.D. diss., City University of New York, 1997); Susan Platt Noyes, "The Jersey Homesteads Mural: Ben Shahn, Bernarda Bryson, and History Painting in the 1930s," in *Redefining American History Painting*, ed. Patricia Burnham and Lucretia Griese (Cambridge: Cambridge University Press, 1995); and Frances K. Pohl, "Constructing History: A Mural by Ben Shahn," *Arts Magazine* (September 1987), 36–40.
44. Frances K. Pohl, "The Artist and the Politicians: Ben Shahn, 1947–1954," Ph.D. diss., University of California, Los Angeles, 1985, 6. Pohl's dissertation and subsequent book, *Ben Shahn: New Deal Artist in a Cold War Climate, 1947–1954* (Austin: University of Texas Press, 1989), offer the best discussions of Shahn's career during this seven-year period, his 1947 exhibition at MoMA and at the 1954 Venice Biennial.
45. Shahn's relationship with the institution dated back to 1930 and MoMA-owned *Bartolomeo Vanzetti and Nicola Sacco*, (1931–32) a gift from Abigail Rockefeller, along with *Handball* (1939) acquired in 1943.
46. To review Shahn's early career, see Frances K. Pohl, *Ben Shahn (with Ben Shahn's Writings)* (San Francisco: Pomegranate *ArtBooks*, 1993).
47. See James Thrall Soby, *Ben Shahn* (Middlesex: Penguin, 1947), 6-8, and *Museum of Modern Art Bulletin* (Summer 1947).
48. Carlyle Burrows, "Shahn Exhibition on at Museum of Modern Art," *New York Herald Tribune* (October 1, 1947) clipping, MoMA.
49. Edward Alden Jewell, "Art by Ben Shahn Shown at Gallery," *New York Times* (October 1, 1947) clipping, MoMA.
50. Betty Chamberlain, "The New Season Opens at The Museum of Modern Art," *Art News*, (October 1947): 41, 54–55. As Pohl points out, Chamberlain charts the shifts in Shahn's use of architectural elements, yet doesn't comment on the significance of the change. See Pohl, "The Artist and the Politicians," 95–96.
51. Ralph M. Pearson, "A Modern Viewpoint: Ben Shahn at the Modern," *The Art Digest*, (December 1, 1947), 36.
52. "Current Exhibitions: Extensive One-Man Show by Ben Shahn at the Modern Museum" *New York Sun* (October 3, 1947) clipping, MoMA.
53. Further, the assessment that people had forgotten the case was not entirely accurate, as it was soon revisited by Louis G. Joughin and

Edmund M. Morgan who asserted the men's innocence and the unfairness of the proceedings. See their *The Legacy of Sacco and Vanzetti* (Princeton, NJ: Princeton University Press,1948).

54. Clement Greenberg, "Art," *Nation* (November 1, 1947) 481–82.
55. Joseph Solomon, "The Art of Ben Shahn," *New Masses* (November 4, 1947) clipping, MoMA.
56. Ibid.
57. Selden Rodman, *Portrait of the Artist as an American* (New York: Harper and Row, 1951), 116–121.
58. Howard Fast clearly titled his impressionist novel in debt to Shahn's work. See Howard Fast, *Passion of Sacco and Vanzetti: A New England Legend* (New York: The Blue Heron Press, 1953).
59. 1954 was the year after the execution of the Rosenbergs and the year the Army-McCarthy Hearings began.
60. James Thrall Soby, "Ben Shahn," 1953 manuscript, MoMA.
61. Alfred Barr, Jr., "Gli Stati Uniti alla Biennale: Shahn e De Kooning, Lachaise, Lassaw e Smith," *Biennale di Venezia*, n. 19–20 (Aprile-Giugno 1954).
62. Ibid., 65.
63. Young and Kaiser, *Postmortem*, 7.
64. Robert Montgomery, *Sacco-Vanzetti: The Murder and the Myth* (New York: The Devin-Adair Company, 1960).
65. James Thrall Soby, *Ben Shahn Paintings* (New York: George Braziller, Inc., 1963), 11.
66. Bush, *Ben Shahn: The Passion of Sacco and Vanzetti,* 28.
67. Ibid.
68. Bernarda Bryson Shahn, *Ben Shahn* (New York: Harry N. Abrams, Inc., 1972), 127.
69. Morris Dorsky, "Ben Shahn's Passion of Sacco and Vanzetti: A Note on its Reception," *American Imago* (Spring-Summer, 1978): 146–50.
70. See Hilton Kramer, "Publicizing Social Causes on Canvas," *New York Times* (November 7, 1976) D 23 and Harold Rosenberg, "The Art World: Ben Shahn," *New Yorker*, December 13, 1976, 156–59.
71. Pohl, *New Deal Artist*, 158. The politics and agenda behind having Shahn represent the United States is a complex discussion, one beyond the scope of this essay but treated in full by Frances K. Pohl. Her works are the key sources for understanding Shahn's 1947 and 1954 exhibitions.
72. Young and Kaiser, *Postmortem*, 1985.
73. Francis Russell, *Sacco and Vanzetti: The Case Resolved* (New York: Harper and Row, 1986).

Alejandro Anreus
Ben Shahn and The Passion of Sacco and Vanzetti

1. Edmund Wilson, *The Twenties*, ed. Leon Edel (New York: Farrar, Straus and Giroux, 1975), 388–89. Wilson letter to John Peale Bishop (who was living abroad at the time), October 22, 1928.
2. Edna St. Vincent Millay, *Selected Poems*, (New York: Harper Collins, 1999), 76–77.
3. Julio Antonio Mella, *Julio Antonio Mella en El Machete*, ed. Raquel Tibol (Mexico: Editorial Penelope, 1984), 143–44. Translation from the Spanish by the author.
4. John D. Morse, "Ben Shahn: An Interview," *Magazine of Art* (April 1944):136–141.
5. Gardner Jackson letter to Ben Shahn, October 13, 1931. Ben Shahn Papers, Archives of American Art, Washington, D.C.
6. Wilson, *The Twenties*, 405–406. Wilson wrote down verbatim what e.e. cummings told him, under the heading "Cummings on Sacco and Vanzetti."
7. The Museum of Modern Art, Advisory Committee Meeting Minutes, May 1932. Unpaginated. The Museum of Modern Art Library, New York, N.Y.
8. Alfred H. Barr, Jr., telegram to A. Conger Goodyear, April 28, 1932. A. Conger Goodyear Papers. The Museum of Modern Art Library, New York, N.Y.
9. Bernarda Bryson Shahn, interview by author, Roosevelt, N.J., October 12, 1993.
10. John Dos Passos, *U.S.A. The Big Money*, (Boston: Houghton Mifflin Company, 1946), 414.
11. Morse, "Ben Shahn: An Interview," 137.

Profile of Essayists

Alejandro Anreus
has been the curator at the Jersey City Museum since December of 1993. He is the project manager of this exhibition and the editor of this catalogue. Dr. Anreus is the author of *Orozco in Gringoland: The Years in New York* (University of New Mexico Press, 2001).

Laura Katzman
is Assistant Professor of Art and Director of the Museum Studies Program, Randolph-Macon Woman's College, Lynchburg, Virginia. Prof. Katzman was co-curator of the traveling exhibition, *Ben Shahn's New York: The Photography of Modern Times* (Arthur M. Sackler Museum, Harvard University).

Diana L. Linden
Prof. Linden was a contributing essayist to the catalogue of the exhibition, *Ben Shahn: Common Man, Mythic Vision* (Jewish Museum, NYC). Her monograph on Shahn's New Deal murals is forthcoming.

Nunzio Pernicone
is Associate Professor of History at Drexel University in Philadelphia. Prof. Pernicone is the author of *Italian Anarchism* (Princeton University Press, 1993). His biography of Carlo Tresca is forthcoming.

Frances K. Pohl
is Professor of Art History and Associate Dean of the College, Pomona College, Claremont, California. Prof. Pohl is the senior scholar on Ben Shahn, and the author of *Ben Shahn: New Deal Artist in a Cold War Climate 1947–1954* (University of Texas Press, 1989) and Ben Shahn (Pomegranate ArtBooks, 1993).

List of Illustrations

1. Ben Shahn
Villa Felleto, Vanzetti's Home Town
1931. Watercolor and gouache
on paper, 9 x 13 in. Kennedy Galleries,
New York, New York

2. Ben Shahn
Bartolomeo Vanzetti & Nicola Sacco
1931–32. Gouache on paper mounted
on composition board, 10 7/8 x 14 5/8 in.
The Museum of Modern Art, New York,
New York. Gift of Abby Aldrich
Rockefeller

3. Ben Shahn
Bartolomeo Vanzetti, 1931-32.
Gouache on paper, 14 1/2 x 11 1/2 in.
Private Collection and R.D.Schonfeld
& Co., Inc.

4. Ben Shahn
In the Courtroom Cage, 1931–32.
Gouache on paper, 11 1/2 x 14 1/2 in.
The Art Museum, Princeton University,
Princeton, New Jersey
Gift of Dr. Walter E. Rothman

5. Ben Shahn
*Nicola Sacco, His Wife and
Their Son Dante,* 1931–32.
Gouache on paper, 13 x 10 1/2 in.
Frederick R. Weisman Art Museum
Gift of Gertrude Lippincott. University
of Minnesota, Minneapolis, Minnesota

6. Ben Shahn
*Mrs. Sacco and Elizabeth Glendower
Evans,* 1931–32.
Gouache on paper, 10 x 12 1/4 in.
Frederick R. Weisman Art Museum
Gift of Gertrude Lippincott
University of Minnesota,
Minneapolis, Minnesota

7. Ben Shahn
Three Witnesses, 1931–32.
Watercolor, gouache and ink
on paper, 9 1/2 x 13 in.
The Montclair Art Museum,
Montclair, New Jersey
Bequest in memory of Moses
and Ida Soyer

8. Ben Shahn
Judge Webster Thayer, 1931–31.
Gouache on paper, 13 x 6 1/2 in.
Collection of Mr. and Mrs. Jonathan
Wittenberg, Tocahoe, New York

9. Ben Shahn
Sacco's Family After the Verdict
1931–32. Gouache on paper, 10 x 10 in.
Collection of Mr. and Mrs. Harry Spiro,
New York

10. Ben Shahn painting *The Passion
of Sacco and Vanzetti,* 1932.
Courtesy of Bernarda Bryson Shahn,
Roosevelt, New Jersey

11. Ben Shahn
The Passion of Sacco and Vanzetti.
1932. Tempera on board, 21 x 48 in.
Private Collection (not in exhibition)

12. Ben Shahn
The Passion of Sacco and Vanzetti
1931–32. Tempera on canvas,
84 1/2 x 48 in. Whitney Museum of
American Art, New York.
Gift of Edith and Milton Lowenthal in
memory of Juliana Force

13. George Grosz
Sacco & Vanzetti, 1927.
Ink on paper, 12 x 9 inches
Courtesy of Peter Grosz, Princeton,
New Jersey

14. George Biddle
*Our senses will applaud this world again,
But who can clap life with murdered
men?,* 1930. Lithograph, 24 x 18 in.
Private Collection, New Jersey

15. Hugo Gellert
Sacco and Vanzetti, 1932.
Crayon on paper, dimensions unknown
Location unknown

16. Ben Shahn
Sacco and Vanzetti, 1952.
Black ink on cream wove paper,
5 3/4 x 8 1/2 in. Fogg Art Museum,
Harvard University Art Museums
Gift of Meta and Paul J. Sachs

17. Ben Shahn
The Passion of Sacco and Vanzetti
1958. Serigraph, 25 3/4 x 17 1/2 in.
Gift of the Lessing and Edith Rosenwald
Foundation. New Jersey State Museum,
Trenton, New Jersey

18. Ben Shahn
The Passion of Sacco and Vanzetti
1967. Left panel. Mosaic. Syracuse
University, Syracuse, New York. Gift of
Mr. and Mrs. Jacob Schulman, and
Mr. and Mrs. Richard Evans, III

19. Ben Shahn
The Passion of Sacco and Vanzetti
1967. Middle panel. Mosaic. Syracuse
University, Syracuse, New York
Gift of Mr. and Mrs. Jacob Schulman,
and Mr. and Mrs. Richard Evans, III

20. Ben Shahn
The Passion of Sacco and Vanzetti
1967. Right panel. Mosaic
Syracuse University, Syracuse, New York
Gift of Mr. and Mrs. Jacob Schulman,
and Mr. and Mrs. Richard Evans, III

21. Ben Shahn
Detail of left panel of *The Passion of
Sacco and Vanzetti*, 1967. Mosaic.
Syracuse University, Syracuse, New York
Gift of Mr. and Mrs. Jacob Schulman,
and M. and Mrs. Richard Evans, III

Checklist

1. Ben Shahn
Villa Felleto, Vanzetti's Home Town
1931. Watercolor and gouache on paper, 9 x 13 1/2 in.
Kennedy Galleries, New York, NY

2. Ben Shahn
Bartolomeo Vanzetti and Nicola Sacco
1931–32. Gouache on paper mounted on composition board, 10 7/8 x 14 5/8 in.
The Museum of Modern Art, New York
Gift of Abby Aldrich Rockefeller

3. Ben Shahn
Bartolomeo Vanzetti, 1931–32
Gouache on paper, 14 1/2 x 11 1/2 in.
Private Collection and R.D. Schonfeld & Co., Inc.

4. Ben Shahn
In the Courtroom Cage, 1931–32
Gouache on paper, 11 1/2 x 14 1/2 in.
The Art Museum, Princeton University, Princeton, New Jersey
Gift of Dr. Walter E. Rothman

5. Ben Shahn
Nicola Sacco, His Wife and Their Son Dante, 1931–32
Gouache on paper, 13 x 10 1/2 in.
Frederick R. Weisman Art Museum, University of Minnesota, Minneapolis, Minnesota. Gift of Gertrude Lippincott

6. Ben Shahn
Mrs. Sacco and Elizabeth Glendower Evans, 1931–32
Gouache on paper, 10 x 12 1/4 in.
Frederick R. Weisman Art Museum
University of Minnesota, Minneapolis, Minnesota. Gift of Gertrude Lippincott

7. Ben Shahn
Three Witnesses, 1931–32.
Watercolor, gouache and ink on paper, 9 1/2 x 13 in.
The Montclair Art Museum, Montclair, New Jersey
Bequest in memory of Moses and Ida Soyer

8. Ben Shahn
Judge Webster Thayer, 1931–32.
Gouache on paper, 13 x 6 1/2 in.
Collection of Mr. and Mrs. Jonathan Wittenberg, Tocahoe, New York

9. Ben Shahn
Sacco's Family After the Verdict
1931-32. Gouache on paper, 10 x 10 in.
Collection of Mr. and Mrs. Harry Spiro, New York, New York

10. Ben Shahn
The Passion of Sacco and Vanzetti
1931–32. Tempera on canvas, 84 1/2 x 48 in.
Whitney Museum of American Art, New York, New York. Gift of Edith and Milton Lowenthal in memory of Juliana Force

11. Ben Shahn
Sacco and Vanzetti, 1952.
Black ink on cream wove paper, 5 3/4 x 8 1/2 in. Fogg Art Museum, Harvard University Art Museums
Gift of Meta and Paul J. Sachs

12. Ben Shahn
The Passion of Sacco and Vanzetti
1958. Serigraph, 25 3/4 x 17 1/2 in.
New Jersey State Museum, Trenton, New Jersey. Gift of the Lessing and Edith Rosenwald Foundation

13. Ben Shahn
Portrait of Sacco and Vanzetti, 1958
Serigraph, 12 3/4 x 17 3/8 in.
New Jersey State Museum, Trenton, New Jersey

14. Ben Shahn
Immortal Words, 1958.
Serigraph, 12 3/4 x 17 3/8 in.
Jersey City Museum, Jersey City, New Jersey

15–18. Ben Shahn
Photographs of *The Passion of Sacco and Vanzetti* mosaic mural, 1967
Syracuse University, Syracuse, New York
Gift of Mr. and Mrs. Jacob Schulman, and Mr. and Mrs. Richard Evans, III

19. George Biddle
Our senses will applaud this world again, But who can clap life with murdered men?, 1930, Lithograph, 24 x 18 in.
Private Collection, Plainfield, New Jersey

20. Nicola Sacco, his wife and their son Dante

21. Sacco and Vanzetti just before sentence is passed

22. Vanzetti, early period of his detention

23. Sacco and Vanzetti, during trial

24. Vanzetti and Sacco in the courtroom cage

25. Sacco, early period of his detention

26. Sacco and Vanzetti, boarding the van

27. Sacco and Vanzetti en route to Court House

28. Sacco and Vanzetti

29. Sacco and Vanzetti's bodies taken to the mortuary

30. Sacco and Vanzetti's death masks

31. Hearses bearing Sacco and Vanzetti's bodies

32. Sacco and Vanzetti Funeral procession

33. Deadham Court House

34. Judge Webster Thayer

35. District Attorney Frederick G. Katzmann

36. Fred H. Moore, Chief Counsel, Sacco and Vanzetti Defense

37. Rosina Sacco with Mary Donovan

38. Governor Alvan T. Fuller

39. A. Lawrence Lowell

41. Gov. Fuller's Advisory Committee

41. And workers came in thousands

42. Armbands, "Remember! Justice Crucified"

43. Edna St. Vincent Millay

44. John Dos Passos
Photographs. Boston Public Library, Boston, Massachusetts. Aldino Felicani Papers

45. Sacco and Vanzetti Rally Poster
Photolithography, 13 1/4 x 10 1/4 in.
Alfredo Sinibaldi, Montclair, New Jersey

Miscellaneous Sacco and Vanzetti materials (pamphlets, books, etc.)
Dr. Nuzio Pernicone, Newtown, Pennsylvania

Bibliography

BIBLIOGRAPHY BOOKS

Allen, Frederick Lewis. *Since Yesterday: The Nineteen Thirties in America: 1929–1939.* New York: Harper and Brothers, 1939.

Amfitheatrof, Erik. *The Children of Columbus: An Informal History of the Italians in the New World.* Boston and Toronto: Little, Brown and Co., 1973.

Avrich, Paul. *Sacco and Vanzetti: The Anarchist Background.* Princeton: Princeton University Press, 1991.

Baigell, Matthew. *A Concise History of American Painting and Sculpture.* New York: Harper Collins, 1996.

Barthes, *Roland. Image, Music, Text.* New York: Hill and Wang, 1977.

Beger, Meyer. *The Story of the New York Times, 1851–1951.* New York: Simon and Schuster, 1951.

Blumfield, Harold. *Sacco and Vanzetti: Their Story in Pictures.* New York: Scholastic Book Service, 1972.

Buhle, Mary Jo, Paul Buhle and Dan Georgakas, eds. *Encyclopedia of the American Left.* Urbana and Chicago: University of Illinois Press, 1992.

Bush, Martin. *Ben Shahn: The Passion of Sacco and Vanzetti.* Syracuse, NY: Syracuse University Press, 1968.

Charlot, Jean. *An Artist on Art, Collected Essays of Jean Charlot.* Honolulu: University of Hawaii Press, 1972.

Covert, Catherine and John Stevens, eds. *Mass Media Between the Wars: Perceptions of Cultural Tension: 1918–1941.* Syracuse: Syracuse University Press, 1984.

Creagh, Ronald. *Sacco and Vanzetti.* Paris: Editions La Decouverte, 1984.

D'Atillo, Robert and Jane Manthorn eds. "La Salute e in Voi: The Anarchist Dimension". *Sacco and Vanzetti: Developments and Reconsiderations, 1979.* Boston: Boston Public Library, 1979.

Davidson, James West and Mark Hamilton Lytle. *After the Fact: The Art of Historical Delection: Volume II.* New York: McGraw Hill, 1992.

Denning, Michael. *The Cultural Front: The Laboring of American Culture in the Twentieth Century.* London and New York: Verso, 1996.

Deren Coke, Van. *The Painter and the Photograph: From Delacoix to Warhol.* Albuquerque: University of New Mexico Press, 1972.

Dos Passos, John. *The Big Money.* New York: Harcourt, Brace, 1938.

Dorsky, Morris. *The Formative Years of Ben Shahn: The Origin and Development of His Style.* New York University: M.A. Thesis, 1966.

Ehrmann. *The Case That Will Not Die.* Little, Boston and Toronto: Brown and Co, 1969.

Ehrmann, Hebert B. *The Untried Case: The Sacco and Vanzetti Case and the Morelli Gang.* New York: Vanguard, 1933.

Evans, Elizabeth Glendower. *Outstanding Features of the Sacco and Vanzetti Case.* New England Civil Liberties Committee, 1924.

Fast, Howard. *The Passion of Sacco and Vanzetti: A New England Legend.* The Blue Horn Press, 1953.

Felix, David. *Protest: Sacco and Vanzetti and the Intellectuals.* Bloomington: Indiana University Press, 1966.

Feuerlicht, Roberta Strauss. *Justice Crucified: The Story of Sacco and Vanzetti.* New York: McGraw Hill, 1977.

Frankfurter, Felix. *The Case of Sacco and Vanzetti: A Critical Analysis for Lawyers and Laymen.* New York: Little, Brown and Co., 1927.

Frankfurter, Marion Denman and Gardner Jackson, eds. *The Letters of Sacco and Vanzetti.* New York: Penguin Books, 1928.

Goldstein, Robert Justin. *Political Repression in Modern America: From 1870 to the Present.* Cambridge New York: Schenkman Publishing Co., 1978.

Greenfield, Howard. Ben Shahn: *An Artists Life. Random House. New York. 1998. Marquart, Virginia. Louis Lozowick: Development From Machine Aesthetic to Social Realism: 1922–1936.* University of Maryland. Maryland: Ph.D Dissertation, 1983.

Hill, Patricia and Lucretia Griese, eds. *Redefining American Painting.* Cambridge: Cambridge University Press, 1995.

Joughin, Louis G., and Edmund M. Morgan. *The Legacy of Sacco and Vanzetti.* Princeton, NJ: Princeton University Press, 1948; 1976.

Kadane, Joseph B., and David A. Schum, A Probabilistic Analysis of The Sacco and Vanzetti Evidence. New York: John Wiley & Sons, 1996.

Lynd, Helen and Robert. *Middletown in Transition: A Study in Cultural Conflicts.* New York: Harcourt, Brace Jovanovich. 1937, 1965.

Lyons. *The Life and Death of Sacco and Vanzetti.* New York: International Publishers, 1927.

MacDougall, Curtis. *Interpretative Reporting.* New York: Macmillan, 1938.

Montgomery, Robert. *Sacco and Vanzetti: The Murder and the Myth.* New York: The Devin-Adair Company, 1960.

Morse. *Ben Shahn.* New York: Praeger, 1972.

Mott, Frank Luther. *American Journalism, a History : 1690–1960.* New York: The Macmillan Company, 1941; 1962.

Musmanno, Michael A., *After Twelve Years.* New York: Knoff, 1939.

Orvell, Miles. *The Reel Thing: Imitation and Authenticity in American Culture 1880–1949.* Chapel Hill: University of North Carolina Press, 1989.

Pohl, Frances. *Ben Shahn (With Ben Shahn's Writings).* San Fransisco, CA: Pomegranate Artbooks, 1993.

Pohl, Frances K. *Ben Shahn: New Deal Artist in a Cold War Climate* 1947–1954. Austin: University of Texas Press, 1989.

Robertson, Bruce. *Representing America: The Ken Trevey Collection of American Realist Prints.* Santa Barbara, CA: University Art Museum, 1995.

Rodman, Selden. *Portrait of the Artist as an American: Ben Shahn. A Biography with Pictures.* New York: Harper and Brothers, 1951.

Rodman. *Conversations with Artists.* New York: Capricorn Books, 1957.

Rosten, Leo. T*he Washington Correspondents.* New York: Harcourt, Brace, 1938.

Russell, Francis. *Sacco and Vanzetti: The Case Resolved.* New York: Harper and Row Publishers, 1986.

Russell. *Tragedy in Dedham.* New York: McGraw Hill, 1962.

Schudson, Michael. *Discovering the News: A Social History of American Newspapers.* New York: Basic Books, Inc., 1988.

Shahn, Ben. *The Shape of Content.* Cambridge, MA: Harvard University Press, 1957.

Shahn, Bernarda Bryson. *Ben Shahn.* New York: Harry N. Abrams, Inc., 1972.

Sinclair, Upton. *Boston: A Documentary Novel of the Sacco and Vanzetti Case.* Cambridge, MA: Robert Bentley, Inc., 1978.

Sloan, John. *Gist of Art.* New York: American Artist's Group, Inc., 1939.

Soby, James Thrall. *Ben Shahn.* New York: Museum of Modern Art. 1947.

Soby, James Thrall. *Ben Shahn.* Middlesex: Penguin, 1947.

Soby, James Thrall. *Ben Shahn Paintings.* New York: George Braziller, Inc., 1963.

Stebbins, Theodore and Norman Keyes. Charles Sheeler: *The Photographs.* Boston: Museum of Fine Arts, 1987.

Stott, William. *Documentary Expression and Thirties America (1973).* Chicago: University of Chicago Press, 1986.

Sussman, Warren. *Culture as History: The Transformation of American Society in the Twentieth Century.* New York: Pantheon Books, 1973; 1984.

Trachtenberg, Alan. *Reading American Photographs: Images as History: Matthew Brady To Walker Evans.* New York: Hill and Wang, 1989.

Vaizey, Marina. *The Artist as Photographer.* New York: Holt, Reinhart and Winston, 1982.

Vanzetti, Bartolomeo. *Background of the Plymouth Trial.* Boston: Road to Freedom Group, 1926.

Wald, Alan M. *The New York Intellectuals: The Rise and Decline of The Anti-Stalanist Left From the 1930's to the 1980's.* Chapel Hill and London: University of North Carolina Press, 1987.

Whiting, Cecile. *Antifacism in American Art.* New Haven, CT: Yale University Press, 1989.

Young, William and David Kaiser. *Postmortem: New Evidence in the Case of Sacco and Vanzetti.* Amherst: University of Massachusetts Press, 1985.

BIBLIOGRAPHY JOURNALS

Abell, Walter. "Art and Labor." *Magazine of Art*. 39. October 1946, P 260.

Amishai-Maisels, Ziva. "Ben Shahn and the Problem of Jewish Identity." *Jewish Art*. 1986-1987, P 304-319.

Argon, Louis. "Painting and Reality" *Art Front*. Vol. 2, No. 12. January, 1937, P 9.

Buckley, William F. Jr. "Sacco and Vanzetti, Again." *American Legion Magazine* 69. October 1960, P 50.

Chamberlain, Betty. "The New Season Opens at the Museum of Modern Art." *Art News*. October 1947, P 41, 54–55.

Charlot, Jean. "Ben Shahn." *Hound and Horn*. Vol. VI, No. 4. July–September 1933, PP 633-634.

Clark, Kenneth. "The Relations of Photography and Painting" (1953). Reprinted in *The Aperture*. Vol. 3, No. 1. 1995, P 13.

De Hart Mathews, Jane. "Art and the People: The New Deal Quest for a Cultural Democracy" *The Journal of American History*. Vol. 62, No. 2. September 1975. P 337.

Dorsky, Morris. "Ben Shahn's Passion of Sacco and Vanzetti: A Note On Its Reception." *American Imago*. Vol. 135, Nos 1–2. 1978, P 146.

Foner, Eric. "Sacco and Vanzetti: The Men and the Symbols." *The Nation* 225, No. 5. August 20–27 1997, P 135.

Frankfurter, Felix. "The Case of Sacco and Vanzetti." *Atlantic Monthly*. March 1927.

Gellert, Hugo. "We Captured the Walls." *New Masses*. June 1932. Also in Art Front. Vol.1, No.1. November 1934, P 6.

Goldsmith, Arthur. "Ben Shahn: An Unfinished Interview." *Technical Photography*. Vol. 1, No. 4. June 1969, P 33.

Greenberg, Clement. "Art." *The Nation*. Vol. 165, No. 18. November 1, 1947, PP 481–482.

Gutman, Walter. "Art: The Passion of Sacco-Vanzetti." *Nation*. April 20, 1932, P 475.

Gutman, Walter. "Ben Shahn: Downtown Gallery." *Art News*. April 9, 1932, P 10.

Hills, Patricia. "Philip Evergood's American Tragedy: The Poetics of Ugliness. The Politics of Anger." *Arts Magazine*. Vol. 54. No.6. February 1980, P 141.

Josephson, Matthew. "The Passion of Sacco and Vanzetti" *The New Republic*. Vol. 70. April 20, 1932, P 275.

Katzman, Laura. "The Politics of Media: Painting and Photography in the Art of Ben Shahn." *American Art*. Vol. 7, No 1. Winter 1993, PP 61-87.

Kirstein, Lincoln. "Art Chronicle: Contemporary Mural Painting in the United States" *Hound and Horn*. Vol. 5, No. 4. July–September 1932, P 660.

Leonard, Ann. "Around the Galleries: Ben Shahn, A People's Artist." *People's World*. December 1, 1948.

McWilliams, Carey. "Massachusetts Pays its Debts." *The Nation* 225, No. 5. August 20–27 1997, P 133–135.

Morse, John. "Ben Shahn: An Interview" *Magazine of Art*. Vol. 37, No. 4. April 1944, PP 138–139.

Newhall, Beaumont. "Photography and the Artist." *Parnassus*. Vol.6, No.5. October 1934, P 24.

Newhall, Nancy. "Ben Shahn." *Photo Notes*. November 1947, P 3.

No Author. "Sacco-Vanzetti Series." *Art Digest*. April 15, 1932. Edith Halpert Papers. Archive of American Art.

No Author. "Ben Shahn: Downtown Gallery." *Art News*. April 9, 1932. Clipping, Ben Shahn Papers, Archive of American Art.

No Author. No Title. *Creative Art*. June 1932, PP 396-397.

No Author. "Massachusetts Refuses a Plaque in Honor of Sacco and Vanzetti." *Life*. September 6, 1947, P 24.

No Author. No Title. *Man!: A Journal of the Anarchist Ideal and Movement*. Vol. 1, Nos. 8–9. August–September 1933.

No Author. "The Passion of Sacco-Vanzetti." *The Nation*. April 20, 1932, P 475.

Pearson, Ralph M. "A Modern Viewpoint: Ben Shahn at the Modern." *The Art Digest*. December 1, 1947,P 36.

Pernicone, Nunzio. "Carlo Tresca and the Sacco-Vanzetti Case." *The Journal of American History 66*, No. 3. December 1979, PP 535-547.

Pohl, Frances. "Constructing History: A Mural by Ben Shahn." *Arts Magazine*. 1987, P 36-40.

Ragghianti, Carlo. "l'artista e il politicismo."*Sele Arte*. No. 9. November/December 1953, P 28.

Rivera, Diego. "The Revolutionary Spirit in Modern Art" *The Modern Art Quarterly*. Vol. VI, No 3. Autumn 1932, P 56.

Rosenberg, Harold. "The Art World: Ben Shahn." T*he New Yorker*. December 13, 1976, PP 156-59.

Sachs, H. "The Passion of Sacco-Vanzetti." *The Road to Freedom: A Monthly Journal of Anarchist Thought and Interpretation*. Vol. VIII, No. 9. May 1932, P 5.

Shahn, Ben. "Art: Angry Eye". *Time*. Vol. 50, No. 15. October 13, 1947, P 63.

Shahn, Ben. "The Artist and the Politicians." *Rights*. 1. 1953. PP 4, 8. Also *Art News*. 52. September 1953, P 7.

Shahn, Ben. "Henri Cartier Bresson." *The Magazine of Art*. Vol. 40, No. 5. May 1947, P 189.

Shahn, Ben. "Photos For Art" *US Camera*. Vol. 9, No. 4. May 1946, P 33.

Solomon, Joseph. "The Art of Ben Shahn." *New Masses*. November 4, 1947. Clipping, MoMA.

Starrs, James E. "Once More Unto the Breach: The Firearms Evidence in the Sacco and Vanzetti Case Revisited." Parts 1, 2. *Journal of Forensic Sciences* 31, Nos. 2 and 3. 1986, PP 630–654 and 1050–1078.

Strand, Paul. "Correspondence of Argon." *Art Front*. Vol. 33, No. 1. February 1937, P 13.

BIBLIOGRAPHY NEWSPAPERS WITH AUTHORS

Alden-Jewll, Edward. "Art By Ben Shahn Shown at Gallery" *New York Times*. October 1, 1947. Clipping, MoMA.

Appleton Reed, Helen. "American Murals." *Brooklyn Daily Eagle*. May 8, 1932. Clipping, Goodyear Papers, MoMA.

Burrows, Carlyle. "Briefer Comment on Current Art Attractions in NY: Ben Shahn." *New York Herald Tribune*. April 10, 1932. Section VII, P 10.

Burrows, Carlyle. "Shahn Exhibition on at Museum of Modern Art." *New York Herald Tribune*. October 1, 1947. Clipping, MoMA.

Clements, Robert. "Knights Errant in Error?." *New York Times Book Review*. January 30, 1966, P 3.

Fisk, Rose Mary. "Murals by Americans is Dull Show." *Chicago Evening Post*. May 10, 1932. Clipping, Goodyear Papers, MoMA.

Grillo, Thomas. "Sculpture to Remind of Sacco, Vanzetti." *The Boston Globe*. Metro Section. August 20, 1997, P B3.

H.L.B. "Reviewer Discusses Ben Shahn's Portrait Work." *Harvard Crimson*. October 18, 1932. Stephen Lee Taller/Ben Shahn Archives, Berkeley, California.

KGS. "Sacco-Vanzetti: Case in Art." *New York Times*. April 6, 1931, P 23.

Kramer, Hilton. "Publicizing Social Causes on Canvas." *New York Times*. November 7, 1976. D 23. McBride, Henry. "Attractions in the Galleries". *New York Sun*. April 16, 1932, P 110.

Scacheri, Mabel. "Your Camera." *New York World Telegram*. October 2, 1947.

Burrows, Carlyle. "Briefer Comment on Current Art Attractions in New York: Ben Shahn." *New York Herald Tribune*. April 10, 1932. Section VII, 10.

Vaughan, William. "Young Shahn Turns From Ivory Tower." *New York American*. April 16, 1932, P 32.

BIBLIOGRAPHY NEWSPAPERS WITH NO AUTHORS

Untitled. *Boston Evening Transcript.* February 1, 1912.

"This is Art—Not Caricature." *Boston Herald.* October 17, 1932. Stephen Lee Taller/Ben Shahn Archives, Berkeley, California.

Untitled. *New York Evening Journal.* July 31, 1900.

"Exhibit Accepts Murals Caricaturing Notables." *New York Herald Tribune.* February 1, 1932. Clippings, Goodyear Papers, MoMA.

"Insurgent Art Stirs Up Storm Among Society." *New York Herald Tribune.* May 2, 1932. Clippings, Goodyear Papers, MoMA.

"Sacco-Vanzetti Exhibit of Art Arouses Harvard." *New York Herald Tribune.* October 18, 1932. Stephen Lee Taller/Ben Shahn Archives, Berkeley, California.

"Attractions in the Galleries." *New York Sun.* April 16, 1932. Edith Halpert Papers, Archive of American Art.

"Current Exhibitions: Extensive One-Man Show By Ben Shahn at the Modern Museum." *New York Sun.* October 3, 1947. Clipping, MoMA.

"Opening Exhibition of Murals at Museum of Modern Art Proves Disappointing." *New York Sun.* May 7, 1932. Clipping, Goodyear Papers, MoMA.

"A Roster of Recently Opened Shows" *New York Times.* Section VIII. April 10, 1932, P 10.

"The Week in New York: A Roster of Recently Opened Shows." *New York Times.* April 1 0, 1932. 10X.

Untitled. *New York Times.* July 31, 1900.

"Sacco and Vanzetti Story Told at Young Artist's Show." *New York World-Telegram.* April 6, 1932. Clipping Ben Shahn Papers, Archive of American Art.

BIBLIOGRAPHY MISCELLANEOUS CORRESPONDENCE

Edith Halpert to Ben Shahn. Correspondence. November 2, 1932; October 2, 1932. Downtown Gallery Papers. *Archives of American Art.* Smithsonian Institution. Washington D.C. Artists File Ben Shahn.

Edith Halpert, Van Deren Coke and Ben Shahn. Correspondence, 1963. Between Reels 5006 and 5027.

Ann Henry to Ben Shahn. Correspondence. June 13, 1940. Ben Shahn Papers. Between Reels 5006–5027.

Beaumont Newall to Ben Shahn. Correspondence. June 27, 1958. Ben Shahn Papers. *Archive of American Art.* Roll D146:1352.

Ben Shahn to Edith Halpert. Correspondence. June 8, 1932; August 3, 1932. October 27, 1932 and November 5, 1932. Downtown Gallery Papers. *Archives of American Art.* Smithsonian Institution. Washington D.C. Artists File Ben Shahn.

Ben Shahn to Ann Henry. Correspondence. June 13, 1940. Ben Shahn Papers. Between Reels 5006-5027.

Ben Shahn to Gardner Jackson. Correspondence. October 13, 1931. Ben Shahn Papers. Reel 5006:718.

Pete Sekaer to Ben Shahn. Correspondence. November 18, 1947. Ben Shahn Papers. Reel 5007:503-504.

James Thrall Soby to Ben Shahn. Correspondence. December 16, 1946. Ben Shahn Papers. Reel D147:1433.

James Thrall Soby to Ben Shahn. Correspondence. September 18, 1947. Ben Shahn Papers. Reel D147:1450.

Frank Zachary to Ben Shahn. Correspondence. November 30, 1944. Ben Shahn Papers. D146:535.

BIBLIOGRAPHY MISCELLANEOUS

Catania, Franco. *Corriere de Sicilia*. MoMA. August 24, 1954.

Dondero, George: Modern Art Shackled to Communism". *U.S. Congressional Record*. 81st Congress. 1st Session. August 16, 1948. PP 11585–86.

Dorsky, Morris. *The Formative Years of Ben Shahn: The Origin and Development of His Style*. M.A. Thesis. New York University, 1966–1976.

Doud, Richard. Interview with Ben Shahn. April 14, 1964. *Archive of American Art*, PP 7–8.
Forrest, Selvig. Interview with Ben Shahn. Unmicrofilmed Transcript. Ben Shahn Papers, PP 3–6

Halpert, Edith. Exhibition Brochure. "Practical Manifestations of American Art". Downtown Gallery. December 13–31, 1934. Ben Shahn Papers.

Halpert, Edith. "The Passion of Sacco and Vanzetti". Exhibition Press Release: Downtown Gallery; March 30, 1932. James Thrall Soby Papers. The Museum of Modern Art, 135, 7B.

Halpert, Edith. Press Release. March 30, 1932. Edith Halpert Papers, Archives of American Art, Smithsonian Institution, Washington D.C.

Katzman, Laura. *The Politics of Media: Ben Shahn and Photography*. Ph.D. Dissertation. Yale University, 1997.

Lester, Henry M. "Evaluating Reader's Interest in Pictures". *19th Art Director's Annual of Advertising Art*, 1941.

Linden, Diane L. *The New Deal Murals of Ben Shahn: The Intersection of Jewish Identity, Social Reform and Government Patronage*. Ph.D. Dissertation. City University of New York, 1997.

Marquardt, Virginia. *Louis Lozowck: Development From Machine Aesthetic to Social Realism: 1922–1936*. Ph.D. Dissertation. University of Maryland, 1983, P 67.

Morgan, Willard, organizer. Symposium: "Photography and Other Arts". April 19, 1944. Willard Morgan Papers, Newhall Files, Department of Photography, The Museum of Modern Art. New York.

"The Sacco-Vanzetti Case: Transcript of the Record of the Trial of Nicola Sacco and Bartolomeo Vanzetti in the Courts of Massachusetts and Subsequent Proceedings, 1920–1927", 6 Volumes. Henry Holt. New York, 1928–1929. V.53781

"Summary of European Press Reaction to the Exhibition 'Two Painters and Three Sculptors from the United States' Shown at the XXVII Biennale, Venice, June 19–October 17, 1954". The Museum of Modern Art. New York. October 1, 1956, P 12.

Photostat Copy of a Photograph Clipping and Source File. Ben Shahn Papers. Reel 5024:1282.

Pohl, Frances K. *The Artist and The Politicians: Ben Shahn, 1947–1954*. Ph.D. Dissertation. University of California, Los Angeles, 1985.

Shahn, Ben. Source File on Tom Mooney. Ben Shahn Papers. Reel 5002.

Shahn, Ben. Transcript of Interview with Walter Rosenblum. "What is Modern Photography". Ben Shahn Papers. 1950. Reel 5019:616-617.

Simmons, Michael L. "Shahn's Way" *The Official Metropolitan Guide*. April 1932, P 11.

Soby, James Thrall. "Ben Shahn." Manuscript. The Museum of Modern Art. New York, 1954.

Soby, James Thrall. Ben Shahn. *Museum of Modern Art Bulletin*. Summer 1947.

Tepfer, Diane. *Edith Gregor Halpert and the Downtown Gallery: 1926–1940: A Study in American Art Patronage*. Ph.D. Dissertation. University of Michigan, 1989, P 98–101.

Tyler, *Francine. Artists Respond to the Great Depression and the Threat of Fascism: The New York Artist's Union and its Magazine* Art Front. Ph.D. Dissertation. New York University, 1991.

Unpublished Manuscript. Ben Shahn Autobiography. The Stephen Lee Taller Ben Shahn Archive. c. 1965. Part I; Part II PP 13–14.

Jersey City Museum

STAFF

Alejandro Anreus, Ph.D.
Curator

Rocío Aranda-Alvarado, Ph.D.
Assistant Curator

Charles Thomas Strider
Collections Manager

David Silletto
Director of Finance and Administration

Akram Miam
Bookkeeper

Anne Kneuer
Director of Development

Anne De Vivo De Mesa
Development Officer

Jennifer Smiga
Membership and Development Manager

Barbara Schauwecker
Museum Educator

Nichette Meusa
Assistant to the Director / Assistant Office Manager

But even without a definite answer, the Sacco-Vanzetti case will continue to rank as the most notorious political trial in the twentieth-century American history, "the case that will not die."